MIRACLE
at
MERION

MIRACLE
at
MERION

The Inspiring Story of Ben Hogan's Amazing Comeback
and Victory at the 1950 U.S. Open

DAVID BARRETT

Skyhorse Publishing

Skyhorse Publishing books may be purchased in bulk at special discounts for sales promotion, corporate gifts, fund-raising, or educational purposes. Special editions can also be created to specifications. For details, contact Special Sales Department, Skyhorse Publishing, 555 Eighth Avenue, Suite 903, New York, NY 10018 or info@skyhorsepublishing.com.

www.skyhorsepublishing.com

Pictured on back cover, left to right, George Fazio, Ben Hogan, and Jimmy Demaret

10 9 8 7 6 5 4 3 2

Library of Congress Cataloging-in-Publication data is available on file.
ISBN: 978-1-61608-082-2

Printed in the United States of America

To Luda, Michael, Sophia,
and mom and dad

CONTENTS

INTRODUCTION

BEN HOGAN'S BALL sits four feet from the cup on the 18th hole at Merion Golf Club. Four lousy feet. If he knocks the ball in from that distance, he still has a chance to complete one of the greatest comebacks from injury in sports history. If he misses the putt, he instead completes a back-nine collapse and throws away a U.S. Open that was firmly in his grasp.

The large crowd looks on in silence. If ever a gallery could *will* a ball into a hole, this is the time. They have come to see Hogan win the 1950 U.S. Open, not to see him come close.

The putt is a short one, but Hogan missed an even shorter putt four years earlier that would have put him into a playoff in the Masters—and missed another short one later that same year to miss a playoff in the U.S. Open.

Those misses aren't on anyone's mind now, though. Hogan eliminated those memories by winning the 1946 and 1948 PGA Championships and the 1948 U.S. Open, three major victories among thirty titles in a three-year span that lifted him to the top of the golf world and landed him on the cover of *Time* magazine.

All of that past history has been wiped away by a fresh narrative. In February 1949, Hogan was driving on a two-lane west Texas highway when a Greyhound bus crashed head-on into his car. His injuries were severe. A month later, blood clots nearly took his life. There were serious doubts about whether he could even play golf again, let alone play it on the PGA circuit. Returning to his spot at the pinnacle of his profession seemed out of the question.

Then, in January 1950, Hogan shocked the world by not only returning to action at the Los Angeles Open, but nearly winning the tournament (Sam Snead beat him in a playoff). Now it's June, and Hogan is still looking for his first official victory after the crash, though he has shown flashes of his former self and won an unofficial event five weeks earlier.

He entered the U.S. Open as a defending champion of sorts, having won at Riviera Country Club in Los Angeles in 1948 and then being forced to sit out the 1949 championship due to injury. But the Open is not considered one of the likely events for Hogan to return to the winner's circle. Its final two rounds are conducted in one marathon day, and that could be too much strain for Hogan's legs to endure.

Vascular surgery saved Hogan's life after the blood clotting, but it also hampered the circulation in his legs. Walking a golf course is difficult for him, and 36 holes in one day is agony. At the Open, Hogan has taken a hot bath for two hours every evening to soak and soothe his legs. Still, during the final round, he felt his legs buckle after hitting his tee shot on the 12th hole and in order to keep from falling needed to grab onto a friend who was standing next to the tee box. At the time, he wasn't sure if he could even make it the rest of the way.

The owner of a three-stroke lead at that point, Hogan has managed to walk the rest of the course. But he is limping noticeably and, even worse, his score has suffered, too. Three bogeys during a stretch of six holes left Hogan tied for the lead coming to the 18th. The other players in that tie, Lloyd Mangrum and George Fazio, have each completed their rounds, so Hogan knows what he has to do—par to tie and birdie to win.

The long par-four 18th is the toughest hole at a Merion course that has taken a heavy toll on the field. The leading score for the championship is seven-over par, and the final round has produced the highest scores of all. A birdie on 18 is pretty much out of the question.

The brave Texan hits a good drive, but is still left with a long second shot to the green on the 458-yard hole. After some deliberation, he chooses a one-iron and aims to the left of a flagstick that is dangerously close to a bunker.

The shot comes off nicely and bounds onto the green to about 40 feet from the hole. The crowd swarms around the putting surface, with everyone desperately trying to get a view.

Hogan misreads the green a bit and hits his long putt a little too hard, watching the ball swing four feet left of the hole. Now he faces what golfers call a "tester"—this is more like a brutal final exam. Undoubtedly, there are spectators who are afraid to even watch. Hogan's playing partner on the final day, Cary Middlecoff, expects Hogan to miss.

As Hogan walks toward his second putt, everyone is all too aware that real life does not always produce storybook endings. A prime example was Hogan's return to competition at the Los Angeles Open. Hogan looked like he would be the winner there, but Snead birdied the final two holes to force a tie and spoiled the story with his playoff victory.

Hogan does not let the suspense linger in the air for long. Playing more quickly than usual, he barely surveys the putt. He just walks up to it and knocks the ball into the hole.

"I wanted to get it over with," he would say later.

Hogan has survived to play another day. And so has one of the greatest stories ever to unfold in golf.

1

1948 U.S. OPEN/BANTAM BEN

AT 10:28 A.M. on Saturday, June 12, 1948, Ben Hogan set off in pursuit of a U.S. Open title in the company of fellow competitors Lloyd Mangrum and George Fazio. Remember that threesome: Two years later, they would again tee it up with the U.S. Open on the line, in an 18-hole playoff at Merion.

This time it was at Riviera Country Club in Los Angeles, in the third and fourth rounds of a championship that called for 36 holes on the final day (it didn't change to a four-day format until 1965). Hogan was tied for second after two rounds, but Mangrum and Fazio were further back; in those days, pairings for the final day were not based on scores and the leaders did not go off in the final groups.

The idea was to spread the leaders, and thus the galleries, throughout the field. Players who were in contention for the title were usually paired together, but not strictly by scores. Hogan entered the final day in the thick of things with a stroke total of 139, three under par, one behind leader Sam Snead. Mangrum and Fazio were more on the fringe of contention, Mangrum tied for 13th at 143 and Fazio tied for 18th at 144.

So far, this U.S. Open was notable for low scoring. On the championship's first trip to the West Coast, longtime Riviera pro Willie

Hunter had convinced United States Golf Association Executive Secretary Joe Dey that with the course's wiry Kikuyu grass the originally planned six-inch rough would be too severe. Three inches, Hunter felt, would be enough.

After winning the Los Angeles Open at Riviera in January with a total of 275, Hogan wrote in his syndicated newspaper column, "The course is certain to play six to eight strokes harder in the Open." But when he arrived and played a couple of practice rounds, Hogan said the course wasn't playing any tougher than it did for the Los Angeles Open.

Hogan shot out of the gate with a 31, four under par, on the front nine of the first round, and finished with a four-under 67 to share the lead with Snead. Hogan slipped a little with a 72 in the second round, enabling Snead to move in front with a second straight 69.

The *Los Angeles Times* reported that Snead had the galleries "oohing and woohing" at his long drives, including one that rolled to within 40 yards of the green on the 385-yard eighth hole. But while he had been one of the best players in the game since he emerged from the West Virginia hills in 1937, Snead had never been able to win the Open despite several close calls.

This is the history Snead was trying to overcome on Saturday at Riviera. He started like gangbusters, making an eagle on the 513-yard par-five first hole and a birdie on the difficult second hole. He admitted a few weeks later that he felt he had the tournament "well in hand" at that point. Then the demons returned, particularly on the greens, where Snead had struggled for much of the past year.

Snead slowly faded from view with rounds of 73 and 72 and finished fifth.

"Snead's fine putting of the first two days was just a myth," wrote Charles Curtis in Sunday's *Los Angeles Times*. "He returned to form yesterday, became the Sam Snead of old and couldn't putt."

Hogan's playing partners Mangrum and Fazio were strictly bit players, falling back to finish 21st and 25th, respectively, while Ben battled for the title. Mangrum had also been paired with Hogan in the first two rounds. That might have not pleased Mangrum as the two reportedly were not fond of each other, but it wouldn't have fazed Hogan. His focus on the task at hand was so absolute it didn't really matter who he played with.

Fazio later recounted an incident in the third round that showed Hogan's focus. At the par-four second hole, Fazio holed out his second shot from the rough for an eagle two. After the round, Fazio noticed that Hogan, who was keeping his scorecard, had marked him down for a three on the second hole instead of a two. Not only that, but Hogan at first refused to change the score because he didn't remember that Fazio made an eagle.

"You S.O.B., I hit my career shot and you don't even remember it," Fazio said to Hogan.

Hogan's own third-round scorecard showed a 68 that gave him a two-stroke lead over Jimmy Demaret in a tournament that had essentially become a two-man race.

The thirty-five-year-old Hogan had won exactly as many U.S. Opens as Snead—zero. Hogan owned 43 tournament victories, but only two majors, the 1946 and 1948 PGA Championships, the latter coming just three weeks before the Open. While he did not have a tale of Open woe to match Snead's, Ben was hardly considered "Mr. Clutch" at this point in his career.

Hogan's worst Open moment came in 1946, when he had an 18-foot birdie putt to win on the tournament's final hole but instead three-putted, missing a three-footer in the process. That dropped him into a tie for fourth, one stroke out of a three-way playoff for the title between Mangrum (the eventual winner), Byron Nelson, and Vic Ghezzi.

To his credit, Hogan did win a "sort of" U.S. Open in 1942 in a tournament called the Hale America Open. There was no U.S.

Open that year because of World War II, but the USGA helped to run the Hale America event along with the Chicago District Golf Association. Hogan won with a 17-under total of 271, a score which indicated that the course didn't provide the rigorous test a U.S. Open usually provides. Still, it was the closest thing to a national championship that year—it had sectional qualifying, just like the U.S. Open—and Hogan did receive a medal from the USGA for his victory. He always claimed it as a U.S. Open title.

Despite appearing to be opposites, Hogan and Demaret were regular partners in the team events on the PGA tour (there were a couple a year in those days), and on this day they staged quite a battle for the U.S. Open championship. Demaret was known for his wild, colorful attire and gregarious personality; Hogan dressed impeccably but conservatively and was known for his taciturn expression and sometimes blunt comments to reporters. One similarity was that each had won two previous majors, with both of Demaret's coming at the Masters.

Demaret kept the heat on Hogan in the final round at Riviera, making a run with three birdies in a row starting at the 10th hole. He looked like he was going to make it four straight, but missed a four-foot birdie putt at the 13th, ending his charge.

Hogan was playing the nearby eighth hole when Demaret was on the 13th. He must have gotten a report, because after the round, he said, "Sure, I knew how Jimmy was doing. And that birdie of mine at the 10th seemed awfully good."

That was Hogan's third birdie against no bogeys to that point in the round, enabling him to preserve his advantage. From there, he made all pars except for a three-putt bogey on the 15th (his only three-putt all week) to match Demaret's final-round 69 to win by two.

Hogan's 72-hole total of 276 shattered the record of 281 set by Ralph Guldahl in 1937, with Demaret and third-place finisher Jim Turnesa also breaking the mark. It was the second time in less than a month that Demaret played great golf only to lose to Hogan. In the semifinals of the PGA Championship, then held at match play, Hogan won their scheduled 36-hole match by a two-and-one margin; both would have been 10-under in stroke play.

Hogan's sweep of the 1948 PGA and U.S. Open made him the only player other than Gene Sarazen in 1922 to capture those two prestigious titles in the same year. If there was any doubt before, Hogan had now surely arrived at the top of the golf world.

It was a long way from Dublin, Texas—a cattle town with no golf course—where William Ben Hogan was born on August 13, 1912, the son of a blacksmith. Young Ben had a lot to overcome, including the trauma of his father's suicide when Ben was nine years old. Accounts differ, but it is very possible that Ben was in the room when his father, Chester, shot himself in the chest.

His father's suicide was virtually unknown during Hogan's playing career; he kept it under wraps. A cover story on Hogan in *Time* in 1949 did not mention it, neither did profiles of Hogan in *Sport* in 1953 and *Sports Illustrated* in 1955, nor did Demaret's book, *My Partner Ben Hogan,* in 1954; they simply stated that Hogan's father died when he was nine. Even Ben's wife, Valerie, did not learn of the suicide until the late 1940s when they had been married for more than a decade, and then only by accident when another relative mentioned it. She later wrote in an essay for the book *Ben Hogan: The Man Behind the Mystique* that Ben talked about his father's death only a few times.

Surely, it must have had a deep impact on his psyche. Biographers Curt Sampson and James Dodson have speculated on how it turned Ben into a driven individual. The immediate impact was that it forced him to work to help support his family, which included an older brother and sister who also went to work. (His brother, Royal, quit school at age thirteen shortly after the suicide to work full-time; Ben ended up dropping out after his sophomore year of high school.)

The Hogans had moved to Fort Worth, about eighty miles from Dublin, when Ben was eight so Chester could get treatment for depression. Five months later, Chester moved back to Dublin. About a month after that, he traveled to Fort Worth to try to persuade his wife, Clara, to bring the family back to Dublin. An argument ensued, and Ben's father skulked off into an adjacent room and shot himself.

For a couple of years, starting at the age of nine, little Ben (then known as Bennie) sold newspapers at the Fort Worth train station. Then he heard that caddies at Glen Garden Country Club earned sixty-five cents a round, which sounded like a better deal to him. The club was six miles from his home, but that didn't stop Bennie; he didn't mind walking long distances.

The caddie yard was a rough place. On the summer day that he first arrived at the club, he was put through an initiation where he was rolled down a hill in a barrel and then had to fight a bigger boy. Bennie was pretty good with his fists, and was accepted into the fraternity.

Bennie was quickly captivated by the game, perhaps because of its individual nature. In a piece of serendipity for the world of golf, Glen Garden had a practice range, not a standard accoutrement for a course in those times. It wasn't used by the members all that much, so the caddies were free to hit balls while they were waiting for a bag to carry.

No caddie hit more balls than Bennie Hogan; later, no pro would hit more balls than Ben Hogan.

When he started, Bennie briefly swung left-handed, because somebody had given him a left-handed club. Glen Garden pro Ted Longworth quickly convinced him that in the long run, right-handed would be the better way to go. Longworth also gave him a couple of pointers on such basics as the grip, but other than that Hogan learned the game on his own, partly by watching the players he caddied for (particularly a very good golfer named Ed Stewart) and partly by trial and error on the range.

Despite his small stature, he developed a swing that would propel the ball pretty far. He did so out of necessity, as the caddies had a game in which the shortest hitter had to go out and pick up all the balls.

Despite limited opportunities to actually play the game (caddies could play only one morning a week at Glen Garden; later Hogan sometimes walked ten miles to a nine-hole course with sand greens), Hogan improved rapidly. While he was not as much of a natural as Snead or some other sweet swingers, Hogan clearly had an aptitude for the game and an unmatched work ethic to make the most of his talent.

By a strange coincidence, there was another caddie at Glen Garden also destined to become one of the greats of the game, Byron Nelson, who was just six months older than Hogan. The two fifteen-year-olds competed just before Christmas 1927 in the club's annual caddie tournament, Hogan unexpectedly tying the more refined Nelson in the nine-hole contest before losing a nine-hole playoff.

By the following Christmas, Hogan had graduated from the caddie shack to the golf shop, where he repaired and polished clubs. That year, his mother, who until then had tried to discourage Bennie from golf because she didn't see any future in it for him, scraped together $40 and bought the sixteen-year-old a set of clubs for Christmas (before then, he used clubs he bought for a buck apiece out of a barrel at a dime store). She later told a newspaper reporter that on receiving the gift, Bennie told her, "Mama, I'm going to be the greatest golfer that ever lived." Ben didn't remember it that way, saying in a 1955 *Sports Illustrated* interview, "I never did decide that golf was going to be my life."

In the summer of 1929, Hogan ventured to Shreveport, Louisiana, to play in the Southwestern Amateur, surprising even himself by finishing second in the match-play event. He hocked the watch he won as a prize to pay his caddie, then hitched his way back home to Fort Worth.

Soon after, at age seventeen, Hogan turned professional when he got a job as an assistant at Oakhurst, a humble nine-hole course near downtown. Ben (as he now called himself) made his pro tour debut at that age in February 1930, traveling with another young player, Ralph Guldahl of Dallas, to play in the Texas Open in San Antonio and the Houston Open. Nowhere near ready for prime time, a nervous Hogan shot no better than 75 in four rounds, withdrawing after two rounds of each tournament despite making both cuts. It was a similar story when he went with Guldahl to a tournament in St. Louis in the summer of 1931.

Still believing in himself, though, the nineteen-year-old Hogan headed west in December 1931 to play the winter circuit with $75 in his pocket—$50 given to him by department store owner (and later developer of Colonial Country Club) Marvin Leonard and $25 from his brother Royal. He earned his first paycheck ($50) at the Phoenix Open, but came up empty in some other tournaments, and with the tour in California had to ask Leonard for more money. While waiting for the money order to arrive, Hogan later told *Sport* writer Kerr Petrie, he "bought sixty cents worth of oranges and lived on them for three days." Hogan stayed with the tour as it headed east to Texas and New Orleans, then returned home in February 1932, broke in his wallet and shaken in his confidence.

Hogan moved on to become the pro at an 18-hole course, Nolan River Country Club in Cleburne, about thirty miles south of Fort Worth. He supplemented his income with other jobs, including a stint as a croupier and dealer at a hotel gambling establishment. Once he made it as a golfer, Hogan didn't like to talk about that part of his past, but he did enjoy showing his manual dexterity by performing card tricks. Ben also worked at a restaurant, as a hotel bellhop, as a maintenance worker at a bank, and for an oil company (some said in the fields; according to Valerie, it was in an office).

Hogan qualified for the U.S. Open in 1934 and 1936, heading northeast (to Merion outside Philadelphia and Baltusrol in New Jersey, respectively) and making the long drive back after missing the cut both times. That first trip to Merion, made with fellow Fort Worth pro Jack Grout (later to become well-known as Jack Nicklaus's teacher), resulted in consecutive rounds of 79.

Between those two Opens, he married Valerie in 1935. All the while, Ben was saving as much money as he could. Apart from his various jobs, Hogan made money by winning bets on the golf course. Like many pros of the time, Ben generally didn't put up his own money but had backers in big-money action and was given a share of their proceeds. After winning one particularly large bet, he was able to buy a car.

By July 1937, Hogan had accumulated $1,450 and was ready to try his luck on the tour again just before his twenty-fifth birthday, this time with Valerie along to keep him company, provide encouragement, and act as "secretary, treasurer, and wardrobe mistress," as she later wrote.

In his first tournament after rejoining the tour, Hogan won $60 for finishing second at the General Brock Open in Niagara Falls, plus an additional $50 for finishing second in a long-drive contest (despite his small size and his later reputation for control, Hogan was a long hitter).

Ben earned just $1,164 in the ten tournaments he played in for the rest of the year, leaving the Hogans with less money than they started with. It's not like Hogan played poorly, though. He finished 12th or better in eight of those ten tournaments, was in the money in all of them, and posted a third-place finish at Lake Placid. It was just that hard to make money on tour in the 1930s.

A few days after Christmas, back in Fort Worth, Ben and Valerie were sitting at a table in the dining area at Blackstone Hotel, where he had worked both as a bellman and a card dealer, debating whether they could afford to go on the tour's western swing. Valerie said that, considering the finances, she would stay home and get a job while Ben played the tour; he insisted that he wouldn't go unless Valerie went with him.

It so happened that Hogan's old friend Jack Grout and Henry Picard, then one of the best players on tour, were passing through Fort Worth on their way to the Los Angeles Open and spied Ben and Valerie when they stopped in at the Blackstone. Seeing the couple in animated conversation, they asked what it was about. Upon hearing their dilemma, Picard told Ben to take Valerie with him and play on the West Coast. "If you run out of money, I'll take care of you," he said.

Picard didn't even know Hogan well, but from what he had seen he liked the newcomer's game and determination. In 1948, Hogan dedicated his book *Power Golf* to Picard in appreciation of the gesture. "Knowing that help was there if I needed it enabled me to forget about my troubles," Hogan wrote.

Hogan never needed to ask Picard for assistance. While they came oh so close to running out of money, Ben and Valerie actually planned to sell their car for train fare home if it came to that rather than asking for Picard's help. That discussion came after Hogan finished in the money in only two of the first five tournaments in 1938, leaving him with less than $100 to his name. Ben and Valerie considered going home right away, but decided Ben would give it one last shot at the Oakland Open. Another bad tournament and Ben would have little choice but to leave the tour, at least temporarily.

As bad luck would have it, on the morning of the first round Hogan went to the lot across from the hotel where he had parked his car only to find the wheels jacked up and the tires stolen. Near the end of his rope, Hogan caught a ride to the tournament and barely made his tee time, somehow regaining his composure to shoot a 70 and earn a share of fifth place. Once the tires were replaced, he was left with $14.

Sometimes pressure brings out the best in a man, and that was the case in Oakland. After slipping in the middle rounds, Hogan shot a 67 in the final round to tie for sixth with a 280 total and earn $285. "It was the biggest check I'd ever seen in my life," he told Ken Venturi of CBS in a 1983 television interview. "And I'm quite sure it will be the biggest check I'll ever see." The next week, he finished third in Sacramento, earning $350. Even better, at least in terms of financial security, around this time he received and accepted an offer to be an assistant professional at Century Country Club just north of New York City in Purchase, New York. A friend of a club member on the West Coast met with Hogan and gave a favorable recommendation, saying he "makes a nice appearance."

The tide had turned. Following a string of top-ten finishes, Hogan was even invited to the Masters. He only finished 25th, but it was still a heady experience for a man whose golf career had so recently been in doubt.

In September 1938, Picard played a role in another turning point for Hogan. Then pro at Hershey Resort in Pennsylvania, Picard unexpectedly invited Hogan to be one of the sixteen players in an elite field at the Hershey Four-Ball Invitational, a decision questioned by chocolate magnate Milton Hershey himself. Picard told his boss that he had never played with Hogan, but had watched him practice and was impressed. Hogan's dedication to practice was not only making him a better player, it opened a door for him that he walked right through.

Originally scheduled to partner with former U.S. Open champion Tommy Armour, Hogan ended up with a fellow young pro, Vic Ghezzi, when Armour withdrew. That was probably another break, since Ghezzi had won on tour that year while Armour was past his prime. Rated as the longest shots in the field, Ghezzi and Hogan cruised to victory, giving Ben his first tour win, albeit a shared one.

To Ghezzi, Hogan's determination—even desperation—to win was evident.

"Maybe I was imagining things, but his face seemed to turn gray from the almost violent effort he put into every shot," Ghezzi said later. "I knew from that day on nobody, but nobody was going to stop Hogan."

After years of starts and stops, Hogan had finally established himself as a legitimate tour player. But his trials weren't over. The next step was winning an individual tournament, and Hogan couldn't seem to manage it. He finished second three times in 1939 and three more times in the first two-and-a-half months of 1940. He may have just been trying too hard, and perhaps he hadn't acquired the experience yet to make his fierce desire to win work for him instead of against him. But a certain impediment to victory was the nasty hook that had always plagued his game.

From his days taking part in driving contests as a young caddie, Hogan developed a right-to-left draw that gave him more roll and helped him hit it as far, or farther, than bigger kids. Now the five-foot-eight, 135-pound Hogan, who would be given the moniker "Bantam Ben" by the newspaper writers, was still competing against opponents much bigger than he. Exceptionally strong wrists helped compensate for his lack of size, as did a very long backswing—he took the club well past parallel. And he still had that right-to-left action.

In his early forays on the tour, that gentle draw too often turned into an ugly hook that sent Hogan home to Fort Worth with no money in his pocket. He had learned to control it much better, but in pressure situations the hook still reared its head.

Before the 1939 PGA Championship, Hogan was so desperate to stop hooking the ball that he did something that he rarely, if ever, did, before or since—he asked somebody for help with his swing. That somebody was his old benefactor, Picard.

Picard's solution was for Hogan to learn to slice the ball, and his tip couldn't have been simpler. He merely had Ben weaken his left-hand grip on the club, turning his hand toward the left.

When Picard related the story a few decades later, he said the lesson took place in Miami in March 1940, two weeks before Hogan broke through with his first individual victory at the North and South Open. That makes for a better story, but Picard did not play in the Miami Biltmore Four Ball that took place two weeks before the North and South. A wire service photo caught Picard working with Hogan on the range at the 1939 PGA, placing the incident in July of that year. So, it wasn't a quick fix that led to immediate results, but it was a significant step on the road to Hogan eliminating his troublesome hook and developing his trademark left-to-right fade.

The last of Hogan's six runner-up finishes in 1939 and early 1940 was the most frustrating of all, as Hogan lost to Nelson in a playoff at the Texas Open—shades of the Glen Garden caddie tournament a little more than twelve years earlier. What's more, while Hogan was showing improvement, he was lagging well behind old running mates like Nelson, who had won the 1937 Masters and 1939 U.S. Open (and soon the 1940 PGA Championship) and Guldahl, who had won the 1937 and 1938 U.S. Opens, the 1939 Masters, and three Western Opens all before turning twenty-eight years old.

Hogan later said that he decided the only way to reach the winner's circle "was to get so far out in front that no one could catch me." It was a simple thought, but that's exactly what he did. And the quick fix came not in the form of a swing tip, but a driver that was given to him by Nelson in March 1940, just before the North and South Open.

After opening with a course-record-tying 66 to lead the field by three at the famed No. 2 Course at Pinehurst, Hogan told reporters, "Main trouble with my game has always been driving. I could hit 'em far enough, but they had a tendency to hook right at the end. But this new driver Nelson gave me—heck, I never hit tee shots like that before. Clothesline drives, every one of them, and not a hook in the lot."

A second-round 67 stretched his lead to a whopping seven strokes, and he held on to beat Snead by three.

"I was beginning to think I was an also-ran," he said after the final round. "I needed that win. They've kidded me about practicing so much. I'd go out there before a round and practice, and when I was through I'd practice some more. Well, they can kid me all I want because it finally paid off."

It's often said about a promising young player that once he wins the first tournament, the floodgates open. Hogan was a classic example of that axiom. He went on to win the next two tournaments, in Greensboro and Asheville, for a North Carolina triple. Hogan finished 1940 as the leading money winner on tour, but he wasn't completely satisfied. Though he added one more victory at the Goodall Round Robin in New York, Hogan finished no better than fifth at the Masters, U.S. Open, and PGA Championship.

"This year has been really gratifying," he said at the end of the campaign, "but until I win a major tournament, I won't really be happy."

Hogan led the money list again in 1941, winning five times. But he hadn't entirely whipped his runner-up blues. He finished second an extraordinary eleven times that year and still couldn't win a major.

Hogan took over that spring as the professional at Hershey for Picard, who was moving to Cleveland's Canterbury Country Club and—in yet another benevolent gesture—recommended Hogan for the job. This time, Milton Hershey was completely in agreement. It was a great move for Hogan, not only because it offered much better pay ($8,000 a year) but because he didn't have to give lessons, which was his least favorite part of the job at Century. In fact, he didn't have to be in residence all that much; mainly, he was hired for the publicity he would generate by being listed as playing out of Hershey.

The 1942 schedule was somewhat reduced as the United States entered World War II, but the game went on, since the majority of pros had not yet gone into the service. It was more of the same for Hogan: six wins, a third straight money title, no majors (unless you count the Hale America Open), and a frustrating playoff loss to Nelson at the Masters.

Hogan's quest for a major would have to wait until after the war was over. But in one sense, his quest was complete. The boy from humble origins with an incredible drive to succeed had persevered through rough times as a young man and emerged as one of the best players in the game.

Looking back on his life in his interview with Venturi in 1983, Hogan said, "My family wasn't rich; they were poor. I feel sorry for rich kids now. I really do! Because they're never going to have the opportunity that I had. Because I knew tough things and I had tough days all my life, and I can handle tough things. They can't! Every day that I progressed was a joy to me. And I recognized it every day. I don't think that I could have done what I've done if I hadn't had the tough days to begin with."

2

1948 WORLD CHAMPIONSHIP/
PURPLE HEART

THE U.S. OPEN was the country's most prestigious tournament, but Chicago's Tam O'Shanter Country Club hosted the game's richest events in the middle of the twentieth century.

In August 1948, that meant a six-day extravaganza featuring two tournaments, the All-American Open followed by the grandly named World Championship of Golf. The former had a purse of $30,000, by far the biggest of the year. The latter, with a field of only twelve players and a winner-take-all format, had by far the largest first prize of the year, $10,000.

The impresario of both tournaments was the flamboyant George S. May, owner of an eponymous national business consulting company and also of Tam O'Shanter. He used his tournaments as a way of promoting both his company and his club, running the events in a way that produced maximum publicity.

It began with the purse. When starting the Tam O'Shanter Open in 1941, May asked the PGA what the largest purse was; told it was $10,000, he made his $11,000. Since then, he widened the gap, and it would only become greater. By 1954, the World Champion-

16

ship of Golf offered a $100,000 purse and first prize of $50,000 at a time when winners of most other events were getting between $2,000 and $5,000.

May was the first to erect grandstands on a course, including permanent stands behind the 18th green. He was at the forefront of getting golf on television. As early as 1948, the final round of the World Championship was shown on the DuMont Network in select cities in the Midwest and East. In 1953, the World Championship was the first to be telecast nationally.

Some of his ideas were less successful, notably his notion of pinning numbers on the back waistbands of players so that fans could identify them by looking in the program. Many, like Sam Snead, went along. Others, like Ben Hogan, objected, and refused to wear them. May docked the prize money of players who didn't wear numbers by fifteen percent in 1946 and fifty percent in 1947. In 1948, he tried bribery, saying he would double the purse in 1949 if everyone wore a number, but there were still a few holdouts, including Jimmy Demaret. By 1950, May gave up on having players wear numbers and put the numbers on the caddies instead.

May, usually wearing a Hawaiian shirt, would walk around the course making bets with players, giving them favorable odds—such as 100–1 for hitting the green from the rough or making a birdie on a hole. During an 18-hole playoff for the World Championship in 1949, Demaret was constantly engaging in side bets with May even while losing to Johnny Palmer.

In 1946, May turned the Tam O'Shanter Open into the All-American Open, a large carnival of an event with divisions for men and women professionals and men and women amateurs. The next year, he added the World Championship of Golf, and in 1948 scheduled them back to back. The World Championship was expanded from 36 to 72 holes in 1949, and in ensuing years had its purse pumped up to monstrous proportions while the All-American purse was scaled down to something closer to a typical tour event.

Hogan didn't compete in the All-American in 1947 because he didn't want to wear a number, but played in and won the World Championship, where he didn't need to. In 1948, he skipped both.

Every other top player was on hand that year, though, including Tam O'Shanter's own pro, Lloyd Mangrum. May hired Mangrum after he won the 1946 U.S. Open, and he fit right in at the "Tam." With his hair parted down the middle and a thin moustache, Mangrum had the looks of a riverboat gambler, and was known to enjoy card games and playing for money on the golf course.

Tam O'Shanter was anything but a genteel club. It was full of nouveau riche types who loved some action. The clubhouse featured slot machines, keno, a roulette wheel, and no fewer than thirteen bars, according to a 1955 *Sports Illustrated* story by Jack Mabley, who wrote, "Nobody who can walk or crawl can possibly be thirsty for more than a few minutes at Tam O'Shanter."

The week of the 1948 All-American Open and World Championship would provide Mangrum with the biggest payout in the history of golf to that point.

First, he won the All-American Open and its $5,000 first prize. Next, he set a course record of 63 in the second round of the World Championship to earn a $2,500 bonus May was offering for that feat. Then, he won the World Championship in a playoff to earn the $10,000 first prize. On top of that, May, in his role as Mangrum's employer, paid him a $5,000 bonus for leading the PGA tour money list through the All-American. That's $22,500. And if you take Mangrum's word that May bet him at 1,000-to-1 odds that he wouldn't win the World Championship, you can tack on $1,000 to that total.

Mangrum selected a day from that week for the 1950 book *My Greatest Day in Golf* by Darsie L. Darsie rather than his playoff win at the 1946 U.S. Open.

"It isn't surprising that winning a national open championship did not seem as important to Lloyd Mangrum as winning a lot of money, for to Mangrum the playing of championship golf is a means of livelihood, a source of income, a profession—and he measures his success not by his low scoring and not by the titles he holds—but by the cash he is able to put in the bank by virtue of his fine play," Darsie wrote.

Lady Luck was certainly on Mangrum's side that week. In the final round of the All-American, he holed a bunker shot for a birdie on the 16th hole, posted a 277 total, and waited to see if Bobby Locke could match or beat it. Locke came to the 18th hole needing a par to force a playoff. His approach shot caught a tree to the right of the green and ricocheted back into a water hazard, leading to a double bogey that handed the title to Mangrum.

In the World Championship, Mangrum reached an 18-hole playoff with Snead and Dutch Harrison thanks to his spectacular 63 in the second round, setting up a seventh straight day of tournament golf at Tam O'Shanter. He and Snead were tied going to the 18th, where Snead hit his drive behind a lone pine tree and made a bogey. For the second time in four days, Mangrum was the beneficiary of a poor finish by a fellow competitor, and once again he had one of the trees on his home course to thank for it.

Mangrum turned thirty-four on the eve of his Tam O'Shanter double. The victories were his fifth and sixth of the year. He had an interesting backstory that included being awarded two Purple Hearts in World War II action in Europe. He had dashing good looks, was a sharp dresser, and was, in many ways, a fascinating character. Yet, for all of this, he came across as thoroughly dull, and never quite caught the fancy of the golf-watching public.

Mangrum loved to play cards perhaps even more than he loved to play golf. Maybe that's where he developed the poker face that he always displayed on the golf course. In a 1952 profile in *Sport* magazine, Al Stump called Mangrum a "mystery," writing, "He dislikes handshaking. Crowds and cheers leave him cold. Interviews give him a pain he takes little trouble to disguise . . . During matches he looks past galleries as if they didn't exist. Opponents get steady and unsettled silent treatment . . . Other pros look reflective when you mention his name. Nobody knocks him but the attitude is: 'Why doesn't he just loosen up and have fun? We've seen him crack about a dozen smiles in that many years.'"

Much the same could have been said about Hogan, and sometimes was. Somehow, though, it seemed that Hogan's ability to focus was almost superhuman, and that became his defining quality, one that was fascinating in its own way because it was so extreme. But when the tournament was over, Hogan would flash a brilliant smile at the awards presentation. By comparison, Mangrum just looked like a guy who wasn't having any fun on the course, and not a whole lot of fun off it, either.

"In his relations with the press and public, Mangrum almost made Hogan a bright and witty raconteur," wrote Al Barkow in a 2006 *Golf World* profile of Mangrum. "But when Hogan did speak, it was in measured tones and proper language. Mangrum was abrupt, profanely direct, and unequivocal in his opinions."

Once, a reporter at a tournament, desperate for an angle, was asking players for their instructional tips. "Monkey see, monkey do," was Mangrum's offering. He declined to elaborate. It was a typically blunt answer.

He could also be confrontational. Late in his life, Mangrum recalled that when he was a rookie on the tour, veteran star Gene Sarazen hit into his group twice on the front nine, apparently because he thought they were playing too slowly. Mangrum's group was delayed getting off the 10th tee, and Sarazen, sitting on a bench waiting for his turn, said something like, "Get moving."

"I turned to him and said, 'Mr. Sarazen, you'll probably win this tournament. I'm trying to make $100 to get out of town on. But if you play into me again, I'm gonna take your bleep-bleep ball and hit it back over your bleep-bleep head,'" Mangrum related.

Some of his coarseness could be traced to his rough-and-tumble upbringing. Mangrum was born on a farm in Trenton, Texas, a small town near Dallas, and then moved with his family to Dallas, where his father operated a boarding house. Mangrum's father abandoned the family when Lloyd was eight years old.

To this point, Mangrum's childhood arc was remarkably similar to Hogan's Dublin-to-Fort Worth/loss-of-father trajectory. But Lloyd's path would be even more difficult. He had seven siblings, and his overwhelmed mother essentially left them to raise themselves.

Lloyd got into golf because of his older brother, Ray. The two of them used to hit shots at a makeshift green on the other side of a creek behind their house. When Ray got a job as an assistant pro at Cliff-Dale Country Club in Dallas, Lloyd caught on as a caddie there.

When he was fourteen, Lloyd followed his brother west to Los Angeles, where Lloyd lived with an older sister and supported himself. Over the next few years, he bounced back and forth between Los Angeles and Dallas, earning money by caddying, parking cars, driving a taxi, cleaning golf clubs, and gambling on the golf course and at the card table at municipal courses.

At the age of nineteen, he settled down in an unusual way, marrying Eleta Hurst, who was ten years older and had three children by a previous marriage. The oldest child was twelve, just seven years younger than he was. Eleta ran a beauty parlor, which provided a steady income while Mangrum continued his golf hustling and halting steps toward becoming a tour pro.

He also did some caddying at PGA tour events, unusual in those days because there was no corps of tour caddies traveling around the country—players couldn't have afforded to pay them. But with his brother Ray now playing on the tour, Lloyd had connections. He didn't caddie on a regular basis, but did so in some big tournaments—always for top players.

Mangrum developed his own game by copying players he admired—he really did believe in "monkey see, monkey do." For putting, he emulated Horton Smith; for the short game, Johnny Revolta; and for the long game, Snead.

Lloyd began to play in regional events like the Southern California Open, where he finished sixth in 1936, earning $50. Ray had a summer job as a pro at a club in Pittsburgh, so Lloyd listed himself as being from Pittsburgh and played in the 1937 Pennsylvania Open, held that year at the East Course of Merion Cricket Club, where he would play the U.S. Open thirteen years later. He finished fifth.

Lloyd qualified for the U.S. Open at Oakland Hills that year and missed the cut. But the winner, Ralph Guldahl, credited a Tuesday gambling session with fellow Dallas product Mangrum on the practice green for turning around his putting. Guldahl had been struggling on the greens in recent tournaments, and he quickly fell four dollars down to Mangrum before finding the touch—almost out of necessity—to match Lloyd, always an excellent putter.

"Every time I had a tough one in the tournament, I just looked it over as if I were four bucks down to Lloyd," Guldahl said later.

Mangrum's efforts to play the tour in 1937 ended ignominiously at the St. Paul Open. When the tournament ended, Mangrum said to an acquaintance, "What does a guy do when he's flat broke and two thousand miles from home?"

That acquaintance was Scotty Chisolm, an editor, author, and sometimes tournament announcer (he always wore a kilt in that role), a fellow Southern California resident who, fortunately, happened to be heading home. "You go back and get together another few bucks, laddie. Then you hit the circuit again," Chisolm replied. It could have been the credo for the tour in the 1930s.

After the St. Paul tournament, Chisolm later recalled, "I had a few dollars and the loan of a car. To save buying food, we drove back to L.A. almost nonstop. We rolled up to Lloyd's modest little joint in Monterey Park with $1.70 left in the kick, dead-beat, dirty, and hungry."

Chisolm asked Mangrum if he was going to quit. "Quit like hell," Mangrum replied. "I can beat these guys. Just give me a little time."

The next summer Lloyd headed east again, and this time he won the Pennsylvania Open, which had moved to a different site. It wasn't a tour event, but it was something. In 1939, he captured two more minor events, the Central New York and Santa Anita Opens.

Mangrum took his first club pro job, as an assistant at Oak Park Country Club outside Chicago, in 1939 and hated it. Giving lessons and performing menial tasks in the pro shop wasn't for him, and he didn't last long. Fortunately, by then his game had developed to the point where he could make it on tour full-time (supplemented, no doubt, by winnings from card games and golf bets).

His first official title came at the Thomasville Open in Georgia in March 1940, and he received a Masters invitation only four days before the start of the event. The relative unknown shocked everybody with a course record 64 at Augusta National in the first round and finished second, sandwiched between fellow Texans Demaret and Byron Nelson.

When he took the first-round lead at the Oakland Open in 1941, the Associated Press report described Mangrum as "a little fellow with a moustache and not much of that intangible something called 'color.'" He did have enough game, though, to post 36 top-ten finishes and four victories in 1941 and '42, establishing himself in the top echelon of players on tour.

Then came the war, which for Mangrum would be a very different experience than for other golfers. Nearly all of the pros went into the service, but only a few went overseas, and Mangrum was the only top pro to see real combat.

He could have gotten out of it. Shortly before he was due to be shipped from Fort Meade, Maryland, to Europe as an infantryman, Mangrum was told that the base's golf course was in need of a pro and he could have the job. He declined.

Mangrum landed in Normandy soon after D-Day. He had gotten himself into a reconnaissance unit that went out ahead of the troops in jeeps to scout out enemy positions. As the Allies broke out of Normandy, Mangrum had a jeep overturn on him near the Falaise gap. His upper left arm and shoulder were broken, and he suffered damage to his deltoid muscle, too.

"It's very doubtful that you can play golf again," the surgeon told him, "but you'll be well enough to go back to active duty."

The doubt about playing golf arose out of uncertainty regarding Mangrum's ability to raise his arm high enough to make a golf swing. Mangrum remained in a cast for much of his six-month stay in the hospital, not sure if his golf career was finished. Then the cast came off and "not even the thrill of winning the Open equaled the one I had that day I found I could lift my arm," he said later.

In a sense, the jeep accident might have been fortuitous. He missed six months of dangerous action in a war in which he was only one of two enlisted men from his original unit to survive. (For the rest of his life, he kept half of a dollar bill he had split with a buddy with a pact to put the two halves together if both made it through the war.)

As it was, he had some close calls in the remaining months of the war. Returning to action near Frankfurt, Germany, he was hit in the chin by shrapnel. "I didn't even go to the first-aid station," he said. "We were too short of men."

Then in Czechoslovakia, he faced his closest call yet. His unit was under sniper fire, and a bullet whizzed past his head, missing him only because he had just turned to ask a buddy what he'd just said. When one of their men went down across the road, Lloyd went out to drag him back, and the sniper, shooting from about three hundred yards away, clipped him in the side of the knee.

"He must have been a lousy shot," Mangrum later said, flexing a dry wit. "Imagine only nicking a guy from that distance. I could have done better with a driver and a rabbit ball."

With Hitler defeated, Mangrum set about seeing whether he could play golf again. He could lift his arm, but felt pain every time he swung as he made his first tentative efforts in the Bavarian hills. But the pain wore away, and in August 1945, at the same time other tour pros were back playing tournaments in the States, Mangrum won the Army Victory Open in St. Cloud, France. Shortly thereafter, he won the GI championship at St. Andrews, Scotland. It wasn't the British Open, but for Mangrum it was a major championship of a different sort.

Finally, he was able to come home to a relieved Eleta and rejoin the tour in 1946. He hadn't found his way back to the winner's circle entering that year's U.S. Open at Canterbury, where he was tied for first after 72 holes with Nelson and Vic Ghezzi. All three shot 72 in an 18-hole playoff and returned to the course for another 18 holes that same afternoon.

In retrospect, the key moment for Mangrum was holing a 60-foot putt for a bogey on the ninth hole of the second 18-hole playoff after sending his drive out of bounds. But he was three strokes behind with six holes to play when a storm rolled in and the thunder started crashing like cannon fire.

"The former corporal was just another G.I. again for a minute," wrote Oscar Fraley for United Press International (UPI). " His cream-colored sports shirt seemed to turn to khaki and to him it was no longer a golf course. That rumble was too familiar and it meant trouble. And that's when Mangrum looked up at the flashes, laughed, and really started to play."

Mangrum birdied three of the next four holes and shot a 72, one stroke ahead of both Nelson and Ghezzi, finishing in a driving rainstorm.

While he had always prided himself at being cool under pressure on the golf course, Mangrum was even more so after the war. Frank Stranahan remembered playing with Mangrum when he was in contention at Phoenix in 1947 and got a bad break when his ball got caught in a tree and he had to take a lost-ball penalty.

"Lloyd never said boo. He just went about his business," Stranahan later told Mark Stewart of the *Arizona Daily Star*. "I said,

'Jeez, Lloyd, I never saw a tough break like that, under pressure, handled so well.' He said, 'Frank, after surviving a jeep rollover and getting out of World War II alive, I promised myself I'd never get upset about anything in golf ever again.'"

On the other hand, the war seemed to adversely affect Mangrum off the golf course. He developed a tough-guy image, hanging out with unsavory characters away and sometimes getting into fights. It was said that he carried a revolver, and Snead remembered Mangrum hitting a man in the face with a sugar bowl at a restaurant.

Even in his early days, Mangrum lived on the edge sometimes. Johnny Bulla remembered rooming with him in Thomasville, Georgia, one year.

"One night, Lloyd said, 'I'm going to a poker game. It's crooked, but it's the only one in town.' When he got back at 2 a.m., I asked him how it went. He said, 'I was a better cheater than they were.'"

It's easy to imagine that kind of lifestyle getting someone in trouble. Some of the stories about Mangrum may have been exaggerated, though one very real fight knocked him off the tour for four months. Still, the "tough guy" picture isn't a complete one when it comes to Mangrum.

His stepdaughter, Reina, later remembered that with her mother busy running a business, it was Lloyd who taught her how to cook and iron in those early years of the marriage when he wasn't yet a tour regular. "He was one great guy," she said. "All three of us thought the world of him."

Bob Mangrum, the stepson who was only seven years younger than Lloyd, and who later took his name, concurred. In 1999, he told Brad Townsend of the *Dallas Morning News*, "I hadn't had one before, but he was the best damned dad anybody could have asked for."

Bob bristled when asked if his stepdad was a barroom brawler.

"That's a bunch of bull," he said. "He was a really sweet guy. If he liked you, he'd do anything for you. Of course, he didn't like too many people."

That was the rub. Bob Toski was a good friend of Mangrum's on the tour, and he echoed that thought. "If he loved you, he loved you. If he didn't like you, forget it," Toski said in a 2009 interview.

Another player of that era, Doug Ford, recalled Mangrum as a player willing to give you a tip ("he gave me a very important bunker lesson in my second year") and one of the guys you could go to if you needed somebody to lend you a buck.

Mangrum was a family man, whose marriage to Eleta was considered one of the most solid on the tour, though oddly he always called her "maw." (He also had a habit of addressing fellow players as "pro.") His brother, Ray, in contrast, reportedly saw his career end when his fourth wife shot him in the arm.

Toski, an admitted carouser when he first came out on tour, said Lloyd told him he needed reform. "He always told me, 'You're gonna make it out here, but you have to change your lifestyle. It's a business, not a circus.'"

Mangrum was happy when Toski got married a couple of years later. "He always told me if I hadn't married that redhead, I wouldn't have done anything."

Lloyd's love for his wife and his sarcastic humor shone through in his dedication to his book *Golf: A New Approach*, published in 1949:

"To my wife Eleta, who has made my golfing career possible by her willingness to sacrifice the pleasures of home life in favor of a steady diet of indigestible food in strange restaurants, boardlike beds in unique hotels, and laundering facilities in bathroom wash basins."

Mangrum also had a wry take at golf instruction. In the book's preface, he wrote, "The easiest shot in golf to learn is undoubtedly a one-inch putt. And your problems will increase as the distance from the cup increases."

He may have played in crooked poker games, but on the golf course Mangrum had a sense of honor about the rules. At the 1948

Masters, Lloyd led after the first round. On the eighth hole of the second round, while preparing to hit a shot from the woods, he stepped on a twig and his ball moved. Mangrum called the one-stroke penalty on himself.

Mangrum took full advantage of the opportunities that came his way from winning the U.S. Open. He took a lucrative pro job at Tam O'Shanter that didn't require giving lessons, got the book deal, and increased his endorsement contracts for equipment and golf shoes. Mangrum was known to keep a cigarette in his mouth as he was swinging or putting, so it's only natural he landed a cigarette endorsement. There was even a Lloyd Mangrum Table Golf game.

Still, he was fourth fiddle in the public's eyes, well behind Hogan, Snead, and Demaret.

Perhaps it was just that he didn't *look* as impressive as the sweet-swinging Snead, the intense Hogan, or the colorful Demaret. His on-course personality didn't resonate with the public, and neither did his game, really. He was perhaps the best putter of his time, but that doesn't draw in the fans like the long ball does.

Mangrum had an extremely narrow stance, which worked well with his irons but not so well with the driver. "There must be fifty pros that can outdrive me, and maybe a hundred who can hit it straighter," Mangrum once said. "But golf doesn't seem to come to them the way it does to me."

3

THE TOUR

TO **UNDERSTAND WHAT** life was like on the PGA tour around the midpoint of the twentieth century, you have to consider the money. Or rather, the lack of it.

In 1950, nearly every PGA tour event offered prize money totaling either $10,000 or $15,000. Now let's take inflation into account. In 2010 dollars, that translates into purses of about $90,000 or $135,000. First prize was $2,000 or $2,600 (in 2010 dollars, about $18,000 or $23,500). In 2010, the typical purse is $6 million, with a winner's check of around $1.1 million.

Only the PGA Championship and World Championship of Golf offered more than $15,000 in prize money, though a few tournaments, including the U.S. Open, paid more than $2,600 to the winner. But the PGA Championship had only a slightly higher purse ($17,950), leaving the World Championship as an outlier at $50,000. That's about $450,000 in 2010 dollars, which is less than the lowest purse on the secondary Nationwide Tour today.

Clearly, nobody was in it to get rich back then. Why play the tour, then? The simplest answer is pride. If you were one of the best players in the country, this was a chance to compete and show that you belonged among the best. There was also the camaraderie.

The tour had a "we're all in this together" kind of feeling, with the players being friends as much as competitors. They often drove from town to town together and sometimes roomed together, they ate dinner together, and they sat around in hotel lounges drinking and telling stories.

"It was a close fraternity. We would go out there and try to help each other on the practice tee," said Bob Toski in a 2009 interview, looking back on the time when he joined the tour sixty years before. "There was a lot of socializing. We would get a group of six to ten guys for dinner, tell war stories and lies, and get drunk."

Not everybody got drunk or hung out with the boys, though. In fact, some of the best players tended to stay to themselves. Ben Hogan traveled with his wife, Valerie, and didn't hang out with the other players much. Sam Snead was a teetotaler when he was on the road. Lloyd Mangrum, as noted in the last chapter, steered Toski away from the party aspect of the tour. Jimmy Demaret, on the other hand, was the life of the party.

Nearly all the players felt a connection on some level.

"A lot of guys were on a short bankroll," said Doug Ford, who joined the tour in 1949. "If you needed to borrow $100 to get to the next tournament, there were a lot of guys you could go to who would lend you the money. It was a friendly group. We used to say the hardest putt was one to win $100 and get you to the next tournament."

Those putts arose because only the top twenty players finished in the money, with the final prize being $100. It would be less, though, if there was a tie for twentieth—a three-way tie, for example, would earn two players $33.33, while the lucky one of the trio would get $33.34.

As a form of insurance, players would even sometimes make deals with each other to split not only expenses but also any prize money either earned. Johnny Bulla declined such an offer from an as yet unproven Snead in 1937, to his regret when Sam went on a victory tear. And it was a common practice for playoff participants to agree ahead of time to split the prize money equally, no matter who won.

It seems anomalous that in such an atmosphere some players supplemented their income by betting in practice rounds. But for the most part, they weren't betting much against their brothers in arms, but against local players who'd entered the tournament or local pigeons—rich amateurs who thought they could beat the pros if given strokes, but who usually couldn't. In their weeks off the tour, a lot of players supplemented their income in this way, probably none more than Dutch Harrison and Al Besselink.

Prize money was so small in those days, Besselink reflected in 2009, that "we had to gamble. I hung around millionaires, and had big bets with millionaires." For Besselink, there never was such a thing as a casual round, before, during, or after his tour career. "I don't know how you can play golf and not gamble."

Tour players supplemented their income more conventionally with club pro jobs and sponsorship contracts with equipment manufacturers.

But even though most players were affiliated with clubs in some capacity, the tour had evolved past the point where the pro shop was their primary occupation. Top players like Hogan and Mangrum got positions where they didn't have to give lessons, fix clubs, or in Hogan's case, show up much (he reportedly went a couple of years in the late 1940s without even setting foot in Hershey). Others managed it so that they were able to spend twenty-five or thirty weeks on tour. Johnny Bulla was one of the first pros to forge a new path, supporting himself by promoting a golf ball sold in Walgreens drug stores.

What struck the British press after losing the 1947 and '49 Ryder Cups to the Americans was this new breed of tour professional.

After the United States won by an 11–1 margin in 1947, an article in Scotland's *Golf Monthly* said the "American opponents were bulky men of exceptional physique, inured to tackle the occasion nonchalantly in their stride, confidence cultivated by sustained experience in the strenuous test of tournament play. The Americans have brought into the game over the years a corps of super-professionals."

It was a circuit that developed toughness, both on and off the course.

For the most part, travel was done by car. That's even harder than it sounds. There were no interstate highways, so even long-distance driving required stopping at traffic lights. Roadside motels hadn't yet sprung up in any great numbers. That meant finding in-town hotels—and not the most expensive ones, either. Some of them were establishments that put the "flea" in the term fleabag.

Toski later told writer Randall Mell about sharing a car and hotel rooms with Doug Ford and Ted Kroll. Toski, the smallest, had to sleep on a cot. "With the snoring, the farting, and the belching, you did your best," Toski remembered. "And Ted used to grind his teeth in his sleep."

So did Hogan, as Byron Nelson found out in the late 1930s when they roomed together. Nelson was awakened by a sound he thought was rats scurrying, but turned out to be Ben's teeth grinding.

Over half of the players traveled regularly with their wives, which added to the expenses. But the veteran players had developed a network of friends around the country, and often stayed at friends' homes during tournaments.

The drives through the open spaces of the Southwest were especially boring. Once, Mangrum was with a couple of other pros driving across the Texas panhandle. They stopped for gas, driving past the station, turning around, and coming back to it. Mangrum, asleep in the backseat, didn't notice; taking his turn to drive, he pulled out of the station and started heading in the wrong direction. They drove a hundred miles before anyone realized it.

Driving was dangerous, as the golf world found out in the fall of 1947. George Payton, a very promising twenty-four-year-old pro from Virginia, was killed in Chicago when the car in which he was a passenger slammed into a railroad abutment. After his own near-fatal accident in 1949, Hogan often rode the train.

In fact, he also rode the train at times before his crash. The problem with that was getting around once you got to your destination—unless you were staying at a friend's home. Courtesy cars weren't even a distant dream. There were no spreads of food in the locker room and range balls weren't provided.

"Nothing was free," Toski said. "We stood in line to buy hot dogs for lunch like everybody else."

By the late 1940s a few pros began to fly on occasion, especially on long trips. Bulla even bought a plane and flew some of his fellow pros from stop to stop for a while. Bulla had flying in his blood, and worked as a pilot for Eastern Airlines during World War II after so many commercial pilots were called into the service. Hogan, who learned to fly in the Army Air Corps during the war, was Bulla's co-pilot on one of those tour trips. But Hogan summarily retired from flying after that flight ended in an emergency landing.

With such a hard life and so little financial reward, it's no wonder that parents in those days didn't want their boys to grow up to be tour pros. Many pros joined the tour over the objections of their moms and dads.

Julius Boros didn't turn pro until he was twenty-nine years old, leaving behind a comfortable position at an accounting firm where where his boss let him off to play in amateur events. "You'll starve," his worried mother told him.

Doug Ford's mom felt the same way. "My father was a pro, and she saw how hard it was to make money at it during the Depression. She didn't want me to go through that," said Ford, who turned pro just short of age twenty-seven in 1949, the same year as Boros.

Cary Middlecoff's father was a dentist and country club member who at first wanted his son, who was also a dentist, to be another Bobby Jones and stay an amateur for life, though in the end he supported Cary's decision to turn pro. Jim Ferrier's father, the secretary of a golf club in Australia, also wanted his son to remain an amateur.

The players who came of age in the 1930s faced similar objections. Hogan's mother did not share Ben's enthusiasm for golf. George Fazio's immigrant parents knew nothing about the game. Bulla's Quaker parents were avowedly against their son even playing the game in the first place, let alone becoming a pro.

"They just thought it was wrong, frivolous," Bulla said later. "I'd tell my father I was going to the woods to meditate, and I'd go off to caddie."

If their loved ones had their doubts about them joining the tour caravan, the players themselves harbored doubts about staying on it. Nelson got out at age thirty-four after his sensational play of 1944–46 earned him enough money to buy a ranch and not have to put his nervous stomach through any more torment. He wasn't the only one.

Henry Picard was the best player in the game from 1935 to '39, but he halved his schedule after that. A slumping Sam Snead announced in 1947 that he would quit the tour next spring to work full-time at The Greenbrier Resort in West Virginia, playing only the majors. Of course, when he started playing better again, he left The Greenbrier and resumed a full schedule.

Oscar Fraley of UPI reported in the summer of 1947 that Hogan was on the verge of retiring, though he did not quote Hogan. It didn't happen, but at the end of the 1948 season, Hogan told journalist Bob Lee that he was "dead tired" and "if something good comes along, I'd like to quit golf for keeps."

Some players avoided burnout by pursuing other interests on the side. Fazio had a scrap metal business. Bulla, besides his own stint at piloting tour players, was the vice president of and second leading investor in Arizona Airways. Joe Kirkwood Jr. went back and forth between playing the tour and an acting career in which he played boxer Joe Palooka in movies and, later, on television.

The players who went at it full-time often complained of the grind. Just a week after his double win at Tam O'Shanter in 1948, Mangrum told a writer in St. Paul, the next tour stop, that he was sick and tired of tournament golf and just wanted to go fishing. "This golf day after day is enough to kill anybody," he said. "It's beginning to affect my concentration . . . It's wearin' me down." Mangrum played in 38 tournaments that year. (In 2009, the top ten players on the money list played in an average of 22 tournaments.)

Starting in 1947, Hogan took a week off now and then to try to remain fresh. In fact, when his car was smashed by a bus in 1949, he was heading back home to spend some time in Texas instead of going from Phoenix to Tucson for the next tournament.

In the immediate post-war era, players who cut their teeth during the Depression still formed the bulwark of the tour. Nearly all of them came from less than privileged backgrounds and had gotten into the game as caddies as a way to earn a bit of money either for themselves or to help the family. They had scraped by in the Depression, playing the tour with little money in their pockets or working at country clubs where they were second-class citizens. Just when they were in their primes, the tour stopped because of World War II and nearly all went into the service (albeit most of them not into combat.)

It was a hard life, and they were hard men. But things got better after the war. The tour began to expand and purses rose a bit, more because of a general post-war economic boom than a specific golf boom. And when golf returned to full swing, these men in their thirties found themselves pretty much unchallenged by any new guard. While they had lost a couple of their prime years to the war, development of young players had come to a standstill. There were Middlecoff, Johnny Palmer, Skip Alexander, and . . . well, that was about it, except for George Payton, who died tragically.

"We don't have any future Sarazens, Nelsons, and Hogans on the way up," said the tour's former promotion man, Fred Corcoran, in 1948. "Where they'll come from, nobody knows. Maybe it'll be necessary to take a tip from baseball—scout around for youngsters with talent, let our top pros instruct them in clinics, and then give them a solid start in competition. Nowadays, how many youngsters are going to walk 10 or 15 miles a day for a small caddie fee when they can get good folding money doing a softer job?"

He was right about the caddie yards drying up as a source of players. And there weren't any Hogans or Nelsons (though Middlecoff came reasonably close) until Arnold Palmer came along in the late 1950s. The charismatic Palmer arrived at the dawn of the television age, fueling a dramatic jump in prize money that in turn drew more youngsters to the game—future pros would come more from the ranks of country club kids and college golfers.

Some new blood did finally begin to come on the scene. Turning pro in 1949 or 1950 were Ford, Besselink, Boros, Skee Riegel, Dick Mayer, Jay Hebert, and Art Wall. Ford and Besselink both turned pro pretty much under pressure from the United States Golf Association, which was questioning their amateur credentials.

"I was making more money playing amateur golf in Westchester County than I made in prize money after I turned pro. There was a lot of action there," said Ford, perhaps the only tour pro ever to grow up in Manhattan, where his father ran an indoor golf school in the winter. "The USGA was investigating how I was making a living. When I qualified for the 1949 U.S. Open at Medinah, I just told [USGA official] Joe Dey to register me as a pro."

Besselink grew up in New Jersey but stayed in Florida after graduating from the University of Miami, and in the summer he moved north and registered himself as playing out of Tam O'Shanter Country Club near Chicago. Considering that club's reputation as a gambling hotbed, that was enough to raise eyebrows, and Besselink subsequently turned pro in the fall of 1949.

At that time, the PGA had a probationary period, which meant that after declaring yourself a pro you had to wait six months before you could collect any money from playing in tournaments. That was the downside to joining the tour. The upside was that there was no qualifying school. All you needed was to show up and register for tournaments, and you were on tour. That's how rough the life of a tour player was at the time. There weren't enough people desiring to play the tour to necessitate any kind of qualifying system.

According to newspaper reports, tournaments drew anywhere between 6,000 and 15,000 spectators for the final round—and those were probably overestimates. With the exception of Tam O'Shanter, there were no grandstands. The only parts of the course to be roped—if any—were the tees and the greens. The gallery was free to walk down the fairway with the players.

It could be distracting to have the gallery walking so close, and even carrying on conversations with the players.

"What throws a player off when he has a chance [to win] is for somebody to rush out of the gallery and ask the player if he remembers Cousin Joe from Grunting, Nebraska, and slap his back, telling him Cousin Joe said to 'get in there and pitch,'" Mangrum told writer Herb Graffis in 1948.

But when it wasn't crunch time, players usually didn't mind interacting with the gallery.

In a 2007 issue of *Golf World*, writer Dave Anderson recalled watching a tournament in the early 1950s as a college-age spectator when Mangrum made a hole-in-one.

"After his drive on the next hole, I walked off the tee with him," Anderson wrote. "'Great shot, Mr. Mangrum,' I said. 'How many holes-in-one have you had in your career?'

"I forget the number he told me—maybe seven or eight—but I was still talking to him walking up the fairway when, very cordially, he said, 'Excuse me, son. We're almost to my ball.'"

Tournaments were mostly sponsored and put together by local civic organizations, the idea in many cases being to get the name of the town mentioned in wire service stories across the country and thus boost tourism. Corporate sponsorship of tournaments was nearly unheard of, but Goodall, a clothing company, was ahead of the curve. It sponsored an event in New York first called the Goodall Round Robin and later the Palm Beach Round Robin (Palm Beach being one of the company's clothing lines).

There were enough fanatics deeply interested in the tour for Bob Harlow to launch *Golf World*, a weekly magazine, in 1947. Television hadn't yet developed to the point where it could deliver golf to the masses. Not many people had television sets, and national network broadcasts weren't technically possible until 1953. The 1947 U.S. Open was televised locally in St. Louis and the 1949 and 1950 Opens were broadcast in a number of cities in the East and Midwest. But most sports fans knew of Hogan and other pros only by reading about them, or by hearing radio coverage of the major tournaments, unless they lived in a city where the tour came to town.

The U.S. Open was the most coveted and highest profile championship in the middle of the century, but by the late 1940s the Masters was probably second. *Golf World* noted that the 1948 Masters drew 149 press representatives—96 newspaper reporters, 43 radio representatives, 11 still photographers, and five newsreel photographers. The record was believed to be 267 for the 1946 U.S. Open in Cleveland, but the Masters was a clear second in press coverage.

The PGA Championship had prestige, of course, but not quite the same coverage. The British Open was an interesting case. Very few Americans made the transatlantic trip—Bulla and amateur Frank Stranahan were the only ones to regularly do so in the late

1940s—so it wasn't a "major" for most guys on the tour. But whoever was the top American player was under some pressure from the golf media to play the British Open and prove himself in historic terms. Hogan received some criticism for not playing the British Open in 1948; eventually, he would make his only appearance in 1953, at Carnoustie in Scotland, and win.

So for most players, there were just three majors. Looking back at this era, some observers point to the Western Open as a fourth. But press accounts from the time don't support placing it quite at that level, the tournament's prestige probably having peaked in the teens and twenties. In 1950, when it was held on the West Coast at an inconvenient time for players to head out west, most of the top players didn't even play. If players are skipping an event, it can't be considered a major.

The tour was not without controversy in the late 1940s. Tournament manager Fred Corcoran was punched by player Dick Metz in 1947; two players, Henry Ransom and Norman Von Nida, had a physical altercation after a round in 1948, with Ransom throwing a punch and then being wrestled to the ground by Von Nida following a disagreement over whether Ransom whiffed a short putt or was merely waving his putter in frustration.

A sort of Wild West atmosphere prevailed. Running their own show, the pros decided to go against USGA rules in some cases. Whereas the rules of the game called for a 14-club limit, the PGA allowed players to have 16 clubs in their bags. For a while, players were allowed to clean the ball on the greens. Winter rules were invoked at even a hint of adverse conditions. There was talk that players were deepening the grooves on their irons to impart more backspin. Many of an older generation said that the low scores being posted were more the result of easy courses than the current golfers' skills. As 1948 dawned, British golf writer Henry Longhurst (later a television commentator in the United States) lamented that "golf in the United States has gone to seed."

The grooves issue was spotlighted at the 1947 U.S. Open. The PGA had done nothing to stop the practice of players altering their clubfaces, but the U.S. Open was (and is) run by the USGA. Before the start of the 1947 Open, the USGA posted a notice that "players in doubt about markings on iron clubs may consult the USGA committee."

While voluntary, the notice seemed ominous enough that most pros had their clubs checked, and many were declared illegal and sent to the pro shop to be ground into legality. At the Ryder Cup that same year, British captain Henry Cotton had the U.S. players' irons inspected before the event, and six players on the 10-man team were found to have illegal clubs.

The PGA began to crack down on irons in 1948, declaring that it would enforce USGA standards. It started to inspect clubs with a gauge to determine if the grooves were legal in terms of the depth and space between them.

In February, a dispute arose in New Orleanswhen some players felt that the irons of third-round leader Fred Haas should have been declared illegal. Demaret withdrew from the tournament in protest and Bobby Locke raised a fuss with tournament manager George Schneiter, who had measured Haas's clubs before the tournament and pronounced them legal. Locke measured them himself with the same gauge and came to a different conclusion.

The USGA inspected clubs again at the 1948 U.S. Open, this time with a more precise measuring device. Some players (Hogan included) were told they needed to grind down their clubs to make them legal, but championship chairman Richard S. Tufts laid the blame on manufacturers, stating that the clubs they produced did not meet USGA specifications and hadn't been altered by players.

Various controversies had caused some to call for the PGA to hire a "czar" to run its tournaments. Corcoran was no longer around, having been fired by the players at the end of 1947. The new tournament manager, Schneiter, played in the tournaments he was running. He was paid a fee, but it was doubtful that the PGA had the money that would have been required to bring in a powerful czar from the outside.

It frankly didn't seem a very likely moment for bringing things under control. But the grooves situation was being taken care of, and within a year the PGA would return to USGA standards with a 14-club limit and prohibiting the cleaning of balls on the greens. Against the odds, the PGA was getting its shop back in order.

4

HOGAN TRANSCENDENT/
BLAZIN' BEN

BEN HOGAN SERVED stateside during World War II in the Army Air Corps, starting in March 1943. He learned to fly, rose to the rank of lieutenant, and entered a program where he would train young pilots.

That duty never materialized, as by 1944 experienced combat veterans were ready to take over that task. Hogan was allowed to return from Tulsa, Oklahoma, to his Fort Worth home, still a member of the Air Corps but free to dress in civilian clothes and do pretty much as he pleased. Naturally, he chose to practice and play golf. While the tour had resumed, Hogan mostly stayed in Fort Worth during his inactive duty, heading out for only three tournaments in 1944 and two in 1945 before he was discharged in August of the latter year.

Shortly before his discharge, he played in the Tam O'Shanter Open, the richest tournament of 1945 by more than a factor of four. While Hogan had been practicing and biding his time, Byron Nelson (excused from military service because of a blood disorder) was in the process of tearing up the tour, and he made the Tam

O'Shanter his tenth straight victory in a phenomenal winning streak that would be stopped at 11.

The fields Nelson was beating were not as weak as might be supposed. Sam Snead got out of the service in November 1944 (he had entered it earlier than Hogan, enlisting in June 1942) and played 28 tournaments in 1945, though he missed five tournaments during Nelson's winning streak due to an injury. Others, except for Lloyd Mangrum, returned to the tour at various points during the year.

Even with Hogan out of the Army and Snead back from injury, Nelson won five times after mid-July to finish the year with 18 victories, a record which still stands to this day and will likely never be broken. The streak was so spectacular that the newspapers had taken to calling Nelson "Mr. Golf."

That didn't sit well with the intense, prideful Hogan. Winning the Portland Invitational with a tour record 261 score, Hogan saw Jimmy Demaret in the locker room and said, "Well, that's enough of that 'Mr. Golf' stuff."

Not exactly. Nelson came back two weeks later and broke Hogan's record with a 259 in Seattle. He also handed Hogan a painful defeat in the Glen Garden Invitational, played on the very course where young Byron had beaten young Ben in a caddie tournament. On a more encouraging note, Hogan notched five victories since returning to the tour, matching Nelson's total during that period.

The bad news for the rest of the tour was that only at the end of 1945 did Hogan feel like he was getting back into his accustomed tournament mode after a couple of years away from the action. Of those first six months back, he said a couple of years later, "I couldn't concentrate. I was always thinking of something other than my next shot."

Hogan was fully locked in the next year, producing one of the greatest campaigns in the history of the tour. He won 13 times in

1946, a number that ranks second in tour history to Nelson's 18 the year before. What's more, Hogan finished second seven times, giving him 20 top-two finishes in 32 starts. In November, *Time* proclaimed that he had become the new "Mr. Golf."

The old Mr. Golf, Nelson, retired in the summer of 1946 to a ranch he bought near Fort Worth. Hogan didn't force him there, but the pressures of competition did.

Tommy Armour, the 1927 U.S. Open champion and still sometime competitor on tour, couldn't picture Hogan opting for the easy life. "He'll never quit until they carry him out," Armour said. "They may be able to beat this boy in the muscle, but not in the mind."

Yet 1946 did include a couple of notable disappointments, as Hogan threw away chances to win the Masters and U.S. Open in identical fashion. Ben had a chance to win both tournaments on their 72nd holes if he could sink birdie putts from 12 feet (Masters) and 18 feet (U.S. Open). Not only did he miss the birdies, he ended up three-putting both times, missing comeback putts described in various accounts as between two and four feet, depriving him of chances for a playoff.

What's worse, to this point in his career, Hogan, at the age of thirty-three, *still* hadn't won a major, since the USGA didn't count the 1942 Hale American Open as a real U.S. Open. Shades of Sam Snead, but even he had been able to win a PGA Championship (in 1942).

The PGA would be Hogan's last chance in 1946. Due to the slow start to his career, and the war, he had only played in the event four times, never advancing past the quarterfinals. This time, he whipped Demaret, ten and eight, in a scheduled 36-hole semifinal, the second most lopsided margin in the history of the championship. When reporters asked Demaret what the turning point was, he replied, "Ten o'clock this morning, when the match started."

On the other side of the bracket, Ed "Porky" Oliver defeated Nelson in the quarterfinals on his way to the final. That might have been a break for Hogan, who had lost to Nelson in playoffs at the 1927 Glen Garden caddie tournament, 1940 Texas Open, and 1942 Masters, and in the quarterfinals of the 1941 PGA. Or it might have been a lost opportunity to finally beat his old rival head-to-head. In any case, Hogan claimed his first major with a comfortable six-and-four victory over Oliver.

His fellow competitors were impressed. And perhaps a bit discouraged.

Said one late in 1946, "With Hogan, the age of golfing man ended, the age of golfing machine began."

There were a few bugs in the machine in 1947, however. Hogan's troubles in majors continued; in fact, he lost in the first round of the PGA and didn't seriously contend at the other two majors. He won "only" seven tournaments, and two of those were team events. Hogan was plagued by shoulder and back aches and slid to third on the money list, which was led by Demaret. The best player in the game was suddenly not Hogan, but South African sensation Bobby Locke, who came to America for the first time and won six of the fourteen events he entered.

Rather than explicitly denying a midyear report that he planned to retire, Hogan gave indefinite answers like, "You'll know when I know."

Hogan's outlook changed drastically for the better late in 1947 when he found "the secret" that finally rid him of his hook for good.

When Hogan revealed the secret in a *Life* magazine cover story in 1955, he placed its discovery in 1946. This was a case of faulty memory.

For one thing, that article reported he was at a point of desperation before his discovery, but in 1946 Hogan was winning nearly every other tournament he played and never had anything close to a poor stretch. Also, he said that after divining the secret, he went out and won at Tam O'Shanter. Hogan didn't win at Tam O'Shanter in 1946.

He did win at Tam O'Shanter in September 1947, taking the World Championship of Golf at the end of a frustrating season. Moreover, he took two weeks off before that World Championship, which fits in with what he said in *Life* about going home to Fort Worth to figure things out.

After the World Championship, Hogan, presumably working on solidifying the changes, played only in the Ryder Cup in the last three months of the year. He headed out for the tour in 1948 with his confidence sky high. *Golf World* reported from the Phoenix Open that Hogan "backed up his boast that he had made a startling discovery about the golf swing. He hit the ball straighter and longer than he has for some time here."

When Hogan's book *Power Golf* came out in April 1948, *Golf World* noted that "a few months ago Hogan remarked that he had discovered something so sensational about the swing that he refused to divulge it to anyone, not even his wife." A *Time* cover story in January 1949 also places the discovery in 1947.

Power Golf didn't say anything about the secret; Hogan considered it so valuable that he didn't want to give it away to his competition.

What was the secret? According to the *Life* article, which came out when Hogan said he was close to retiring from competition, it was pronation of the wrists (rolling them to the right on the backswing), combined with two other moves, all three of which contributed to having an open clubface at the top of the backswing. From this position, Hogan said, no matter how hard he swung or how much wrist action he used on the downswing, he could not hook the ball, but instead produced a power fade. (He could still work the ball from right to left, when required, by not using the secret.)

To this day, some people consider this a lot of hooey. They either think the secret was something other than what he told *Life* (golf periodicals and books are full of claims by various people that Hogan told them the real secret) or that there was no real secret and Hogan was just being mysterious or playing a psychological game with his competitors—and cashing in on it by getting a large fee to write the article, to boot.

Hogan might have been trying to give *Life* its money's worth, for he clearly was overdramatizing in the article when he wrote that before figuring out the secret, "I was having trouble getting the ball in the air. I had a low, ducking, agonizing hook, the kind you hang your coat on." That sounds like Hogan in the early 1930s when he couldn't make it on tour, not the player in the midst of a year when he won seven tournaments. Still, Hogan was clearly bothered by the fact that, despite the adjustment he had made with Picard years before on his grip, the hook kept turning up like a bad penny, especially when he was tired at the end of a tournament.

Also, he wanted to find a way to stop hooking without losing distance. He said that conventional cures such as weakening his grip or opening his stance "all worked, but in the process they cut down my distance from five to 10 yards. Five yards is a long way. You can't give anybody five yards. You can't cure a fault with a fault."

Hogan said he went three days without picking up a club—which must have been torture for him—and then found the answer while lying awake one night. After not being able to sleep for the rest of the night, he rushed to the range and found that the adjustments worked right away. After pounding balls for a week, he found that it worked under pressure in a tournament, too, as he won at Tam O'Shanter.

Whether it was the absolute truth, an exaggeration, or mere hogwash, *that's* a secret Hogan took to the grave.

In any case, Hogan was a changed man in 1948. The self-doubt that had crept in during the previous year was gone and Hogan was on the offensive, his game better than ever and his troublesome hook finally overcome. (We should not, though, fall into the trap of painting Hogan as a suddenly superhuman golfing machine who hit every shot exactly where he wanted and never hit another hook in his life. As we will see, he hit a drive out of bounds to the left during the 1950 U.S. Open. It can't be said that Hogan took the left side of the course entirely out of play.)

Not that 1948 started out like it would be better than 1947. Hogan won the season-opening Los Angeles Open, but then went eleven straight events without a victory. He was hitting the ball well, but his putting was letting him down. It began to appear as if his body was letting him down, too.

Hogan withdrew after he and Demaret won their first-round match at the Miami Four-Ball Invitational, where it was reported that Hogan had "more trouble with his physical condition" and "could not go on." Incidentally, this was the only team event that Hogan and Demaret did not win in 1946–48. Other than this withdrawal, they went five-for-five at the Inverness and Miami Four-Balls in those years.

Golf World reported that Hogan didn't play the next week in Jacksonville, Florida, reportedly suffering from "the miseries" in his back. He also skipped Greensboro and Charlotte in North Carolina before returning for the Masters, where he finished sixth.

In three events leading into the PGA Championship in May, Hogan finished third, second, and third. He was getting closer. What followed was nothing short of one the greatest stretches of sustained excellence in the history of the game. Over the remainder of 1948, Hogan entered 12 tournaments and won nine of them.

It began in the PGA, held at Norwood Hills outside St. Louis, where Hogan started relatively slowly, squeaking through in some close matches. Then he defeated Demaret two and one in a semifinal shootout and ended up overwhelming Mike Turnesa seven and six in the final.

Following a second-place finish at Colonial, Hogan prevailed over Demaret at the U.S. Open at Riviera to finally earn that title. It was the first of six straight victories, the third best winning streak all-time after Nelson's 11 in 1945 and Tiger Woods's seven in 2006–07.

Victories followed at Inverness (with Demaret), Motor City, Reading, the Western Open, and Denver. There were also six tournaments along the way Hogan didn't enter, as he chose to pick his spots and rest his body—and shoot a film short in Los Angeles after the U.S. Open and do some exhibitions.

The Western Open was noteworthy in the press for making a "terrific triangle" with the U.S. Open and PGA titles. The Denver Open was noteworthy in the press for less pleasant reasons—Hogan skipped out on the awards ceremony.

He later explained that he left the course to catch a train for the tour's next stop, Salt Lake City, thinking that Fred Haas had the tournament wrapped up. When he got to his hotel, his wife, Valerie, told him that she heard on the radio that Haas stumbled at the end, giving Hogan the victory. Hogan called the course and apologized to a tournament official for not being there, but the message was never relayed to the assembled media.

The Denver papers and the wire services all ripped Hogan. Those writers didn't know Hogan's explanation, but frankly, even if they did, the criticism was warranted. Hogan's excuse was a pretty weak one. And the *Rocky Mountain News* pointed to more examples of Hogan's uncooperativeness, stating he flatly refused to appear in a Wednesday clinic, refused a radio interview, refused a request from photographers for a posed shot with a willing Haas and Cary Middlecoff after an earlier round, and told a seven-year-old boy asking for an autograph to "go away."

Hogan might have found the secret to the golf swing, but the secret to public relations eluded him. Perhaps bothered by the bad press (or the press itself), Hogan finished ninth in Utah. He then wrapped up his extraordinary campaign with a win at Reno, a playoff loss at Portland, and a win in California at Glendale.

His final tally for 1948 listed 10 victories in 24 tournaments, with a scoring average of 69.3. The winning percentage (41.7) surpassed his rate when he won thirteen times in 32 events in 1946. From 1946 through 1948, Hogan won 30 tournaments. If you throw in the five events he won after getting out of the Army in 1945, it adds up to a remarkable 35 wins in three-and-a-half years. Some perspective: Tom Watson and Gene Sarazen, two of the greats of the game, each won 39 events in their entire careers on the tour.

The world noticed Hogan's dominance, and not just the golf world. The January 10, 1949, issue of *Time* featured Hogan on the cover, with a lengthy story dropped in among the important international and national news.

The *Time* article, largely researched by future Pulitzer Prize-winning *Los Angeles Times* sports columnist Jim Murray, portrayed Hogan as a sort of super golfer who left his foes demoralized. In it, a player identified as "a frank Chicago pro" was quoted saying, "It's no fun to play with Hogan. He's so good and so mechanically perfect that he seems inhuman. You get kind of uneasy and start to flub your shots."

The article calls Hogan "the fiercest competitor in the game," one who prevails because of the soundness of his swing, the meticulousness of his planning, and the intensity of his concentration. And the key to all of it was Hogan's rule: "If you can't outplay them, outwork them."

Back in 1942, famed sports writer Grantland Rice looked at what made Hogan tick in a *Collier's* magazine article titled "Ice Heart."

"Hogan came up the hard way and he is on the hard side. He is about as soft as a hydrant," Rice wrote.

"I thought I was a tough competitor," Sarazen was quoted as saying after teaming with Hogan to win a four-ball tournament. "I'm just a violet compared to Hogan."

On the importance of the mental side of the game, Hogan told Rice, "In golf, mind must be superior to matter, no matter what happens. Having worked hard to get a golf swing, golf to me means an iron grip on my mental and nerve side, in the thought that I can't afford to play even one careless, slipshod stroke."

Indeed, Hogan tried not to play any careless strokes on the *practice range*, let alone the golf course.

Nobody questioned that practice was the key to Hogan's success. Asked how he developed his game, he once responded, "I dug it out of the ground," and that's about right.

Hogan has (at least) a couple of other famous quotes about practice:

"There isn't enough daylight in any day to practice all the shots you need to."

"Every day you miss practicing, it takes one day longer to be good."

Hogan told Ken Venturi in a 1983 television interview, "My swing wasn't the best in the world and I knew it wasn't and I thought, well, the only way I can win is to outwork these fellows. So, they might work two hours a day and I might work eight. Then, after I won a couple of tournaments, I noticed these fellows were practicing longer."

Doug Ford, then a teenager with connections in the New York area thanks to his golf pro father, used to watch Hogan hit balls at Century Country Club when Ben was the assistant pro in the late 1930s. "He would hit balls all day," Ford recalled. "I asked a caddie, 'Does he ever stop?' He said, 'Only to get a Hershey bar and a Coke.'"

Hogan didn't neglect the short game in his practice, though he probably would have liked to. He was never fond of putting, once telling an interviewer that golf and putting were two separate games. It was clear which he preferred. Late in his career, in the mid-1950s, he was a terrible putter, one who was so fearful on short putts that he could hardly bring the putter back. That's the image that has survived of Hogan's putting. But, in fact, he was a very good putter throughout the 1940s. He couldn't have won so many tournaments otherwise.

Hogan wasn't so good on the greens when he joined the tour, and his improvement in that area, where a natural touch is generally so important, astounded Demaret.

"Most good putters are born that way, not made. But Ben made himself into a great putter," Demaret said. "To me, that will always be one of the most amazing parts of his success. He tried everything. Tapping the ball, stroking the ball, sending it on its way with a prayer, I guess. And then suddenly, the touch came to him. He was off and running."

It was the same kind of trial-and-error process with his golf swing.

"There's no such thing as a natural golf swing," Hogan told *Time*.

After spending countless hours finding something that worked, Hogan did not rest. Instead, what came next would be countless more hours on the range, grooving the swing so that it would work under pressure.

"The swing must be committed to muscle memory so it's secondary," Hogan told *Sports Illustrated*'s Joan Flynn Dreyspool in 1955. "I've practiced hard enough . . . so in a tournament my swing will remain just as good as it was on the practice tee."

The importance of a repeating swing has become axiomatic at the highest levels of golf, but Hogan was the first to talk about it.

While to some this might seem a life of drudgery, it wasn't for Hogan. "The truth is, I was enjoying myself," Hogan said in a *Golf* magazine interview in 1987. "I couldn't wait to get up in the morning so I could hit balls . . . When I'm hitting the ball where

I want, hard and crisply—when anyone is—it's a joy that very few people experience."

Armed with a reliable swing, Hogan's other weapons when he arrived at a tournament were preparation, determination, and concentration.

Hogan was also a trailblazer in course management, spending his time in practice rounds plotting the best way around the course. A caddie at Riviera, where Hogan had so much success in the Los Angeles Open and 1948 U.S. Open, said that Hogan would sometimes take three hours for nine practice holes.

It was all part of getting the most out of his ability. "I call Ben's unceasing struggle for perfection his 'inside game,'" Demaret wrote in the book *My Partner, Ben Hogan.* "Other professional golfers just can't equal it. We're all serious about golf, make no mistake about that, but Ben has a single-mindedness of purpose that makes the rest of us look like carefree schoolboys."

That single-mindedness didn't allow for idle chitchat either with his fellow competitors or galleries during a tournament round. Or smiling, for that matter.

"As I walk down the first fairway, I try to get all my thinking within me and obliterate every outside influence, the people, everything, even the fellow I'm playing with . . . I can't remember ever knowing what my playing partner has shot on the round," Hogan told Dreyspool.

Hogan walked the fairways with an icy stare that may have intimidated some of his foes. It was part of what came to be called the Hogan Mystique. Everyone wanted to win, of course. But no one wanted to win quite as much as Hogan did. And no one else had figured out how to make it happen the way Hogan had.

This might have been the one thing that Hogan *was* a natural at. He was small in stature, and he didn't have the grace of a natural athlete. But he had the ingrained qualities of a battler and a winner. If Hogan had been introduced to formal boxing at a young age, it's easy to imagine him becoming a bantamweight champion. Instead, he became "Bantam Ben," a determined little man who brought a boxer's mentality to the links.

Hogan was tagged with many nicknames. The most common in newspaper articles during his prime were "Blazin' Ben" and "Beltin' Ben," for obvious alliterative reasons. Other nicknames were born out of his size, his personality, or both.

Time called him "Little Ice Water." There were also the "Mighty Atom," the "Mighty Mite," and even the "Frigid Midget." When he played in the British Open in 1953, the Scots called him the "Wee Ice Mon." The nickname that seems to have worn best to the present day is the "Hawk," which Demaret coined, but it does not appear that he was ever referred to that way in the media in the time up to 1950.

The nicknames reflect that Hogan was anything but a warm and fuzzy person. His relationship with the press was rocky. His relationship with his fellow players was aloof. His relationship with the fans was distant, and from their end involved admiration—even awe—more than warmth.

Hogan certainly could be brusque. A writer asking what Hogan thought was a dumb question would receive little more than a stare. Doug Ford once asked him a question on the driving range, and Hogan said, "I don't talk when I'm practicing."

When Dreypool was researching her story on Hogan, a fellow player asked if Ben and Valerie would like to come over for dinner one night. "No," was all Hogan said (though at least he said it with a smile). He explained to the writer, but only after the player left, "I don't go out to dinner anymore unless the people are very close friends. Otherwise I find although there's supposed to be another couple there, about twenty people show up and I spend the whole evening answering questions."

Perhaps that gets to the heart of Hogan's "aloofness." Those close to him say that he was more shy than cold.

Dan Jenkins, who grew up in Fort Worth and covered Hogan for the *Fort Worth Press* and later for *Sports Illustrated*, was one of the few writers—and one of the few people—to get to know Hogan well. "Ben's image around me, or his close friends at Colonial and Shady Oaks [Hogan's home club in his later years], was quite different from the legend," Jenkins said in 2009. "He was mostly a shy man and had a closet sense of humor. During his whole career, he sought out tour friends that had 'personality'—Demaret, Snead, [Tommy] Bolt, Jackie Burke—because he felt that he didn't. He thought he could only talk with his golf clubs."

His circle of friends was very small, though, and arguably didn't include any of his fellow tour players. Even his frequent four-ball partner Demaret said, "Nobody gets close to Ben Hogan."

If his own generation of players was somewhat intimidated by him, the younger generation who came up while Hogan was established was in awe of him. Bob Toski, who joined the tour in 1949, said he was fascinated with Hogan, and used to watch him practice.

"I probably watched him practice a dozen times for about an hour, and he never said a word to me," Toski recalled in 2009. "One time my white shoes must have gotten a little too close, and he just waved his hand. Later, in the locker room, he looked at me and said, 'You were out there a long time today. Did you learn anything?'

"I said, 'Every time I watch you hit a golf ball, I learn something.'

"He said, 'Good.' And that was it. He walked out."

Hogan probably had only one real confidante, and that was Valerie. That was all he needed. She was the one who believed in him when no one else did. She was the one he had always wanted to travel with rather than spending time with the boys on the road. They formed a team in those early days that carried through Hogan's entire career.

In the fall of 1948, Ben and Valerie bought a new house in Fort Worth. Ben was quoted in *Time* saying, "Anyone who doesn't live in California is a victim of circumstances." But as much as Ben loved that state, Valerie preferred to stay near their roots. Besides, Fort Worth provided a better base for heading out to the tour in various parts of the country.

During the year, he had made some cryptic comments about his future, such as saying after winning at Inverness that he wouldn't be back next year. He also said that he wouldn't defend his PGA title; the grind of 36-hole matches was just too much. "I want to die an old man, not a young man," he said.

But that was just tiredness talking. In October, he intimated that he would play the PGA Championship in the future. And in November, according to biographer James Dodson, the thirty-six-year-old Hogan told friends that he fully expected to go on playing and winning until he was fifty.

He wouldn't play every tournament; he would continue to take some time off to rest as he had done in 1947 and '48.

The reason for the reduced schedule, Hogan told *Time* in January, "isn't the golf, it's the traveling. I want to die an old man, not a young man."

It was the same thought he expressed at the PGA Championship, in a different context—a thought that was more true than he realized.

5

THE CRASH

RIVIERA COUNTRY CLUB came to be known as "Hogan's Alley" after Ben Hogan won the 1947 and '48 Los Angeles Opens and 1948 U.S. Open there, so it was surprising when he finished 11th in the Los Angeles Open to open the 1949 season.

That was just a temporary blip, though. Hogan won the next two tournaments, the Bing Crosby Pro-Am and Long Beach Open, the latter in a playoff over Jimmy Demaret, giving him 11 victories in 15 starts. The next week, at the Phoenix Open, Hogan birdied the 72nd hole to tie Demaret, just as he had done at Long Beach, but this time Jimmy turned the tables and won the playoff.

Both playoffs were at 18 holes on Monday. The Phoenix playoff delayed the Hogans' trip back home to Fort Worth by a day; Ben was skipping the Tucson Open in order to rest a bit and spend some time with Valerie in their new home, which wasn't even completely furnished yet.

It was a trip of 1,040 miles, which meant two long days of driving. Just past the midpoint, and 120 miles southeast of El Paso, was the small town of Van Horn, the only outpost of civilization in a desolate region of west Texas. The Hogans stayed at a favorite stop in that town, the El Capitan Hotel. The room cost $4.50 for the night.

The Hogans pulled onto U.S. Highway 80 at around 8 a.m. on February 2. Today, the Van Horn-to-Fort Worth trip is a smooth one on I-10 and I-20, but in 1950 it was made on two-lane Highway 80, rolling through a stark, arid landscape. Upon leaving Van Horn, there were just a few isolated ranches along the way until the small village of Kent 37 miles to the east.

About 10 miles short of Kent, Hogan pulled onto the shoulder and stopped his Cadillac because he thought it might have a flat tire. It didn't, but he noticed some ice on the road (the elevation in this part of Texas, at the southern end of the Rockies, is over 4,000 feet). There was also ground fog, very thick in some places, on an otherwise sunny day. Because of these two factors, Hogan slowed to about 25 mph.

Coming the other direction was a Greyhound bus on the Pecos–El Paso run, driven by a substitute driver named Alvin Logan. In Kent, Logan stopped the bus to deliver a bundle of newspapers to a service station. As he did so, a truck passed on the highway. The part of Highway 80 just ahead was full of blind curves, rises, and dips as it made its way through the foothills of the Apache Mountains. The truck was moving slowly, and after following it for about six miles, Logan was getting antsy.

Already behind schedule, he was afraid of being reprimanded for a late arrival. There was no good place to pass on this stretch even with good visibility, let alone in the fog, but Logan decided to try it anyway. He pulled out into the oncoming lane and gunned his engine. Hidden from Logan by either a dip in the highway or the fog was Hogan's Cadillac.

As Hogan proceeded carefully, he and Valerie suddenly saw four headlights coming at them. Ben's first thought was to swerve off the road, but at just that moment they reached a culvert across a dry wash, with a concrete barrier to the right. There was no place to go.

In a split second, Hogan made a decision that probably saved both his and Valerie's lives. He let go of the steering wheel and dived to his right to protect his wife.

He had been able to steer just enough to his right, and Logan had jerked the bus just enough to his right, that the Greyhound did not plow into the entire front end of Hogan's car. Instead, it caught only the driver's side head-on, sending the steering column into the seat in which Hogan had been sitting only a split-second before. Even the Cadillac's engine ended up in the passenger compartment.

Ben's protective dive kept Valerie from being propelled directly into the dashboard; instead, his upper body took the brunt of that blow while his legs were vulnerable to the destruction on the driver's side.

According to an interview with the Hogans conducted a month later, Ben lost consciousness after the crash, while Valerie was dazed. "The force of the crash left us both hemmed in with our chests against the dashboard," she said. "Somehow, I finally managed to get the door open, squeeze out, and raise Ben to a sitting position. He had come to then, and was moaning."

A driver in a car that came along behind them helped get Hogan out of the wrecked car. There were plenty of people on the scene, including all of the bus passengers (fortunately, none were seriously hurt, nor were Logan or the driver of the truck, which made it off the culvert before jackknifing) and a few cars that came along from each direction. But the closest phone was miles away, and no one took the initiative right away to find one and call for an ambulance. When one finally was called, it had to come nearly 30 miles from Van Horn.

During the 90 minutes between the crash and the arrival of the ambulance, Hogan drifted in and out of consciousness. Meanwhile, an angry Valerie confronted the bus driver.

59

"You coward," she later remembered saying. "Why don't you go over and see what you've done to my husband?"

"Oh, lady," he said.

"Don't 'Oh, lady' me," responded Valerie. "You go look at my husband because you may have killed him."

Logan turned and walked away.

Before the ambulance left, Valerie insisted that an attending police officer get Hogan's golf clubs from the car so they could be brought on the ambulance. Ben had been asking about them.

In his condition, Hogan needed to be brought to a well-equipped major hospital. That meant a 150-mile ride to the Hotel Dieu (French for "Inn of God") hospital in El Paso, after a quick stop for X-rays at a clinic in Van Horn. Hogan finally arrived at the hospital at 1:45 p.m., more than five hours after the accident.

Hogan was fortunate he didn't have more internal injuries, or he never would have survived the long wait. The damage to his body was mostly broken bones: a fractured pelvis, a broken collarbone, and a broken ankle which was not discovered until two days later. He also suffered a deep gash near his left eye and contusions in his left leg. Valerie emerged with only bruises and a black eye.

The first wire report that went out after the accident claimed Hogan had died in the crash. This might have arisen from eyewitness accounts of people who had seen the mangled car, and couldn't imagine how the driver had survived. That report was quickly corrected, and by evening there was much better news.

"The damage isn't as bad as we first thought," said Ben's brother, Royal, on the evening of the crash. "I think Ben's going to be all right."

Pros Dutch Harrison and Herman Keiser were driving together to San Antonio, skipping the Tucson event for an early arrival at the site of the following week's Texas Open, when they drove past the scene of the accident a few hours after it happened and saw the wrecked car, recognizing it as Hogan's. Those two noted hustlers might have had some pigeons lined up in San Antonio, but they turned around to get news on what had happened, and proceeded to El Paso when they found out where Hogan had been taken.

They got in to see him the next day. Keiser later said that his first thought on seeing Hogan was, "He's not going to make it." But he began to feel better about it when Hogan signaled him to come closer and said, "Herman, would you check on my clubs?"

Best wishes poured into Hotel Dieu from all across the country, including many phone calls from Hogan's fellow pros and his Hollywood friends Bing Crosby and Bob Hope. When the Tucson Open ended and the tour headed for Texas, dozens of pros stopped by the hospital. The mailroom was nearly overwhelmed as thousands of cards, letters, and telegrams arrived from people that Hogan didn't even know.

Many had been moved not only by the fact that Hogan was so badly injured, but also by the wire stories that told how Ben had acted to save his wife. The golfing robot who mowed down foes with machinelike efficiency and without a trace of emotion was revealed to be human after all.

"I never realized how swell the American people can be," he told Demaret when Jimmy visited him in the hospital.

"He never got over the letters and wires from people he'd never met, people he probably never would meet," Demaret wrote in *My Partner, Ben Hogan,* published in 1954. "The country's honest concern for his welfare, off the golf course as well as on it, changed his entire outlook. You can see it in Hogan today. Instead of the tight-lipped man who so closely resembled an old-time Wild West frontier sheriff, Ben is a more relaxed and outward-going fellow."

Hogan was in bed with one cast from his chest to his knees, and another on his ankle. But he was making good progress, and there was little question he would be able to play golf again, though still considerable doubt as to whether he would be able to return to the championship level he displayed in 1948.

The doctors were cautiously optimistic. "We all feel that Mr. Hogan will be back playing golf, probably among the greats of golf," wrote Dr. David M. Cameron in a letter to a concerned fan. "However, I anticipate it will be very late summer or early fall before he will be in his stride again."

Hogan was told on February 16, two weeks after the accident, that he could go home the next day. Doctors reversed themselves hours later, when they found that his left leg had swollen due to a blood clot. The massive contusions suffered in the accident were taking a delayed toll, and Hogan would require careful observation.

The concern was that a large clot could move from his leg to a lung, where a blockage would be fatal. Doctors began to consider the possibility of an operation to tie off the vena cava, the large vein that returns blood from the legs to the lungs and heart. It was then a rarely performed procedure, considered risky, and its long-term effects were little known, so it would be resorted to only if the situation became dire.

There were not many surgeons who performed the procedure, and there was no one in El Paso who could do it. The doctors determined that Dr. Alton Ochsner of New Orleans was the best in the country, and the man to be summoned if necessary.

Hogan was administered blood thinners with the hope that they would prevent further clots. But on February 27, a small clot was found near his right lung. Doctors were concerned, calling his condition "moderately serious," but Hogan was feeling well enough that on March 1, reporters were granted their first, brief, interview with Hogan, who asked them to thank everyone for their kindness and interest in his welfare.

Things then suddenly took a drastic turn for the worse. Another clot formed in his leg, causing Hogan intense pain. There was concern that this clot, or maybe the next one, would move to a lung and be large enough to kill him. On the evening of March

2, an urgent call went out to Dr. Ochsner. But he couldn't get a flight out of New Orleans. Some accounts say that it was due to a storm, but Valerie later wrote that it was because of Mardi Gras. The celebration indeed wrapped up on March 1 that year, which might have led to all flights being booked.

Desperate, with Ben in critical condition, either Royal or Valerie (accounts differ) decided to call Brigadier General David Hutchinson of El Paso's Biggs Air Force Base, who earlier had visited Ben in the hospital. Hutchinson arranged for a B-29 to fly from El Paso to New Orleans to pick up Dr. Ochsner to perform surgery on the former Army Air Corps lieutenant.

The next day at around noon, the surgeon arrived at the hospital with a police escort. However, he had been up all night waiting for the plane, and told Valerie, "I just can't operate on your husband now. Let me take a little nap."

Ochsner also had a word with Ben, explaining the surgery to him. "Will I be able to play golf again?" Hogan asked. "I think you will," the doctor replied, and Ben gave the go-ahead.

The operation was set for 6:30 that evening. Meanwhile, the cast was removed from Hogan's mid-section ahead of schedule so that the surgeon could cut through the abdomen and tie off the vena cava.

It was a delicate operation that took two hours to perform. With Hogan's weakened condition, success was anything but a sure thing. Valerie retired to the hospital's chapel to await the outcome.

Ochsner emerged smiling, telling Valerie, and then the waiting press, that the operation was "very successful." Any danger to Hogan's life was "completely removed," said the doctor. The clot that had caused the severe turn in Hogan's condition had apparently broken up, and was no longer a threat, he said. His job finished, Ochsner returned to New Orleans that very evening.

Hogan had survived two brushes with death. But while his life was spared, the prognosis for returning to championship golf had taken a turn for the worse with this latest crisis. With the largest vein, the vena cava, permanently closed off, blood now had to pass through smaller veins to get back to the upper part of the body from the legs. Those veins would dilate enough to do the job, but not to do it as well as the vena cava. Hogan faced a lifetime of poor blood circulation in his legs. At best, that would mean pain and swelling if he did a lot of walking—like playing a round of golf. At worst, he would have difficulty walking at all.

According to biographer James Dodson, Hogan's El Paso doctors were more pessimistic than Ochsner, privately telling Valerie that Ben would be lucky to walk unassisted, let alone play tournament golf again.

It would take months to recover from the operation, and Hogan would not be able to get onto his feet for a while. In the meanwhile, he asked Valerie to buy a couple of rubber balls so he could start exercising his fingers and hands.

On March 14, Hogan got out of the hospital bed for the first time since the accident nearly a month and a half before. He was lifted into a wheelchair to spend 30 minutes sitting in the afternoon sun. Valerie told a reporter she was "overjoyed" with the improvement Ben had shown, and that his spirits were "excellent."

That was the assessment of someone who had seen the worst, but the picture looked different to outsiders getting their first look at Hogan. In late March, Charles Bartlett of the *Chicago Tribune* and Herb Graffis of *Golfdom* magazine visited Hogan and painted a less optimistic picture.

"I left the hospital sick at heart, head, and stomach, but hoping for a miracle," Graffis later wrote.

Bartlett, in the March 29 *Tribune,* described Hogan as "a wan, weary little man who has now spent nearly two months beating death, the roughest player of them all . . . Hogan was always on the lean side, but his gaunt appearance now, after six blood transfusions, a major surgery, and nearly eight weeks of confinement make it difficult to recognize the Hogan of the businesslike walk, the keen eyes, the crisp tongue."

Hogan had lost about 20 pounds from his 135-pound frame and was just beginning to gain some of it back. Doctors considered it an encouraging sign when he started complaining about the hospital food, which indicated that he was getting back to normal. (The finicky Hogan was notorious for sending food back to the kitchen at restaurants.) Fortunately, a local eatery was found that fixed flapjacks just the way Ben liked them for breakfast.

But Bartlett also saw positive signs. "Mention golf, and his eyes light up, his voice, noticeably weak, takes on a new tenor. And don't worry about the Hogan handshake, still given with one of the strongest sets of mitts in golf."

Until now, Royal and Valerie Hogan had requested that reporters not ask Ben about his golfing future. Bartlett, given more time with Hogan, dared to pop the question: "Will you play golf again? Not when, Ben, but will you play?"

Hogan's reply contained equal amounts of resignation, frustration, and determination.

"I'm going to try," Hogan said. "It's going to be a long haul, and in my mind, I don't think that I'll ever get back to the playing edge I had last year. You work for perfection all your life, and then something like this happens. My nervous system has been shot by this, and I don't see how I can readjust to competitive golf. But you can bet I'll be back there swinging."

Valerie was more optimistic.

"Don't believe a word of it," she said. "It's going to take time, lots of it, but I am sure Ben will be himself again, bones, nerves, and all. He has shown me more will power through this terrible spell than he ever did on a golf course."

Bartlett visited Hogan for three straight days. On the second day, he wrote a recap of the accident and Hogan's recovery; on the third, he reported on Hogan's impending departure from the hospital. Ben had gotten back on his feet a little bit, using a walker. He showed Bartlett two large cartons filled with letters, wires, and gifts he had received, and expressed his gratitude.

"So, you're going, eh?" Hogan said to Bartlett. "Well, let's get this straight. There's only one thing on my mind now. That's to get well. Don't go writing that I'll be back playing soon. Sure, I'm going to try to play again, but who knows when? My circulation never was really good, and this hasn't helped it. From now on, if and when I play, it will be in warm, dry weather only. Say hello and thanks to all those folks in Chicago."

Bartlett had a sudden thought.

"Hey, I just remembered," he said. "Byron Nelson once told me that you and Jack Grout once drove to your first National Open in 1934, when it was held at Merion in Philadelphia. Guess where the 1950 Open will be? Merion! So long, Champ, I'll see you at Merion!"

The Open was fourteen months away. Enough time for a comeback—if there was going to be one.

6

1949 MASTERS/SLAMMIN' SAM

WITH BEN HOGAN on the sidelines, the tour found itself without its dominant player and main attraction. Who would fill the void?

A couple of candidates emerged during the winter tour. Lloyd Mangrum, second to Hogan on the official money list in 1948, won in Los Angeles and Tucson and led the tour in earnings through March 1949. The other hot player was Cary Middlecoff, who won the Rio Grande Valley and Jacksonville Opens and teamed with Jim Ferrier to take the Miami Four-Ball, all in a five-week span starting in late February.

Middlecoff had won twice during his first full campaign in 1948, and careful observers of the golf scene watched with interest as the former dentist began to come into his own as a pro. But neither he nor Mangrum had the force of personality or name recognition to draw in casual fans or to garner above-the-fold headlines in the papers.

The most colorful of the top players—literally and figuratively—was Jimmy Demaret. He won three times in 1948, but was a runner-up on six occasions that year. With his wisecracking demeanor and garish outfits, he was a gallery favorite. But, as a player, he seemed destined to hover in the lead pack without ever clawing his way to the top.

South Africa's Bobby Locke created a sensation when he won six tournaments in a half season of play in 1947. But his 1948 record wasn't as impressive, and he only planned to play a couple of months in the United States in 1949. He wouldn't be the man to make the fans forget Hogan.

For years, the triumvirate of Hogan, Byron Nelson, and Sam Snead had carried the freight for the PGA tour. In the latter days and immediate aftermath of World War II, the magnificent trio combined for a remarkable 53 wins in 1945 and 1946 (Nelson with 24, Hogan 18, and Snead 11). Such performances not only helped the tour to get back on its feet after the war, they lifted it to new heights.

But Nelson went into virtual retirement after 1946. Now Hogan was gone from the tour, too, maybe for good. What about Snead? He hadn't disappeared, but his putting touch had. Fighting a case of the yips, Snead didn't win a single tournament in the 1947 season. It's no wonder he missed a two-and-a-half-foot putt to lose the U.S. Open to Lew Worsham that year. For a player struggling on the greens, a short putt for all the marbles was a nightmare scenario.

It got so bad that in December 1947, the thirty-five-year-old Snead announced that he was giving up the tournament trail to become resident pro at The Greenbrier in White Sulphur Springs, West Virginia, which he had long represented on tour. He would play the winter circuit, but then settle into his new role after April 1, playing only the Masters, U.S. Open, PGA Championship, and the All-American Open and World Championship at Tam O'Shanter.

"I'm confident I could make twice as much money playing on the circuit, but it's time to get away from playing virtually every day," he said. "This business of changing water, food, and climate every few days gets you down."

Not to mention missing putts.

Snead managed to win the Texas Open in February 1948, an event where it was so cold he was forced to wear an overcoat between shots. Charles Price wrote in his tournament report for *Golf World*, "It is no secret to anyone who knows a little bit about golf that Snead does not win as many tournaments as he should. Combining the grace of a ballet dancer and the power of a weightlifter into a swing that has no defects noticeable to the naked eye, the Virginian, who astonished the golf world in 1938, has been in a putting slump for several years."

Snead followed through on his plans to sit out much of the 1948 season, playing in only 15 tournaments and finishing 18th on the money list, with only one victory. The low number of events wasn't the only reason he was so far down the list. His scoring average was a lackluster 70.77, nearly a stroke-and-a-half behind Hogan's leading 69.30.

Snead's part-time status was a notable loss for the tour, because he not only had been one of its best players and sweetest swingers but the hillbilly from the mountains was also one of its top personalities. In taking the Greenbrier post, Snead was returning to those mountains. He grew up just across the border in the Virginia hamlet of Ashwood, population 400. The youngest of six children, he spent most of his youth alone in the woods, trapping and shooting, barefoot except for in wintertime.

The Sneads' nearest neighbor was more than a mile away, but just three miles from home was The Cascades resort hotel and golf course in Hot Springs. Little Sam started caddying there when he was a few pounds shy of the required 80.

Sam tried to learn the swing by making a rudimentary club out of a discarded club head and a buggy whip (talk about a whippy shaft!). Then he figured it would work better if he could find the right strength stick in the woods—these were the days when club shafts were still made of hickory, so he wasn't that far off.

Sam sneaked onto the Cascades course every chance he could with his homemade club, trying to play a hole before being shooed off. Later, he got some hand-me-down clubs and played at a nine-hole course. A natural athlete, Snead was a football, basketball, and baseball star at his small high school. But golf would become his game.

After finishing school, Snead turned down an offer from an acquaintance to go into the moonshine business, which he deemed too dangerous. Instead, he found work as a "flunky" in the pro shop at The Homestead, another Hot Springs resort hotel under the same ownership as The Cascades. For the next couple of years, he bounced back and forth between the two courses, repairing clubs and doing odd jobs. For much of this time, Snead later related, he was paid only lunch money and his only real earnings came from giving the occasional lesson.

But he was able to refine his game by playing and practicing, and shot in the 60s fairly often—scores that were just then becoming realistic for ace players after the introduction of steel shafts. When his home course hosted the Cascades Open, an event on the PGA tour in 1935, Snead entered. With no experience playing against top professionals, the twenty-three-year-old stunned everyone by taking a three-stroke lead through 54 holes before closing with a final-round 80, finishing second to Billy Burke.

The next year, Snead got a break when Fred Martin, manager of The Greenbrier, offered him an assistant pro job. Martin saw in the raw talent of Snead the potential to represent The Greenbrier on tour. In the summer of 1936, Snead made a test run up to the Hershey Open in Pennsylvania.

He showed up for a practice round, but with his cornpone accent and a scuffed bag holding just eight clubs, Snead was having trouble getting a game until a kind pro named George Fazio said Sam could join his group. Snead's first drive sailed out of bounds onto the grounds of the chocolate factory. So did his second. His third found a water hazard. The other pros were shaking their heads, wondering what Fazio had gotten them into. Shortly, they were shaking their heads for a different reason—teeing his ball up for the fourth time, Snead drove the green on the 345-yard hole.

Henry Picard, the pro at Hershey, saw to it that Snead was paired with Craig Wood, a top player who represented Dunlop and had a say in who the company signed. "If you can impress Wood," Picard told Snead, "you may wind up with something even more valuable than a few pointers."

Wood was impressed, and Snead got an $800 contract that he intended to use to bankroll an effort to play the tour. But after playing in Miami and Nassau that December, Snead wasn't sure he had enough cash or confidence for the West Coast swing. "Why don't you give it a try?" Wood told him. "If you can't make it, I'll give you enough money to come back home on."

At the first tournament of 1937, the Los Angeles Open, Picard saw Snead hitting balls and told him that the shaft on his driver was too whippy. Picard gave the young pro a new driver, and it worked like a charm as Snead immediately began busting long, straight drives. "How much do you want for it?" Sam asked. "Try it in play, and if you like it, we'll make a deal," answered Picard, who, based on his interactions with Hogan and Snead, must have been the most generous player on tour.

Snead proceeded to finish sixth at Los Angeles and win the next two tournaments, the Oakland Open and a new event, the Bing Crosby Pro-Am, which that year was contested at only 18 holes. Picard asked for $5.50 for the driver. It was the best $5.50 Snead ever spent—he would use the club for more than 20 years.

Snead had taken no time at all to arrive as the tour's newest sensation. It was a fortuitous situation for Fred Corcoran, who at the Oakland Open was working only his second event as the tour's new tournament manager. When a wire photograph of Snead from the Oakland Open appeared in a New York newspaper, Snead asked Corcoran, "How did they get that photo? I've never been to New York."

From then on, Corcoran played up the hillbilly angle for all it was worth.

Snead won five times on tour in 1937 and did even better in 1938, earning eight victories and topping the money list. His long hitting led to the newspaper writers tagging him "Slammin' Sam," though he preferred the "Swingin' Sam" nickname that had been bestowed on him back home. In truth, Snead had the most natural swing action anyone had ever seen. Much later, pro John Schlee would put it best: "Watching Sam Snead practice golf is like watching a fish practice swimming."

A funny thing happened to Snead on his path to stardom, however. While he was winning tournaments by the bushel, he somehow became more known for *blowing* tournaments, especially the big ones. This was mostly due to his failures at the U.S. Open, but he let some other tournaments slip away, too, and through 1941 had not won any of the game's biggest events—the U.S. Open, PGA Championship, Masters, or Western Open.

He finally broke through at the 1942 PGA Championship, defeating Jim Turnesa in the match-play final a week before joining the Navy. After serving stateside, mostly teaching golf, Snead was discharged in late 1944 and immediately started winning tournaments again. In 1946, his equipment sponsor, Wilson, insisted he play in the British Open at St. Andrews, Scotland. He won it, but that was his last appearance at the event. Why make the trip, he reasoned, when travel expenses were greater than the first prize.

The yips struck Snead during a tour of South Africa in the winter of 1946–47 with Locke, against whom Snead managed only two wins and two ties in 16 two-man exhibitions. Locke was a phenomenal putter, still rated today as one of the best ever, and the more Snead saw his opponent's putts finding the hole, the more trouble he encountered with his own putter.

The putting woes continued when Snead got back to the States, leading to his near shutout in the win column in 1947 and 1948. Snead was back on the circuit for the winter swing of 1949, but other than a second-place finish at the Texas Open and a third-place finish at Phoenix he didn't have much of an impact. His putting hadn't gotten any better, as this report on the Los Angeles Open from John Maynard in the *Los Angeles Examiner* dramatizes:

"I stood on top of the steep hill over the 18th green and watched Snead come in. His second shot, a thing of beauty, lay probably seven feet from the cup. The seven-foot effort was a pathetic 18 inches short. The 18-inch effort was a shocking miss . . . I'm sorry I didn't finish the column before watching it."

If there was any place Snead was going to turn it around, it was the Greensboro Open, which was played in March. He had already won the tournament twice, and would go on to win it a total of eight times in his career, still a PGA Tour record for a player at a single event.

Snead loved Greensboro, and the Greensboro fans were crazy about him. Sometimes a little too crazy. Bob Quincy in the *Charlotte News* reported, "Snead is the darling of the crowd here in Greensboro . . . When the bronze idol made one of his frequent bad shots . . . the ball rolled towards a dangerous part of the rough, but still only a few yards from the fairway. Seeing the possible darkness of his hero's lie, one of the more radical members of the Snead-for-president club rushed up, applied the better part of his Cat's Paw to the pill and pitched it as neatly as you please back to playable conditions." Snead and Mangrum tied for first at 276. In the 18-hole playoff on Monday, the difference was putting. Surprisingly, Mangrum, usually the better putter, missed three putts from inside four feet, while Snead was rock solid on the short ones and won by two strokes with a 69.

A year later, Snead told reporters that his putting turnaround beginning in Greensboro was "mostly psychological," that he simply made up his mind that he could putt as well as anybody, and the ball began to roll into the cup. Of course, he went on to say that he changed his putter and his mechanics, too, so the physical element probably came first.

Snead put a new putter in play at Greensboro, one he had found in his locker a month-and-a-half earlier at Tucson. It wasn't until Greensboro that he found out it belonged to fellow pro Stan Kertes. "You want it back?" asked Snead.

"No, keep it for now," replied Kertes. "I'll get it back from you some time or other." Kertes didn't get it back anytime soon.

On the Monday preceding the next tournament, the Masters, Snead demonstrated for reporters on the putting green the tip that had gotten him back on track. "The boys told me to keep the putter head going through straight for the hole, as if the head of the putter was going to follow the ball, in marching order, right into the bottom of the cup," he said. He was able to accomplish that by incorporating more arm action in his stroke instead of using mostly his wrists.

The final piece of the puzzle was a tip that Snead received from Vic Ghezzi. Snead recalled in his book *The Education of a Golfer* that he told Ghezzi his stroke now felt smooth, but that he still couldn't "lay a good line to the hole with my eye. Any ideas?"

"Here's one that works for me," said Ghezzi. "On putts of six feet or less, concentrate on starting the ball on the line you like for the first three inches. Sight an imaginary three-inch line and get the putt started right."

When Snead and the rest of the golf caravan arrived in Augusta, Georgia, for the 13th playing of the Masters, there were two notable absences from the field. Ben Hogan had only just returned to his Fort Worth home after being released from the hospital, and was of course in no shape to participate. The other high-profile player not playing was tournament founder and host Bobby Jones. While Jones retired from competition after winning the Grand

Slam (U.S. Open and Amateur and British Open and Amateur) in 1930, he made an exception for the event he hosted on the course he co-designed with Alister MacKenzie.

Nobody knew it at the time, but Jones would never play another round of golf after undergoing spinal surgery in October 1948. Jones had syringomyelia, a rare condition that leads to gradual degeneration of the spinal cord. He would undergo a second operation in May 1950, but there would be no relief. The rest of his life saw a gradual deterioration in his physical condition until his death in 1971.

While he was not able to play, Jones was on hand in 1949, watching the action through binoculars from the veranda of his cabin near the 10th tee. A couple of weeks after Hogan's accident, Jones wired to Ben in the hospital, "How about coming over to the Masters and sit this one out with me." Hogan's blood clotting problems and subsequent surgery made that impossible.

Hogan was certainly in everyone's thoughts. Byron Nelson told reporters about visiting his friend in the hospital and being struck by the graveness of Hogan's situation as he needed a family member to stay with him at all hours. On Thursday, a Delta Airlines pilot delivered a gift from the Masters competitors to Hogan's front door: a framed photograph of the field and an engraved humidor filled with cigars. The message read, "To our friend Ben Hogan. On the eve of the 1949 Masters, we send you heartfelt good wishes for a speedy and complete recovery."

Among the players present at Augusta, Snead was receiving a lot of attention coming off his victory in Greensboro. "For one of the few times in his professional life Snead is putting well, and that makes him one of the choice picks to win," said an Associated Press story. Actually, Snead had been a perfectly fine putter early in his career, but that had been forgotten with his problems of the last couple of years.

Outside of a runner-up finish to Ralph Guldahl in 1939, Snead hadn't performed very well at Augusta, but he had a couple of interesting experiences. In 1938, he flew in an airplane for the first time so that he could get to Augusta early and play a practice round with Jones.

In 1942, Snead created a stir when he played a couple of holes barefoot on a practice day at Augusta National, at the suggestion of Corcoran. After playing a practice round in shoes, he went out and played the first and ninth holes without them, making a birdie and a par.

Snead told reporters that he used to play barefoot back home. "I feel better when I stand up to the ball in my bare feet," he said. "Those thick-soled shoes keep your toes too far off the ground."

Not everyone was amused. In *The Education of a Golfer*, Snead wrote that when he came back to the clubhouse, 1935 Masters champion Gene Sarazen laid into him. "What are you trying to play around here, Snead—Huckleberry Finn? What we need these days are real 'masters' and not barefoot hillbillies. Can you imagine Walter Hagen or Henry Cotton playing barefoot on this course?" Snead kept his shoes on after that.

Practice wound up on Wednesday with a clinic for the fans, featuring Demaret as the master of ceremonies and a number of pros demonstrating their techniques. Trick-shot artist Jack Redmond put on an exhibition, and there was also a long-driving contest. Chick Harbert won the contest with a poke of 286 yards into the wind. Snead did not compete because he was on the putting green, grooving that new stroke.

It was difficult for anyone's putting stroke or swing to stay grooved in the first two rounds, as winds whipping across Augusta National with gusts up to 35 mph played havoc. Snead shot rounds of 73 and 75, but at 148 was not completely out of it as he was tied for 14th, only five strokes off the lead.

Mangrum shot a steady 69 to hold the first-round lead for the second straight year and the third time in his career. Lloyd shot a 74 in the second round, but his 143 total was still good for a share of the lead with 1946 champion Herman Keiser, who shot an impressive second-round 68.

Snead's newfound putting prowess was on display Saturday. He one-putted the first five greens, collecting three birdies, on the way to a 67 that lifted him within a stroke of leader Johnny Palmer, the North Carolinian who was his playing companion for the third round. Palmer was at 214 after a 70, followed by Snead, Mangrum, and Joe Kirkwood Jr. at 215.

Mangrum would have had the lead except for a double bogey on the par-three 16th hole, which just two years earlier had been lengthened from 150 yards to 190 and had a stream converted to a pond. Mangrum put his tee shot into the water. Still, he fared better than his co-leader through 36 holes, Keiser, who triple-bogeyed the par-five second on the way to a 78.

Snead gave his supporters plenty to cheer about in the final round. He poured in eight birdies in shooting a 67 to sweep to a three-stroke victory over Mangrum and Johnny Bulla, a Snead pal who was his traveling companion on his first trip to the West Coast in 1937. The younger players couldn't keep pace, Palmer managing only a 72 to finish fourth and Kirkwood a 75 for seventh.

Snead again started strong, with birdies on three of the first four holes and a 33 on the front nine. Then he bogeyed the 10th and 11th. Uh-oh. Was another Snead fold job in the works? Not this time. Slammin' Sam birdied the 12th, 13th, 15th, and 18th holes to finish in style.

At age 36, Snead had won only his second big title in America among 44 total victories. His 67–67 finish was the best by far for a Masters winner to that point; in fact, his 134 total for the final 36 holes has been bettered by only two winners since (Jack Nicklaus and Gary Player with 133 in 1965 and 1978, respectively).

Two minutes after his victory, Snead was whisked to a radio interview with Harry Wismer of the American Broadcasting System to tell the country how he'd done it. Then it was back to the 18th green for a ceremony that featured a new twist. Since 1937, Augusta National members had been wearing green jackets, but the tradition of draping a green jacket over the shoulders of the new champion only began in 1949.

When Snead got to the clubhouse, he fielded a phone call—Ben Hogan was on the line to congratulate him. Snead had made a comeback from the yips. Could Hogan come back from even greater problems?

1949 PHILADELPHIA INQUIRER OPEN/JOE PALOOKA

PHILADELPHIA GOLF FANS didn't have to wait for the U.S. Open to come to Merion to see the PGA tour. On an annual basis, they already had the Philadelphia Inquirer Open, which originated in 1944 and was in the top tier of tour events, boasting a $15,000 purse.

The Inquirer tournament was ahead of its time in being staged for the benefit of local charities. Most tournaments didn't make enough money in those days to contribute to charity, unlike today when television revenues, larger gate proceeds, and corporate sponsorships have led not only to skyrocketing purses but also charitable contributions reaching seven figures annually for many events.

Sam Snead didn't enter the Philadelphia event in 1949, but all the other top names—aside from Ben Hogan, of course—were there. So, it was quite a surprise when Joe Palooka won the tournament. More correctly, the actor who played Joe Palooka in the movies—Joe Kirkwood Jr.

Kirkwood followed his father into golf. But like his dad, he didn't pursue the tour full-time. Whereas Joe Sr. drifted into a career as the world's most renowned trick-shot artist, Joe Jr. split his time between Hollywood and the PGA tour.

Joe Kirkwood Jr. played the boxer Palooka in 11 movies between 1946 and 1951, and also in a 1954–55 television series. Churning out two and sometimes three movies a year, Kirkwood had limited time for playing the tour.

He spent February and March 1949 filming *Joe Palooka in the Counterpunch* and did not pick up a club until arriving for the Masters in April. Under those circumstances, his seventh-place finish at Augusta was impressive. A month later, and two weeks before the Philadelphia Inquirer Open, Kirkwood finished second to Cary Middlecoff at The Greenbrier.

While Kirkwood came into Philadelphia playing well, the twenty-eight-year-old did not yet own any tour victories, and had a reputation for faltering late in tournaments. At the Masters, he was one stroke off the lead through 54 holes before closing with a 75.

Kirkwood got off to a good start at the Inquirer tournament with a 68 in the first round to tie Bobby Locke for the lead. Described as a "husky young movie actor on a golfing vacation," Kirkwood had the physique (six-foot-two, 210 pounds) to play a heavyweight boxer in the movies and propel the ball a long way on the golf course. The tricky part was controlling his shots, which wasn't always easy.

After the first round, Kirkwood told reporters, "I prefer the movies. It's easier there, and much more profitable."

He also said that he had never taken a golf lesson from his famous father, and that he had only been playing the game for ten years. The former was true; the latter, an exaggeration. Exaggeration seemed to run in the family. Joe Sr. was a showman who claimed to have played on 6,000 courses and performed his exhibitions in every country except for Russia. Then again, he might have been right. Kirkwood barnstormed the United States and the world in the 1920s and 1930s in a series of tours with Walter Hagen and Gene Sarazen, finding exhibition tours a better way to make money than playing on the fledgling pro tour with its paltry prize money.

The elder Kirkwood was born in Australia in 1897. After winning the Australian Open in 1920, he was called on to perform an exhibition for World War I veterans. A self-taught player, Kirkwood had learned a variety of shots while figuring out how to play the game. "I tried to show them what could be done even though they were amputees," he said later. "I would hit a ball with one hand or standing on one leg."

He found out that people liked watching him hit those and crazier shots. On his way to the 1921 British Open, he played in tournaments across the United States, and at an event in Pinehurst, North Carolina, he gave an impromptu trick-shot exhibition. The spectators collected money by passing a hat, and Kirkwood began to see a potential career.

First, though, he made his mark in the world of conventional golf, nearly winning that 1921 British Open and also contending there in 1923 and 1927. He won nine tournaments in 1923–24 on a U.S. pro tour that was in its infancy. After that, he teamed up with Hagen and concentrated on exhibitions; Kirkwood would do his trick-shot act and then the two of them would go out and play a round, often with a couple of local hotshots.

In 1933, he made another serious run at competition, winning the Canadian Open and North and South Open. "That year of competition convinced me of one thing: Tournament golf is a tough thing," he said about a decade later. "So I went back to the act." Kirkwood is credited with 13 victories on the PGA tour, but the U.S. and British Open titles eluded him.

Joe Jr. was born in Melbourne, Australia, in May 1920. Except that he wasn't Joe Jr. then—his given name was Reginald. His father left Australia when Reginald was an infant, and did not set foot Down Under again until 1928, when he returned on an exhibition tour. A 1950 feature story on Joe Jr. in *Sport* magazine said that he came to the United States when he was six. Given the timing of his father's trip to Australia, it seems more likely that it happened when he was eight, with Joe Sr. taking custody of Reginald and an older brother and bringing them back to the United States.

Kirkwood Sr. had homes in Philadelphia, where he had a long-standing position as the pro at Huntingdon Valley Country Club, and Daytona Beach, Florida. The young Kirkwood split his time between those two locations when he was growing up. In 1939, the *Daytona Beach Morning Journal* reported on Reggie Kirkwood winning an amateur tournament. There was another 1939 report in the *Journal* that "Reg Kirkwood, who prefers to be known as young Joe, plans to enter the Ormond Beach Championship tourney." He entered that tournament as Joe Kirkwood Jr.

The *Sport* profile says that Joe Sr. never tried to interest his sons in golf, and in the case of the younger one, "he figured the lad simply did not have the right temperament to become a great golfer." It was actually a chat with the legendary Bobby Jones at the 1936 Masters, where Joe Sr. was a competitor, that convinced Reggie he should seriously get into the game and have his own set of clubs.

So, while it wasn't true that Joe Jr. had been playing golf for only ten years in 1949, he did start relatively late. He never had a lesson from anyone, including his father, who spent much time away from home with his touring schedule. But the kid was a natural, and turned pro in 1940 at the age of nineteen, serving under his father as an assistant pro at Huntingdon Valley in 1940 and 1941. He played tour events and regional events in 1941 and 1942, sometimes listed as Reginald and sometimes as Joe.

The young Kirkwood had a rather checkered war experience. He tried to enlist in the Army Air Corps, but was rejected. He wanted to enlist in the Royal Canadian Air Force, but his draft board wouldn't let him. Then he failed to report for an Army physical in Philadelphia, where he was registered, landing him in court. He was found guilty in June 1943 of failing to obey a draft board order.

Judge Guy K. Bard called him "a spoiled glamour boy" and told him, "The trouble with you seems to be that you are obsessed with an ego by which you think you can select the branch of service in which you want to serve. You seem to be more interested in golf and Daytona Beach than in serving your country."

Kirkwood received a 60-day suspended sentence and was placed on probation for one year or until he was inducted. He entered the Army later in 1943, where, he told *Sport*, he lasted eight months before receiving a medical discharge for high blood pressure and asthma. Kirkwood said he joined the Royal Canadian Air Force in 1944, but after a few months got another medical discharge.

By January 1945, he was on tour playing in the Los Angeles Open when Warner Brothers director David Butler asked him if he would be interested in taking a screen test. He did, and stayed in Hollywood for a few months, but after landing only a couple of bit parts, he went back to golf.

Then Kirkwood got an unlikely break that led him back to Hollywood. Monogram Pictures held a nationwide Joe Palooka Talent Search in the fall of 1945 to find an actor for a movie based on the Ham Fisher comic strip, and Kirkwood entered the Florida portion of the contest. Based on a brief bio and a photo "in trunks or bathing suit," the ruggedly handsome blond Kirkwood was selected as the Florida winner, receiving a watch as a prize.

Out of all the winners across the nation, four were chosen for screen tests. Hedging its bets, Monogram stated that the winner of the contest, selected on the basis of those tests, would be guaranteed a role in the picture *Joe Palooka, Champ*, but not necessarily the Palooka role. Kirkwood made the final four, passed the screen test in flying colors, and was given the starring role.

A review of the 1946 film in the *St. Petersburg Times* said, "An undemonstrative actor, Kirkwood is highly satisfactory in the part of the Frank Merriwell of the comics, doing far better than is to be expected of film actors who try to play the heroes of the funnies. In the boxing scenes, Kirkwood hardly looks a threat to Joe Louis, but he commits no errors that will offend a sports follower."

The Palooka movies became a franchise for Monogram, certainly not masterpieces of the cinematic art but reliable performers at the box office. Kirkwood earned a reported $12,500 a year making pictures, supplementing that by playing about half the year on the pro circuit.

From 1945 on, he was known only as Joe Kirkwood Jr. Whether he originally started calling himself Joe to honor his father, to give him name recognition as a golfer, or simply because he didn't like his given name, it proved fortuitous when he went to Hollywood. "Reginald Kirkwood" wouldn't have had a ring to it as an actor playing a heavyweight champ.

Being a movie star was good for the ego and, with a string of Palooka roles, good for financial security. (It's a commentary on the shaky prospects of touring pros that even actors were more secure.) But Kirkwood didn't want to give up on his golf ambitions, even if he had a hard time achieving them as a part-timer.

"He could be the greatest player in the world if he had the time to devote to the game," said Joe Sr. in 1950. "He's got the power and the technique. All he lacks is the time."

The Kirkwoods made history at Riviera in 1948 when they became the first father and son to make the cut at the same U.S. Open, a feat that has since been matched only by Jay and Bill Haas in 2004. The senior Kirkwood, fifty-one at the time, didn't play much tour golf anymore. He entered the 1949 Philadelphia

Inquirer Open, but sprained his back changing a tire the day before the tournament and withdrew after nine holes.

Play was stopped in the second round by a rainstorm and strong winds in the afternoon. A few golfers had finished their rounds and most had at least started them (Kirkwood was even par through nine holes), but as was customary in those days all play was washed out and the entire second round replayed the next day.

Kirkwood took control on Saturday with a course-record 66. He took a shower after his round and went out to follow Locke, who entered the day tied with him. The South African only managed a 70, and with nobody else making a move, Kirkwood finished the round with a four-stroke lead.

Because of the rained-out day, the tournament wrapped up with 36 holes on Sunday after the field was cut. Kirkwood turned it into a rout, leading by a ridiculous nine strokes after carding a 68 in the third round. It was too big a lead to blow, even with an utterly careless quadruple bogey seven on the 13th hole leading to a final-round 74. Kirkwood won by four shots over defending champion Johnny Palmer, with Locke another stroke back.

The victory heralded the beginning of the best stretch of Kirkwood's golf career; he would also win a tournament each in 1950 and '51. But his golf career didn't take off after that, and, looking back, Kirkwood blamed his desire to look the part of a heavyweight champion in the movies.

"I was lifting weights and punching the bag so much that I started to get muscle-bound and my game started to drift away," he told *Arizona Daily Star* reporter Mark Stewart in 1994, stating the common belief among golfers that a weightlifter's physique is not good for the golf swing. "My dad and Walter Hagen used to travel together, and they wouldn't even carry their suitcases into a hotel. I thought that was a little extreme, but I developed all these muscles and had no connection to the golf swing."

Kirkwood took advantage of the Hollywood lifestyle, and was a regular in the gossip columns, linked romantically with various starlets. He didn't drink or smoke, so in that sense he was a good fit for the All-American boxer Palooka. However, noted Bob Richelson in *Sport*, "He prefers chocolate milk to liquor, but it can't be said he prefers barbells over movie belles."

Apparently, the apple didn't fall far from the tree. Kirkwood Sr. never drank, but did acquire a reputation in his travels as a womanizer.

Two months after his win in Philadelphia, Kirkwood Jr. landed in the headlines in an unwanted way.

On July 20, 1949, he had to appear in a Worcester, Massachusetts, court on charges of non-support brought by a single mother named Florence Heppenstall, claiming that he was the father of her six-year-old twins. Kirkwood and Heppenstall had both spent the summer of 1942 working at a resort in Jefferson, New Hampshire, she as a waitress and he as a golf pro.

Her lawyer told reporters that during that summer, Kirkwood took Heppenstall riding "constantly" in a "snappy pale blue roadster." Kirkwood denied paternity, saying she was one of "about forty girls" that he met "casually" during the summer. Heppenstall had listed another man as the father at the time of the birth, which her lawyer now claimed that she did to protect Kirkwood's reputation as a golfer. The suit hadn't been filed until now, she said, because they had to wait for Kirkwood to be in Massachusetts in order to serve papers (he had arrived to play in a celebrity softball game at Braves Field in Boston).

Between the pre-trial hearing and the trial, held two days later, Kirkwood and Heppenstall, a movie theater cashier, reached a settlement. The golfer paid her $4,000 for support, plus another $1,000 for legal expenses. The trial was still held to adjudicate paternity, and Judge Walter D. Allen ruled Kirkwood the father.

Kirkwood continued to deny that he was the twins' father, and appealed the ruling, the appeal stating that he paid the money "in order to terminate the matter," and avoid costly delay, "as he had contracts that required his presence in Hollywood and other places." The settlement, his appeal said, did not include an admission of paternity. The appeal was dismissed on October 25.

Kirkwood had two reasons to worry about the adverse publicity from the case.

"My chief worry is that it will hurt the role I play in the movies—that of Joe Palooka, the ideal American boy. That means a lot to youngsters all over the country," he said on the day of the initial hearing.

The studio stuck by Kirkwood, however, and the Palooka series continued unabated.

The other concern was that Kirkwood was engaged to marry actress Cathy Downs in October, but that also turned out to be unaffected. The marriage brought another bit of publicity that Kirkwood wasn't fond of, but it was in a lighter vein.

The November 21, 1949, issue of *Life* included this letter from Kirkwood:

> *In your Oct. 31 issue you ran a picture of my wife Cathy Downs and myself and mentioned in the caption that she was my third bride. This has caused a great deal of embarrassment to both of us, as she is my first wife. I would appreciate it very much if you could correct the mistake made in your last issue.*
>
> *Joe Kirkwood, Jr., Beverly Hills, Cal.*

> LIFE, *which confused Joe Kirkwood, Jr., with twice married Joe Kirkwood, Sr., regrets the error and wishes Mr. and Mrs. Joe, Jr. great and enduring happiness.—ED*

The magazine actually missed a marriage for Kirkwood Sr., who had been married once in Australia and twice in the United States.

Downs went on to play Kirkwood's girlfriend/wife Ann Howe in one of the Joe Palooka movies and in the television series. She also was the Azalea Queen at a 1952 festival in Wilmington, North Carolina, where Joe was playing in the Azalea Open.

However, happiness was not enduring for the couple, as they divorced in 1955. During the divorce proceedings, Downs tearfully testified that she was willing to make every sacrifice to preserve her marriage, even to the extent of taking up golf.

"I tried golf for his sake," she said, "but he just made fun of me."

8

1949 U.S. OPEN/DOC

BEN HOGAN LEFT Hotel Dieu hospital on the evening of March 31, just less than two months after he entered it. He was carried by stretcher into a sleeper car on the "Texas Eagle," a train that left El Paso after midnight and arrived in Fort Worth that afternoon. In the same waiting room where he had sold newspapers as a boy, he was greeted by his mother and other family and friends, then taken by ambulance to his home.

In golf, it is said that the best approach is to take one shot at a time. That's the approach Hogan took to his comeback. But he would be doing it on his own. Today, most anyone recovering from such injuries, and certainly a top athlete, would work on their recovery with physical therapists. Not in 1949. Then again, maybe that's the way this most self-reliant of men preferred it anyway. Doctors told Hogan that the swelling in his legs wouldn't go down for five months, but that he needed to start walking soon in order to build up strength in his atrophied muscles. He started by pushing a walker, but soon graduated to walking around the living room unaided. First, three laps. Then five. Then ten. Eventually, he worked himself up to forty-five circuits around the room. Sometimes, he would get fresh air by walking around the backyard. For his upper body, he squeezed a rubber ball and did chin-ups.

It was drudgery that in some ways mirrored that of hitting balls on the range. Except that for Hogan hitting balls was never drudgery.

Of those early days of building up his leg strength, Hogan told writer Herb Graffis, "That was very hard work, because there didn't seem to be much point to it—just driving yourself. When you hit golf balls hour after hour, you can see where they're going . . . where they land. The improvement in my legs couldn't be seen or felt until weeks later."

At times, Hogan pushed himself too hard. Then his legs would cramp up, and Valerie would have to massage them with rubbing alcohol. Sleeping at night was often not easy. But when the Hogans traveled to New Orleans on April 30 for a follow-up with Dr. Ochsner, Ben was given an encouraging prognosis.

Back in Fort Worth, Hogan graduated to walking down the street in his Westover Hills neighborhood. Sometimes he would go too far, and Valerie would have to go out in the car to find him, usually sitting on the curb somewhere with cramped legs.

In May, officials of the United States Golf Association in New York were stunned to receive a letter from Hogan that read, "Enclosed is my entry for the [U.S.] Open, with the hope that I will be able to play. Up to now I haven't taken a swing, but miracles may happen. Would you please do me a favor and not release my entry to the press? If I can play, I should like it to be a surprise. I hope and pray that I may play in June."

Hogan playing in the 1949 U.S. Open truly would have been a miracle. By the time of the Open in June, he had been to Colonial Country Club in Fort Worth and walked several holes, but without playing. Because of the injuries to his legs and shoulder, he had not yet been able to attempt a full swing. All he had done was chip and putt a little bit. Hogan told a friend that he was so disappointed not to be playing in the Open, he couldn't even bring himself to listen to the radio broadcast.

As the field gathered at Medinah Country Club, outside Chicago, the attention was focused on Sam Snead. On top of winning the Masters in April, he had captured the PGA Championship in May. Could he make it three majors in a row? Could he win the big title that had always eluded him?

Pre-tournament odds listed Snead at 6–1, Bobby Locke at 8–1, and Lloyd Mangrum at 10–1. In the first round, Snead shot a 73—four strokes off the lead held by the obscure Les Kennedy—and the other two favorites each shot 74. Twenty-eight-year-old Cary Middlecoff, owner of four victories since joining the tour a little more than two years earlier, shot a 75 that could have been worse.

"Going to this short little narrow par four, the 15th hole, I told my caddie that if I missed the fairway off the tee, pick up the ball. We were going in," he later remembered. "'Give me the driver,' I told my caddie. 'I'm not going to make the cut if I don't do something.'"

Middlecoff nearly drove the green on the 316-yard hole and made a birdie that turned his tournament around.

If he had picked up his ball and walked in, it would have been in character. A well-liked, gentlemanly sort away from the course, Middlecoff was plagued by a temper on it, which led to the letters WD (withdrew) or DQ (disqualified) often appearing next to his name in tournament results. In the 1947 Atlanta Open, after missing his second putt on the 18th green, incensed by course conditions, he hurled his ball over the heads of the spectators and stormed off. Later, at the 1953 U.S. Open at Oakmont, he intentionally blasted a bunker shot on the 10th hole onto the Pennsylvania Turnpike and withdrew because he wasn't happy with his tee time.

Middlecoff would end up being very glad he stuck around at Medinah. On the second day, he shot a four-under 67 and his 142 total moved him within one stroke of Al Brosch's lead. Middlecoff's decision to leave dentistry, made two years earlier, was looking better all the time.

"Doc" Middlecoff, as he was known, had a different background than most pros of the time. He was a country club kid from Memphis, who attended private school and went to college. His father, Herman, was a dentist, as were two uncles.

Cary learned the game tagging along with his dad at the country club, and at seventeen won the city championship. He decided to follow his father into dentistry, and after graduating from the University of Mississippi in three years (and playing on the golf team) he went on to the University of Tennessee Dental School.

Middlecoff finished his studies as an inactive Army enlistee, then went into duty as an Army dentist in 1943 with the rank of lieutenant. Records show he filled 12,093 teeth during his service at Fort Gordon near Augusta.

It was a strange twist of fate, and a seemingly unlucky accident, that sent Middlecoff on his way to being a pro golfer. In 1945, while working on a patient, a small piece of porcelain popped up and lodged in his right eye. The eye became badly infected, his vision was hampered, and he was sent to Valley Forge hospital in Pennsylvania for a recuperation period that lasted several months.

Still on leave late in the year, he decided to enter PGA tour events in Richmond, Virginia, and Pinehurst, North Carolina, as an amateur. His game had gone into mothballs as he played only about once a month when in dental school, but he played a few rounds with Bobby Jones while being stationed near Augusta. "I'd give the world to have a swing like that," Jones told him.

Lieutenant Middlecoff stunned the pros by winning the North and South Open, becoming the first amateur to win that event. After beating a field that included Hogan and Snead, Middlecoff began to think about a career on the pro tour.

When he got out of the Army in 1946, however, his mother was gravely ill (she would die later in the year), and Middlecoff stayed in Memphis, working for six months in his father's dental practice.

That turned out to be another twist of fate—Cary met his wife, Edie, when she was a patient of his that fall.

Middlecoff played well enough in amateur events in 1946 to be named the next January to play for the United States in the upcoming Walker Cup competition against amateurs from Great Britain. He declined the spot, however, in order to turn pro, explaining his decision in a letter to the USGA:

> *First, I am going to be married March 4.*
>
> *Next thing is that I have planned to turn pro at that time and play the tournaments until I have proved to myself one way or the other if I am good enough to make golf playing a life work.*
>
> *Ever since I can remember I have wanted to play golf without being worried about one thing or another but have never had the chance. I know that I would never be happy practicing dentistry without knowing for sure if I were a good player or a great one, and dentistry is too confining to ever offer me that opportunity.*

At one point during 1946, Dr. Herman Middlecoff asked Jones to try to persuade Cary to remain a career amateur in Jones's own image. But Cary persuaded his dad that he wouldn't be able to realize his potential as a golfer if he remained an amateur, and that week-in-and-week-out competition on the pro tour was what he needed. Herman relented, telling his son that a spot in the dental practice would be waiting should things not work out. Cary's name remained on the door of the dental office for ten more years.

Middlecoff would be strictly a tour pro. He had no desire to ever work in a pro shop. And he would remain on tour only if he proved himself one of the best in the game. "If I can't prove to myself in two years that I can play with the Hogans and the Sneads, then I'll come back to dentistry," was his proviso.

In March 1947, Middlecoff got married and honeymooned in Ponte Vedra, Florida, which just happened to be the site of the Jacksonville Open the following week, where Cary made his pro debut. In just his third tournament, he won the Charlotte Open.

After that promising start, things got dicey. Ten months later, at the Texas Open, he had just enough money to pay the hotel bill and get home. But Cary finished fourth there to collect $800, enough to stay on tour. He had three straight top-ten finishes, followed by a victory with partner Jim Ferrier in the Miami Four-Ball. A month later, he was runner-up in the Masters, and he never looked back after that.

Middlecoff's next individual win came in November 1948 at the Hawaiian Open. He added three more in the winter/spring of 1949, plus an unofficial win at The Greenbrier. Clearly, he was a top-ten player. But was he another Hogan or Snead? A U.S. Open title would go a long way toward showing that, and Middlecoff headed into the 36-hole conclusion at Medinah with a golden opportunity.

Middlecoff got a fortunate pairing for the third and fourth rounds. He went off with Buck White, a fellow Memphian who had once given him lessons, and Clayton Heafner, who Middlecoff could keep an eye on as a fellow main challenger for the title.

Middlecoff started the third round like it might be even better than his second-round 67, making birdies on four of the first five holes. He cooled off after that four-under start, settling for a two-under 69. Unusual for that era, the top three players through 54 holes were together for the final round, Middlecoff at 211, White at 212, and Heafner tied for third with Brosch at 214.

The six-foot-two Middlecoff was a bundle of nerves on the course, even in the best of times. He walked quickly, but had trouble making club selections, and once he stood over the ball he went through an awkward and inconsistent sequence of waggles before he finally convinced himself to pull the trigger. He had developed a reputation, one that he would never shake, as the slowest player on tour.

He was always defensive about charges of slow play, but freely admitted to nervousness. "I have always maintained that a man who is not nervous is either an idiot or has never been close enough to winning to get nervous," he said.

Nerves contributed to a three-over 39 on the front nine in the final round at Medinah. White fared even worse and was almost out of it, but Heafner was now tied for the lead.

Middlecoff did have a couple of things going for him. For one thing, he had a great will to win.

"They say Hogan is a great competitor, and he is," said fellow pro Fred Hawkins. "But Middlecoff is just as tough a fighter, maybe even a little more intense."

Cary also was considered the best driver of the ball in the game, taking into account both distance and accuracy. And that was important on a Medinah course that not only was playing nearly 7,000 yards, but had a claustrophobic feel with trees encroaching on play.

Middlecoff lost the lead when he three-putted for a bogey on the 11th hole, regained it when Heafner double bogeyed the 12th, shared it again when Heafner birdied the 13th, and moved in front by one stroke thanks to a Heafner bogey on the par-three 14th, where he flubbed a chip from behind the green. After that seesaw stretch, both players parred their way in, Heafner missing a six-foot birdie putt on the 18th that would have tied it.

"I made up my mind back on the 15th that if I still held the lead on the final tee, I was going to use an iron instead of a driver," Middlecoff later recalled. "For the first time I realized I was beginning to lose confidence, perhaps choking a bit."

But on the walk to the 18th tee, Middlecoff pulled himself together and decided to hit a driver so as not to leave himself a long second shot to the par four. "I then stepped up and hit the longest, finest tee shot of the entire tournament," he remembered.

Middlecoff had held it together down the stretch, but still he finished the round with a birdieless 75. Greeted after the round by his wife, Edie, Middlecoff told her, "Don't get your hopes up, honey. That Snead's gonna come in like a fire engine and best us out."

It looked like he might be right. Snead, who started the final round six strokes back, with a tee time about an hour behind Middlecoff's, was making a charge. Birdies on the 10th and 11th holes got Snead to two-under for the round, where he remained coming to the par-three 17th hole; two pars would mean a playoff and a chance for a third straight major.

But this was the U.S. Open, which meant that Snead would find a way to lose it. His tee shot on the 17th was held up by the wind just enough to miss the green by a few feet on the right. Electing to use a putter from the fringe, a decision that was much criticized afterward, he knocked it six feet past the hole, and missed the par putt.

Snead missed the green on the 18th, failed to hole his birdie chip, and with a par settled for a tie for second with Heafner, one stroke back. Two more strokes behind came Locke in fourth place. Snead's 70 was the best score of the final round, but it was overshadowed by his bogey on the 17th.

Middlecoff told reporters that his dental career was on hold indefinitely, though he didn't rule out returning to it once his playing days were over, whenever that might be.

By winning the U.S. Open, Middlecoff not only proved himself, he secured his immediate future, because an Open win was one of the few routes to big money in those days. The figure often bandied about in the press was that a U.S. Open title was worth $50,000 in extra income. That figure was probably exaggerated—and it certainly would vary from individual to individual—but there was no doubt that endorsements and exhibitions awaited the Open champ.

Most players in that era had no reason to have an agent. But on the heels of his Open victory, Middlecoff hired a Memphis publicity man, Early Maxwell, to handle his affairs.

Maxwell went to work right away, booking Middlecoff and Snead for a four-city exhibition series in August with scores added together for a 72-hole "championship," culminating in Memphis with "Cary Middlecoff Day." (The pair finished in a tie, and then also tied in match play on a second day in Memphis.)

An ad appeared in *Golf World* in September:

> *Dr. Cary Middlecoff*
> *United States Open Champion*
> *Available for dates in Texas*
> *and Pacific Coast in October*

That fall Middlecoff signed a $5,000 contract to represent the refurbished Ormond Beach Hotel and Country Club in Florida. The marriage didn't last, ending in acrimony the next year with hotel officials saying that Middlecoff had missed opportunities to promote Ormond Beach in radio interviews, hadn't done enough to ensure that he was listed as from Ormond Beach in all tournaments, and neglected to stop by the resort when he had a chance during the Florida swing.

During the U.S. Open at Merion in 1950, *Philadelphia Inquirer* columnist John Webster talked to Maxwell, who estimated that Middlecoff had made $25,000 to $30,000 from winning the 1949 Open, but left some money on the table. He declined offers to tour South America because he didn't want to become over-golfed (a lesson some major winners in recent decades should have taken to heart). He rejected an endorsement for breakfast food because he didn't like the product. (Do today's stars even care if they like what they are endorsing?) The nonpracticing dentist was weighing offers to endorse toothpaste—his manager felt it would be ethical since he would be doing so as a golfer, not a dentist—but had not signed on.

Middlecoff was able to greatly increase his exhibition schedule, but he did not raise his price of $350 weekdays, $500 weekends. "We didn't want anyone to ever lose money through Middlecoff exhibitions," Maxwell said. The golfer had been enticed to overcome his reluctance to author an instruction book, coming out with *Golf Doctor*.

One thing that was not in Middlecoff's future was the 1949 Ryder Cup Matches. The year's second-leading money winner was not eligible for the United States team because he was not a member of the PGA, which required a five-year apprenticeship. (He also was not eligible to play in the PGA Championship.)

"It seems a little ironical because I was chosen on the Walker Cup team in 1947 but passed it up in order to become a pro," Middlecoff complained to the *Washington Post*. "Now that I am a pro, I am NOT eligible for the Ryder Cup team the year I win the biggest title of them all."

As the rule then stood, Middlecoff would not ever become a PGA member unless he did some time in a pro shop. That rule was changed the following winter, in recognition of the new breed of "tour pro," but the five-year apprenticeship remained. Middlecoff wouldn't be eligible for the 1951 Ryder Cup, either.

9

1949 RYDER CUP/DUTCH

ON JULY 6, Ben and Valerie Hogan spiced up his recuperation period by heading out to Los Angeles for a ten-day visit, traveling by train. The taciturn Hogan had a surprisingly close relationship with glittery Hollywood. He once took a screen test, counted actors among his friends, and the day after winning the 1948 U.S. Open in Los Angeles was the guest of honor at a gala dinner hosted by director Sidney Lanfield.

There had been press talk, even then, of a deal for a movie on Hogan's life. Now, after the accident, he was meeting with Lanfield to discuss just that, though he said he was just in town for a rest.

Meanwhile, Jack Curnow of the *Los Angeles Times* was able to interview Hogan. Curnow reported that Hogan walked slowly, with a slight shuffle. "Ben's legs still bother him, especially his left ankle," he wrote. "He sleeps with his legs elevated. They swell during the day."

Said Hogan, "Only time will tell my future golf plans. I putt a little. But that's mighty boring. Otherwise, I haven't touched a club since the accident. Don't know when I will, either."

Hogan was the subject of numerous magazine stories after the crash. Probably the best was written by *Dallas Morning News* sports editor Bill Rives for the September 1949 issue of *Sport.* The editors asked him to give the real answer to the question: "Will Hogan ever play again?"

The general assumption around the country, Rives wrote, was "that he is through, washed-up . . . Followers of golf, who know the rigorous physical demands of the game, shake their heads in sympathy and say, 'It's too bad about Ben. The poor little guy had to hit from the heels when he was at full strength. What can he do now? His accident finished him off.'"

Rives wrote that at first he felt the same way. But as a local sports writer who was able to spend a lot of time with Ben during his recovery, he had changed his mind.

"In all the conjecture about Hogan's future, little consideration has been given to his clear grit and his wild, almost irrational, resolution. Ben Hogan is determined to return to golf. He has told me many times, in recent weeks, of this resolve. He spoke quietly and without visible emotion, but the intense rush of his words, the glow in his eyes, revealed the depth of his feelings."

Rives wrote that Hogan had a putter in his hands every time he talked to him, and that he carried it with him everywhere.

"I was probing for the slightest indication that he was whistling in the dark, that he knew he was only kidding himself," Rives wrote, "but never did Hogan give the slightest indication that in his heart, he knew he was through."

Hogan might have to alter his swing because of the broken collarbone, might have to sacrifice distance because of the condition of his legs, and his nervous system might not be the same. "But you can't write off Ben Hogan. You can't count ten over him until he's had his chance," Rives wrote.

"Ever since my accident," Hogan was quoted, "I've never thought of doing anything else except returning to the tournaments."

Still, the article said that at the time of writing (in August) Hogan was incapable of walking the distance required for 18 holes. He also had yet to swing a golf club.

On August 13, his thirty-seventh birthday, Hogan arrived in New Orleans for another checkup with Dr. Alton Ochsner. He reported that he was feeling pain in his right knee. The doctor found torn cartilage upon examination and recommended surgery to repair it. But Hogan didn't want to have to recover from *another* operation, nor did he want to miss an upcoming trip to England for the Ryder Cup, where he would be the non-playing captain for the United States team. He decided to pass on surgery and see how things worked out.

Ochsner told him it would be another three months before he could swing a club. It's unclear if the knee injury was partly responsible for that, or if it was strictly due to the broken collarbone. That left shoulder would bother Hogan for the rest of his life; he would eventually have three surgeries on it.

"I think I'll swing again. But I don't know when," he told a reporter just before leaving Fort Worth for the first leg of his Ryder Cup journey. "I don't worry much about it. I'm lucky to be here at all."

Hogan was named Ryder Cup captain on August 4 by vote of the players on the team. It was an idea first floated by Jimmy Demaret in February, but awaited the finalization of the team—and Hogan recovering well enough to be able to make the trip—before it was set in motion.

The Ryder Cup was scheduled for September 16 and 17 at Ganton Golf Club in Scarborough, England, but Hogan left Fort Worth on a train on August 23 and did not return until early October. He first traveled to Boston, where the United States team defeated a "scrub team" of American pros who did not make the Ryder squad. Then it was on to New York, where most of the team caught a ship for England on September 3. (Skip Alexander, whose wife was expecting a baby, flew over later.)

On the drive from the port of Southampton to London, where the team spent the night, British golf writer Louis T. Stanley was at the wheel of the car in which Hogan was a passenger. "The road smash in which he had nearly been killed had left its mark," Stanley remembered. "Every oncoming car so tensed his nerves that we reduced our speed at times to a crawling pace."

The team arrived in Scarborough just before midnight on the evening of September 10 after a trip in a fleet of cars from London that was delayed by sightseeing stops. About four hundred people waited for them for five hours, and it was reported that they applauded vigorously when the Americans arrived. Yet even with that warm reception, this was not a Ryder Cup that was conducted in a spirit of gentility and good cheer.

The tension started with the meat affair. Because of food rationing in post-war Britain, the U.S. squad decided to bring its own meat—lots of it. They brought enough sirloin for about six hundred steaks, plus twelve sides of ribs, twelve hams, and twelve boxes of bacon. The Americans felt they were just being practical (the team entourage included wives and guests, and most players planned to stay one or two weeks after the Ryder Cup), but to the Brits it felt like a slight, and it got plenty of attention in the press.

A couple of days after their arrival, Hogan had seen and heard enough. "Every time I pick up a paper, I read about that meat," he said. "I can't even find any golf news. Next time I guess we'll have to leave our clubs at home and just have a meat show." As a sign of goodwill, the Americans shared their meat at a pre-tournament dinner with the British team.

Then came the grooves affair. In 1947, British captain Henry Cotton had asked that the Americans' clubs be inspected on the suspicion of grooves being too deep, and some clubs did have to be filed down. Hogan, who was a playing captain in 1947, returned the favor in 1949 by asking to have the British team's clubs inspected. It was an embarrassment for the home team, as several players had to file down their clubs to be sure they passed inspection. Even after that, Richard Burton's wedge didn't pass and had to be further filed down before it was allowed. He reportedly had used a drill to deepen the holes in his dot-punch wedge.

Once the matches got underway, the crowd was decidedly partisan, with the British fans vociferous in their support of the home squad. Hogan complained that "it was more like an American college football game" than a golf tournament.

The British were primed for this event because they felt playing on their home turf gave them a fighting chance, despite having absorbed an 11–1 defeat to the Americans in Oregon in 1947. "If we don't win this time, we probably never shall," said British captain Charles Whitcombe, an indication of the desperation with which the public saw these matches.

This Ryder Cup was a huge deal. An Associated Press report stated that the course was dotted with "forty tents, housing restaurants and bars, and spectator pavilions." Grandstands were set up at various points, with public address systems to keep the fans, expected to number about 20,000, up to date with the progress of the matches.

Despite the American romp two years before, many observers, including American golf promoter Fred Corcoran, gave the British side a chance in this one. It was partly because Americans weren't accustomed to links courses, especially since most of them had never played in a British Open. Also, the United States squad did not look as strong as it had been in the past, with Hogan sidelined, Byron Nelson retired, and new star Cary Middlecoff ineligible.

Arthur Lacey, chairman of the British PGA, opined that it was the weakest United States team since the competition began in 1927. "They're a nice bunch of fellows, but they're ragged," he said.

Hogan knew that his team would probably face strong competition, but some of his players were overconfident. A member of the American delegation said that when Hogan was giving a pep talk in a team meeting about having a real battle ahead, Demaret interrupted and said, "Benny, you're talking like a football coach. We'll beat these guys easily."

Hogan was decidedly a hands-on captain, especially when it came to making his players practice. He demanded a regimen of an hour on the range before and after each practice round. "Hey, Hawk," Demaret asked. "Are we training for golf or the Army?" Demaret later estimated that the week of the Ryder Cup he practiced twice as much as he wanted to and half as much as Hogan wanted him to.

The Ryder Cup in those days consisted of four 36-hole foursomes matches on Friday and eight singles matches on Saturday. Each team was allotted ten players but, oddly, the injured Hogan was not replaced as a player (he qualified for the team on points in a system that counted 1948 events) and the United States played with nine.

The first day was a disaster for the Americans, as Britain won three of the four matches, highlighted by a fired-up Burton teaming with Arthur Lees to beat the top American duo of Sam Snead and Lloyd Mangrum. Needing only three wins and a draw in the eight singles matches on Saturday to secure victory, British captain Whitcombe brimmed with confidence. "We can beat everybody except Sammy Snead, Lloyd Mangrum, and Jimmy Demaret," he said, "and we might even beat one of them."

Hogan, who carried the same intensity as a captain that he did as a player, wasn't pleased about the Friday result. "When he gave you that look, you knew you were in trouble," said Johnny Palmer of the withering expression on Hogan's face after Palmer lost his foursomes match with partner Dutch Harrison. "I don't remember a whole lot of laughs being had that week. I mostly remember Ben saying we simply had to get the job done."

It can be argued that one mistake captain Hogan made was splitting up the pair of Harrison and Bob Hamilton, each of whom lost their foursomes match with another partner. Harrison and

Hamilton had been partners in countless gambling matches against "pigeon" amateurs and against other pros since they met in 1938 when Hamilton asked Dutch for $50 to get home because he was broke. Hamilton repaid the debt when he made it back on tour, and along with Herman Keiser they formed the "Three Musketeers," often traveling together.

The story has been told about one elaborate hustle where Hamilton showed up in a town and spent a few weeks as a caddie at a local club. Eventually, Harrison rolled into town, and after playing in a few money matches, declared that he could beat a couple of hotshot members even if he took one of the club's caddies as his partner. "Line 'em up, and I'll pick one," Dutch said, and naturally he picked Hamilton (other versions of the story have Keiser as the caddie–hustler).

Whether or not that particular story is true, Harrison and Hamilton had won enough matches together that they could be considered among the leading money winners on tour, counting gambling winnings. Hamilton won the 1944 PGA Championship in an upset over Byron Nelson, but Harrison had won more tournaments and was considered the better player of the two even though he had never won a major.

Hogan would later say that Dutch was "a heckuva good golfer, and I might say he didn't win as much as he should have won."

Some said Harrison could have been a world-beater if he practiced like Hogan. Of that, said Dutch late in his career, "I'm just not built that way, I guess. But if I were just starting now, I'd sure change my ways. I'd work harder, especially on short putts, if I had it to do over again."

Earnest Joe Harrison was named after brothers who were owners of the Conway, Arkansas, plantation where his father was a sharecropper. He later changed his first name to Ernest, but it didn't matter much because on tour he was listed as E.J. Harrison and universally called Dutch. It's a nickname he was given by his fellow caddies as a teenager because they said they could never understand what he was saying.

Harrison's caddie days were spent at Little Rock Country Club after his family moved to the city when he was eight and his father became a Little Rock policeman. One of eight children, perhaps Dutch was barely missed by his parents when he went off to ride the rails around Texas at age fifteen.

"I didn't tell my folks where I was goin' or anybody," Harrison later recalled. "I hoboed a rumblin' freight train outta Little Rock with only a couple dollars in my pocket."

He would hop off the train at various locales and make money by doing odd jobs on a farm or by caddying. He came back to Little Rock a few months later, decked out in cowboy duds after a stint as a ranch hand. Such tales led to Harrison being called the "Arkansas Traveler," a tag applied to him often in newspaper stories during his career.

The traveling eventually was done on the pro tour, though he didn't make an impact there until the late 1930s. Like Mangrum, he married a widow some 12 years his senior whose support helped him to make it on the tour. His marriage had an unhappy end, though. The couple separated after World War II, and Harrison found a traveling companion in a woman he met in a gallery. According to Beach Leighton, the author of *Mr. Dutch: The Arkansas Traveler*, Harrison's wife, Emma, showed up at several tournaments during the late 1940s with a pistol, threatening to shoot Dutch, though the incidents were all defused. Harrison was the only member of the 1949 Ryder Cup team who traveled on the boat unaccompanied; the others all brought their wives.

Harrison won only two tournaments before World War II despite finishing in the top ten 58 times. He found the winning touch during the war, when he was fortunate to have benevolent superior officers in the Army Air Forces who gave him a generous amount of furlough time. He won three tournaments total in 1944 and '45, and by the time of the 1949 Ryder Cup had amassed a total of ten PGA tour victories.

Dutch was an affable person, the type who said that he never met a stranger. He enjoyed talking with the galleries and telling stories in bull sessions with his fellow pros. "One hour after I met him, I felt like he was an old friend," Middlecoff said.

Even the people who lost to him on the golf course came away enjoying the experience, since Dutch had a way of buttering people up while he was beating them. That's exactly what he did in Ryder Cup singles when Hogan sent him out in the crucial opening match against Max Faulkner, one of the top two players on the British team along with Fred Daly. After a few holes of their match, Faulkner said to Dutch, "Mr. Harrison, you've been telling me how well I drive, how well I hit my irons, and how well I putt. How is it I'm three down to you?"

While complimenting Faulkner, Harrison was busy making five threes on the first six holes to take that three-up lead. By lunchtime, Dutch was seven up on the way to an eight-and-seven victory that inspired the Americans.

Still, Britain managed to win two of the next three matches (beating Palmer and Hamilton, losing to Snead) to lead five–three with four matches remaining. They never earned another point. Clayton Heafner, Chick Harbert, Demaret, and Mangrum each won by at least four-and-three margins. All but Heafner shot 68 or better in the morning round. Mangrum had his hands full with Daly in the decisive final match. "This guy is good!" Lloyd said at the lunch break. "I'm around in 65 and only one up!" Mangrum ended up virtually clinching a four-and-three victory by making four straight birdies on the back nine in the afternoon.

British captain Whitcombe had seen all he could stand: "I have suffered the tortures of the damned for the last four hours watching Hogan's team of robots playing golf!"

He probably did not mean it pejoratively, referring rather to the precision of the Americans' play. They were aided in that by the weather. Early in the week, the course was playing extremely fast due to a drought, requiring run-up shots to the greens that the British players were adept at and the visitors unaccustomed to. But rain started on Friday afternoon and continued overnight, softening the course into the type of test more familiar to the Americans.

Fear of captain Hogan's wrath might have played a role, too. Otherwise, it could have been a long boat ride back across the Atlantic.

As it worked out, the team didn't travel back to the States together. Originally, they were scheduled to sail back on October 8 after playing in Britain for three more weeks. That changed when some players decided to make a side trip to Paris before returning. It changed even more when the British government devalued the pound by thirty percent during the week of the Ryder Cup, leaving the prospect of playing tournaments for pounds less appealing (and the pounds they had in their pockets worth less than they had been when they exchanged for them). Eight of the Americans were scheduled to play in the British PGA Championship the week after the Ryder Cup, but the ones who weren't scheduled for the Paris trip the following week tried to book an immediate return.

"What we want most from this country is out," said Demaret. "I feel like a rat leaving a sinking ship, but I want to go back where I can play for those good old American dollars."

When they couldn't arrange an immediate departure, the Americans all started the match-play British PGA. But Demaret, Hamilton, and Hogan booked a departure for two days later. Demaret lost his first-round match, though it is hard to see how he could have been very motivated to win it when he would have needed to withdraw the next day. Hamilton won his match, but withdrew to catch the ship, saying that he had just received word that his child was ill.

Only Palmer and Mangrum advanced as far as the quarterfinals, losing in succession to three-time British Open champion Cotton, who had controversially declined a spot on the British Ryder Cup team, saying that he was semi-retired and not prepared to engage in such a rigorous competition.

None of the Americans stuck around for either of the next two British tournaments. Snead and Alexander, whose baby had been born two days before he left, flew back to the States and the other five headed for Paris. Hogan originally was scheduled to go to Paris as well, but changed his plans for a reason that was not specified.

The American exodus from Britain was noted with displeasure by the host country. The Americans pointed out that they never officially committed to the post-Ryder tournaments, and that players had legitimate reasons for heading back to the United States or wanting to vacation in Paris. Still, the Americans' willingness to pull out of tournaments was ironic considering that less than two months earlier the PGA suspended Bobby Locke indefinitely for failing to honor commitments to play in the Inverness Four-Ball and Western Open.

After winning the British Open and realizing he could make better money following up by playing in British events, Locke wired to the United States that he wouldn't be coming back for the Inverness and the Western. Citing a past history of skipping out on exhibitions that had been set up, the PGA slapped Locke with a suspension. The background was that since first coming to these shores to play in 1947, the South African had earned few friends. He had a prickly personality, and left the impression that he was interested solely in looking out for No. 1, especially when it came to money. He also proved himself to be one of the best players on the tour, winning a total of ten tournaments from his arrival in mid-1947 to mid-1949. The severity of the punishment—why was the suspension indefinite?—made it appear as if the Americans were just trying to rid themselves of a player they had trouble beating.

Earlier in 1949 they had declared Locke ineligible for the PGA Championship after letting him play as an invited guest the previous two years. The Locke decision, plus the five-year eligibility rule that kept Middlecoff from competing in the PGA Championship or Ryder Cup, led Grantland Rice to write in August 1949, "The PGA as a working body, or a committee, can do more stupid things than any other two sports organizations put together."

Even with the Ryder Cup victory, the 1949 season was coming to a rather uninspiring close. Hogan's crash and Locke's suspension had caused the loss of two of the PGA tour's best players, maybe for good. There were fewer tournaments and less prize money than there was in the previous year, due mostly to the length of time required for a Ryder Cup trip in those days, causing the tour to grind to a halt in late August. Still, if the tour was stronger, the lucrative late-year West Coast events could have been delayed by a month instead of canceled.

On the positive side of the ledger were the reemergence of Snead just at the time the tour needed a marquee player (six victories on the year plus a significant unofficial one at the North and South Open) and the emergence of Middlecoff (also with six wins) as a potential star.

Still, this was a tour in need of good news as 1950 loomed on the horizon.

10

1950 LOS ANGELES OPEN/ THE COMEBACK

O N NOVEMBER 25, Oscar Fraley of United Press International suggested that Ben Hogan be inducted into the newly created Golf Hall of Fame because "there is small doubt that he is through as a top flight competitor."

About ten days earlier, unbeknownst to the outside world, Hogan had taken a big step toward proving that commonly held notion wrong. That's when he went out to Colonial Country Club to hit full shots for the first time since his accident.

The Ryder Cup experience had been good for Hogan in that the journey kept him occupied for a month-and-a-half period when he was still not allowed to swing a club. He held up pretty well under the strain of the captaincy, but a doctor had to give him some shots to ease his pain on the trip back aboard the *Queen Mary*.

During the Ryder Cup buildup, British golf writers Leonard Crawley and Henry Longhurst had a chance to talk to Hogan, who told them that he intended to play championship golf again. Crawley wrote four years later, "Longhurst and I looked at one another, and when Hogan left us we said in the same breath: 'How pathetic.'"

After arriving back in Fort Worth, Hogan still had a little more than a month to wait before he could finally venture to the practice range, following his doctor's schedule. During this period he was working on a financial settlement with the Greyhound Corp. and also on a movie deal. Both would be finalized before the end of the year. The Greyhound settlement terms were undisclosed but reported to be $25,000 a year for life; the movie, *Follow the Sun*, would be directed by Sidney Lanfield.

Hogan continued to do his walking, even venturing to Colonial and back, a seven-mile round trip, a few times. His legs were getting better, but he had to wrap them completely in special elastic bandages, and swelling was still a problem. The knee diagnosed with torn cartilage seemed to he holding up well enough.

Finally, in mid-November the day arrived for Hogan to once again take a full swing. Various accounts have him falling down or hitting a shank on his first shot. A Colonial caddie who witnessed the practice session didn't mention either of those occurring, but he did say, "When he started to swing a wood, it was pathetic. I couldn't believe I was watching Ben Hogan."

Those were the effects of going more than nine months without swinging a club, and swinging on legs that had not yet returned to full strength. But Hogan was back home on the range, his favorite place in the world except maybe for the 18th green of a tournament where he was hoisting a trophy.

The man who loved to sort things out on the range now had the chance to do just that. Between muscle memory and experimentation, it didn't take him long to get the swing back.

By December 10, Hogan deemed himself ready to play a full round. He was accompanied by old friend Ray Gafford, a Fort Worth pro and sometime tour player. It went so well that they played the next day, too. During the second round, Gafford asked

Hogan if he had any intentions of entering the Los Angeles Open, which was less than a month away.

"I don't know. Why?" Hogan replied.

"You'd sure shock a lot of people," Gafford said.

He would indeed. Even Hogan's friend Jimmy Demaret showed up at the Miami Open earlier that same week telling people he had recently attended the Notre Dame–Southern Methodist University football game with Hogan in Dallas and that he didn't think Ben would attempt a comeback. Three weeks later, he was playing a practice round with Hogan at Riviera in Los Angeles.

Gafford was so impressed with Hogan's play that he called the local papers and told them that Ben played his first rounds of golf since the crash and shot a 71 and 72. The story was picked up by the wire services and reported nationally.

Golf World termed it a "wild" report after it checked with Hogan, who said that the scores reported were "newspaper scores."

True enough, Hogan used what he termed a "scooter" to get around the course. (The electric golf cart did not hit the market until 1951.) And he wasn't keeping a strict score or putting everything out. But *Golf World*, and the entire world, would find out soon enough that, as wild as it sounded, Hogan was already playing tour quality golf.

Hogan gave mixed signals to *Fort Worth Star-Telegram* writer Jack Murphy. He said that he was going out to the West Coast for the Los Angeles Open, Bing Crosby Pro-Am, and the Phoenix Open (which had been renamed the Ben Hogan Open). But he wasn't sure if he would play in the tournaments or just attend.

"Don't waste your time writing about me," he said. "People are tired of hearing about Ben Hogan. They're interested in the guys who are playing now."

Hogan didn't play his third round until December 20, but this time he walked the course. It took such a toll on his legs that after the round he returned home and went to bed.

Two days later, he told an Associated Press reporter that he was headed west but that he certainly didn't hope to do any competing in California. Of his recent round, he offered only that he shot lower than 80.

"I get awfully tired and sometimes my legs swell on me," he said. "But you know"—and he grinned at this—"I have to get my weight down."

Whether it was relative inactivity, home cooking, or bulking up his upper body with workouts, Hogan now weighed more than 155 pounds—about twenty pounds over his usual playing weight.

"Me trying to take off weight is something to joke about," he said.

Hogan was confident that he would be back playing the tour again. But, he said, "I don't think I'll ever be able to go two rounds in one day in tournament competition. But there aren't many tournaments that have 36 holes in one day anyway."

Unfortunately, two that did were the two biggest tournaments in the United States, the U.S. Open and the PGA Championship.

Augusta Chronicle sports editor Randy Russell was skeptical about the reports of Hogan possibly playing on the West Coast, writing in December that he didn't even expect him to be ready to play in the Masters in April. "He's almost certainly a long way from complete recovery," Russell wrote.

Hogan, meanwhile, was seriously contemplating playing in Los Angeles at the beginning of January. When he boarded a train headed for California on December 28, he sounded a slightly more optimistic note about an immediate return to action.

"There's a possibility that I might play [in Los Angeles]," he was quoted in an Associated Press story, "but right now I can't say. I honestly don't know myself . . . I'll just have to wait to see how I'm feeling and how my game is working. One thing for sure, I'm not going to go out there and shoot in the eighties."

The AP article noted that in practice sessions at Colonial "his game is rounding into form with such ease that even Hogan is astounded."

On the way to California, Hogan stopped in El Paso and visited the Hotel Dieu to thank the staff for the care he received there. He arrived in Los Angeles on the evening of December 29, and was on the course the next day.

This was the Friday before the start of the tournament, so official practice rounds hadn't started yet and Hogan was able to play with Hollywood director Lanfield along with fellow pro George Fazio. Remarkably, Hogan shot a 69. He walked all the way, but his caddie carried a folding chair for him to rest on while the others were playing.

"I was chipping and putting like a madman," Hogan told reporters, saying he really hadn't hit the ball as well as his score indicated. "I wasn't driving very well, or hitting good shots to the green. Some of my drives hit trees and bounced back into good playable positions."

Lucky or not, it was sensational news. In a matter of a few weeks, a Hogan comeback had gone from being unlikely to happen at all (in the minds of many) to being not only probable but imminent. Of course, there was still the question of how his body would hold up under the strain of multiple rounds, which is why Hogan had still not decided whether or not to enter the Los Angeles Open.

Sometime within the next couple of days, Demaret arrived in Los Angeles and found Hogan (where else?) on the practice range. He couldn't believe how well Hogan was hitting the ball.

"Looks like you've been practicing a bit," Demaret said.

"No, I've been out for a long time, Jimmy," Hogan replied. "I'm just going to try my luck here."

Shaking Ben's hand, Demaret noted the calluses. Hogan might have played only four rounds, but he had clearly been putting in a lot of work on the range.

Now he was sharpening his game on the course: Hogan played practice rounds at Riviera on six straight days. In one of those rounds, he was playing with Cary Middlecoff. On the fairway of the 17th hole, a long, uphill par five, Middlecoff asked Hogan if his legs hurt. "They hurt like hell," Hogan responded.

It took Hogan four days from his arrival in Los Angeles before he finally decided to enter the tournament, against the advice of his wife, Valerie, who thought it was too much too soon. "I didn't think he was being fair to himself," she later said, indicating that she thought he was giving in to the pressure of the public and the press to play.

Finally, at around noon on Tuesday, Hogan announced that he would compete. (The Los Angeles Open was played on a Friday-to-Monday schedule, the idea being to maximize the gate. People would come out on the weekend anyway, and then the lure of the final round would encourage fans to make the necessary arrangements to attend on Monday.)

That afternoon, Hogan shot a 72 in a practice round that included a 33 on the back nine. Playing a $10 Nassau bet (separate bets on the front nine, back nine, and entire round) with Ed Furgol as a partner against Jack Burke Jr., and John Barnum, Hogan's team was one down through 14 holes. At that point, Hogan and Furgol "pressed" for $30, meaning an additional bet on the last four holes. Hogan's hot finish enabled his team to win the back nine, the round, and the press.

"It's later than you think," Furgol told Burke and Barnum as he was collecting, meaning that Hogan had somehow avoided the rusty phase after not picking up a club for 10 months and not playing a tournament for 11 months. He had, figuratively speaking, hit the ground running and was in prime form entering his first tournament, as he demonstrated by shooting a 67 in his final practice round on Wednesday. Hogan elected not to play on Thursday, though, instead working on the range in his final preparation for the tournament.

At a sports luncheon that Wednesday, Middlecoff called Hogan "a miracle man." Later in the week, he told reporters, "If he wins this thing, believe me, it won't be with his game. It'll be with his heart. Bennie has more heart than anybody I've ever known."

On Thursday evening, Hogan was the guest of honor at a party for the players, but he ducked out early. The players, no different from golf fans in their curiosity about how Hogan would do, spent the rest of the evening talking about him. They seemed equally divided in their opinions about his prospects.

Was Hogan one of the favorites? Or would tournament rust or his physical condition prevent him from putting forth his best effort for 72 holes?

On Friday, everyone would start to find out. It was probably the most anticipated first round of a tournament ever on the PGA tour, and it turned into somewhat of a circus.

When Hogan's group stepped on the first tee, tournament announcer Scotty Chisolm intoned, "Ladies and gentlemen, this is the greatest event in the history of the Los Angeles Open, but I have been requested by Mr. Hogan to introduce him and say nothing else. On the tee—Ben Hogan!"

The Friday crowd of 9,000 spectators was the largest ever for a first round at the Los Angeles Open. Naturally, they all wanted to see Hogan. So did a larger-than-usual press corps, including photographers.

Hogan posed for photos before playing from the first tee, but requested of tournament officials that no other pictures of him be allowed. His group was accompanied by a boy carrying a hastily made sign that read: NO CAMERAS, PLEASE!!! PLAYER'S REQUEST.

Some photographers ventured out with him anyway, and in the first fairway Hogan said to them, "Can't you fellas read?" as he indicated the sign. An argument ensued, with fans taking Hogan's side, shouting, "Throw them out!" and "Take their cameras away!"

The photographers left, but only to plead their case to tournament director George Schneiter in the clubhouse.

Hogan's no-photo request may seem outrageous. But in 1950 it was unusual for players to be followed by photographers, and unprecedented in the numbers that wanted to follow Hogan on this day. Golf photography then mostly consisted of posed shots of the leaders after the round. Action shots were generally taken by a photographer setting up at a particular spot, usually shooting from a fair distance.

In this case, though, as Herb Graffis pointed out in *Golfdom*, "Each guy figured they might get the Shot of the Year by catching Ben collapsing after making his own shot. That put even the steel-nerved Hogan under the most severe psychological strain borne by any golf tournament contestant." And with galleries and photographers walking down fairways in those days, it would be done from relatively close range.

But, while not outrageous, Hogan's request wasn't exactly reasonable. After all, photographers were allowed to shoot other players, so why should Hogan be exempt?

In previous years, Schneiter had acted as tournament manager while also being a tour player. This year, the PGA no longer allowed him to play that dual role, and it was a good thing at the Los Angeles Open, where there was so much going on. He decided to lift the photo ban, getting word to the course by walkie-talkie. The sign was taken away on the eighth hole. Hogan gave no indication that he noticed, and made no complaint when the photographers reappeared.

After the round, Hogan met with Schneiter and the photographers and reached a truce. Hogan denied saying in the argument on the first fairway that "there are no pictures or I won't play," stating that what he meant were he didn't want any pictures taken before he hit the ball. The photographers agreed not to take any photos until after the shot, and relative harmony reigned for the rest of the tournament.

Schneiter also made a decision for the benefit of the writers covering the tournament. He brought the leading players to the press room for interviews instead of the writers being forced to chase down the players in the locker room or elsewhere, as was usually the case. Not that the print reporters didn't have gripes about their treatment relative to members of the electronic media.

"Writers complained they had to muscle through the mud and crowds while radio guys got classy and comfortable truck and jeep transportation," wrote Graffis. "Jeeps were loaded with some movie and radio hams and a bevy of broads whose interest in golf is limited to barely knowing which end of the caddie to hold."

The movie people were under the direction of Lanfield, gathering material and background for the upcoming movie about Hogan.

Amid all the hubbub, Hogan's first-round score was nothing special as he shot a two-over 73. He shot a one-under 34 on the front nine, but faded on the back nine. The poor finish was understandable for a man whose weakened legs were wrapped not only in bandages but also special rubber support stockings to reduce swelling. The big news was that Ben was back, even if he was in a tie for 16th, five strokes behind leader Ed Furgol.

During the second round, it became clear that Ben was not only back, he was *back*. He again shot a 34 on the front nine, but this time stayed strong with a 35 coming home (aided by holing a 60-foot birdie putt on the 14th) for a 69 that moved him into a tie for third at 142. He was still five strokes off the lead, now held by a red-hot Jerry Barber, who followed an opening round 69 with a 68. But now there was only one other man (Henry Ransom at 139) between Hogan and the lead.

There was a glimpse of a changed Hogan when he heard the voice of radio announcer Bill Stern as he was standing over a two-foot par putt on the fifth hole. Instead of giving Stern a dagger-like stare, Hogan looked up and smiled. Smiled! The terrible accident alone had turned Hogan into a player who fans could root for with their hearts as well as their heads. If he started occasionally showing genuine emotion on the course, he could win them over even further.

Sunday was one of the strangest days ever at the Los Angeles Open. It started out in a drizzle, which turned into a hard rain at around noon. Still, they played on, even as puddles were accumulating on the greens. The rules allow players to move their ball to find a dry path to the hole, but by mid-afternoon many of the greens were completely covered with water and the rest weren't much better.

Willie Hunter, the pro at tournament host Riviera, at 12:30 was the first to protest that play should be stopped because the course was unplayable. When the committee said no, he picked up his ball and stalked off. Over the next three-and-a-half hours, with conditions worsening, 16 other players joined him, including Sam Snead, who shot a 40 on the front nine.

By four o'clock, fifty-seven of the ninety players who survived the 36-hole cut had finished their rounds. Out on the course was Hogan, who after shooting a four-over 39 on the front nine said, "It's idiotic to go on playing, but I'll be as idiotic as the rest of them."

The 11th hole at Riviera is bisected by a normally dry barranca, where there was now a raging torrent of water. When he reached it, Hogan saw that there was no way he could jump across the stream on his battered legs. He could continue, he said, only if there was a rowboat to get him across. Officials were summoned by walkie-talkie, and they finally decided to call off the round.

The way it happened almost made it appear as if the committee was caving in to the tournament's star player, but in retrospect they should have called off the round well before that. If it had gone any further, it would have turned into a farce.

The protocol in those days was that if a round was called by rain, all scores were wiped out and the round replayed. That has since been replaced by the procedure of suspending play, and resuming it at the same point the next day. The philosophy behind a replay was that if a round was played over two days, conditions could be drastically different, and hence unfair to those who played in the worst of it. Eventually, though, it became conventional wisdom that it is more unfair to wash away a player's round, great or poor. The belief now is that every shot should count.

Barber, the smallest player in the field at five-foot-five, was a victim of the policy then in force. The thirty-three-old was just starting his third year on the tour and had yet to post an official victory (he would go on to win seven times, including the 1961 PGA Championship). He was well on his way to the winner's circle after slogging to a 73. Barber's total of three-under 210 for 54 holes was fully ten strokes ahead of anyone else who finished; of the players remaining on the course Ransom was the best at two-over for the tournament through 10 holes and Hogan four-over through the same point.

Those spectators bold enough to go out to Riviera that wet day mostly ended up in the clubhouse watching the local telecast of the tournament. It was showing only the 18th hole, but at least they were able to stay dry. Then, just to add to the chaos, the power went out in that part of town, leaving the television screen blank and the lights off.

The next day the weather returned to normal and Hogan moved closer to the lead. He pulled within two strokes after shooting a 69 that included a blazing three-under 32 on the front nine. Consecutive three-putt bogeys on the 14th and 15th dropped him back, but a seven-foot birdie putt on the 18th hole ended the round on a good note.

UPI's Benson Srere summed up the atmosphere. "So completely does the gallant Texan dominate attention that little heed is paid to other top-notch performances being turned in during the event. There is only one word around the fairways. It's 'Hogan.'"

Barber was a scrambler whose game was fueled by great putting, but the putts weren't falling as often in the third round. He shot a 72 in much more benign conditions than his washed-out 73 of the day before, and the field drew closer to him. Charles Curtis of the *Los Angeles Times* described it as "a pack of hungry hounds closing in on a succulent little bunny." Barber led at 209, followed by Hogan at 211, Burke at 212, Ellsworth Vines at 213, and Snead and Ransom at 214.

The final round was held on a Tuesday, but an estimated 10,500 spectators managed to get off work (or at least slip away early) to see if Hogan could pull off the stunning feat of winning his first tournament back after 11 months of injury-induced inactivity. Barber opened the door by shooting a 79 that left him in a tie for seventh, Sunday's rainout possibly costing him the $2,600 first prize and leaving him instead with $750.

Hogan got off to a great start, reaching the par-five first hole in two shots and two-putting for a birdie. He continued his mastery of the front nine with a 12-foot birdie putt on the eighth hole giving him a two-under 33. Just as he had in the first three rounds, Hogan was resting on a folding chair between shots.

Hogan's only bogey of the day came on the par-five 11th, where he hit "two bad wood shots," according to Curtis's *Times* account. Then it was pars all the way home, except at the 15th hole, where he miraculously holed a putt estimated at 80–90 feet on the two-level green for a birdie. He finished with his third straight 69 for a four-under 280.

A Hollywood scriptwriter might not even dare to have Hogan sink a winning putt that long. If he did, though, it would happen on the 18th green, with all the other contenders sitting in the clubhouse. The real-life scenario was different, which was the first indication that Lanfield's writers weren't scripting the show. Hogan went off about an hour ahead of the threesome of Snead, Burke, and Barber, the first two of whom became his main contenders.

Snead and Burke found out with four holes remaining that they needed to go two-under the rest of the way to tie Hogan. Both parred 15 and 16. As Snead walked to the 17th green, he turned to Burke and said, "We gotta knock a couple of these in to catch the little man."

Snead was already three-under for the day, and he got one of the closing birdies he needed by holing a 10-foot putt on the 17th. The finishing hole at Riviera is a long, difficult par four with one of the best amphitheater settings in golf, a hillside to the left of the green providing thousands with a great view of the finish. Snead planted his approach some 15 feet behind the hole, leaving him a birdie putt to tie Hogan.

As Snead looked over the putt, the tension was broken when a fan fell out of a small tree when the limb he was sitting on broke. The gallery laughed, and so did Snead, who went back to business and holed the curling putt for a great final round score of 66 and a tie with Hogan. The tournament would be decided in a playoff between the 1949 Player of the Year and the 1948 Player of the Year/1950 Comeback Kid.

After finishing his round, Hogan had gone into the shower, presumably to freshen up for the awards ceremony. After emerging and getting dressed, he heard the roar from the spectators on the hillside below the clubhouse, which meant yet another day of golf ahead—the sixth in the tournament (including the day he played 11 holes before the rainout), following six practice rounds in seven days.

"I wish I didn't have to play tomorrow," a weary Hogan told reporters in the locker room. "It would have been better if he had won it out there."

Playoffs then were nearly always 18 holes on the next day, which in this case was now Wednesday. The Motor City Open switched to an innovative sudden-death format in 1949, with Middlecoff and Lloyd Mangrum tying for 11 straight holes before being declared co-winners when the playoff was stopped by darkness.

It's possible that the strangeness of this result (still the record for longest sudden-death playoff on the tour) might have slowed the institution of that format, which for the most part didn't take hold until the 1960s and '70s.

Ten minutes before a scheduled 12:30 start on Wednesday, the playoff was postponed due to rain. With the Bing Crosby Pro-Am scheduled to start on Friday, the playoff was put off until the following Wednesday in order to give Hogan and Snead a chance to travel up to Pebble Beach.

Regarding his physical condition, Hogan told reporters as he packed up at Riviera, "Sure I get tired and have to go a little slower than I used to, but I'll get by."

Unfortunately, in addition to fatigue from the tournament, Hogan was just starting to pick up a nasty head cold. That contributed to a first-round 77 at Cypress Point to open the Crosby, where he ultimately finished out of the money in a tie for 19th. When he was contemplating his return to action, he had said that he would only play where it was warm. But the Crosby was a favorite stop, and Hogan decided that since he had agreed to be on hand, he might as well play, despite the cold wind that often blew in from the ocean on the Monterey Peninsula in January.

"I shouldn't have tried to make two tournaments in a row," Hogan said a few months later, admitting his mistake.

Snead, on the other hand, tied for first at 214 in the 54-hole event. They didn't even bother to have a playoff, with Snead, Burke, Dave Douglas, and Smiley Quick declared joint champions. As Charles Price put it in *Golf World* in 1948, "Any resemblance between Bing Crosby's National Pro-Amateur Championship and a golf tournament is purely unintentional . . . The purpose of the whole thing is for everyone to have a good time."

Now it was back to Southern California for what some were calling the Match of the Century. But even with two days to rest before the Wednesday playoff, Hogan was showing signs of wear.

"Ben is all right, but he's awfully tired," Valerie Hogan told an Associated Press reporter. "The freezing weather during the Crosby tournament took a lot out of him."

The playoff was anticlimactic. The first tee shot was a bad sign for Hogan, as he hooked it out of bounds. He was lucky that the USGA had changed the penalty for an out-of-bounds shot from stroke-and-distance to just a distance penalty in 1948, a change that would last only four years. That meant his second tee shot counted as his second stroke on the hole, instead of his third, and he ended up making a par five. He still lost a stroke to Snead's birdie.

The players were both one over through seven holes, but Snead birdied the eighth and Hogan bogeyed the ninth, where he missed a two-and-a-half-foot putt. The back nine was pretty dull, Snead wrapping up the victory with a string of nine pars while Hogan hit two drives into deep trouble to set up bogeys. Ben didn't make a birdie all day, shooting a 76 to enable Snead to win easily with a one-over 72.

"Snead didn't play too good today, but then neither did I," said a dispirited Hogan after the round. "I'm sorry we didn't play better golf for all these people and I'm also sorry Sam didn't get one more brilliant shot in the last day of the tournament so that we wouldn't have had to go through this playoff."

Grantland Rice summed up the playoff best when, playing himself in the movie *Follow the Sun*, he said that Hogan's "legs weren't strong enough to carry his heart around."

Despite the lack of a Hollywood ending, Hogan's Los Angeles Open performance was inspirational. Pat Robinson of the International News Service wrote that "nobody with the possible exception of the dying Babe Ruth and Lou Gehrig has so stirred the nation's heart as Ben Hogan."

Johnny Bulla, who played the first two rounds in Los Angeles with Hogan, was amazed at how far Ben had come in such a short time.

"It was only last November that I stopped in to visit Ben Hogan at his home in Fort Worth. I took one look at him and was convinced he'd never play tournament golf again," Bulla told Al Abrams of the *Pittsburgh Post-Gazette*. "But, less than two months later, the little son-of-a-gun tees off in the Los Angeles Open and winds up in a tie with Sammy Snead for the lead. No, sir. I wouldn't have believed it if I didn't see it myself."

A far less inspirational story—but one that also involved a car accident—kept defending champion Mangrum from playing in the Los Angeles Open in his hometown. On November 2, 1949, two months before the tournament, Mangrum and his wife were passengers in the rear seat of a car when it was involved in a fender bender with a car driven by a twenty-three-year-old University of Southern California student named Joe Turner. Tempers flared, but the parties got back in their cars without incident.

When the Mangrums arrived home, they were surprised to see the other car pull into the driveway across the street. It turned out that, unbeknownst to each other, the Mangrums and Turners were neighbors.

From there, things went from bad to worse. Joe Turner came to the Mangrums' house to discuss the incident. When the discussion became an argument, Lloyd decided to fetch his gun to persuade Turner to leave. What happened next wasn't clear, but somehow the next act of the play took place on the Turners' front lawn, where Joe Turner and his father, E.J., got into a scuffle with Mangrum. Afterward, Lloyd felt an ache in his right shoulder—the same one he had injured in a Jeep accident in World War II.

He had fractured a shoulder bone, which required surgery, followed by another minor operation on January 3. Mangrum was a spectator at the Los Angeles Open and reported that "it might be March before I could play well enough to pay my hotel bill, so I may be home for some time."

11

1950 MASTERS/TWO JIMS

AFTER THE LOS Angeles Open playoff, Snead headed straight to the Long Beach Open while Hogan went to Palm Springs for a few days before traveling to Phoenix, where the sponsoring Thunderbirds organization had renamed the Phoenix Open the Ben Hogan Open.

Hogan arrived in town with a bout of the flu, but recovered by tournament time and shot a 65 in the first round. He credited it to the best putting of his life, an indication that his ball-striking wasn't what he wanted it to be. The putts stopped falling in the next three rounds, however, as Hogan finished 73–73–72 to tie for 20th and split the last money place with five other players, each earning $16.66.

Jimmy Demaret claimed the title by one stroke over Snead, thanks in part to a favorable ruling on the 18th hole of the final round given by tournament official Bob Goldwater—brother of future United States Senator Barry.

After the end of the Phoenix tournament on January 29, Ben and Valerie headed back to Fort Worth, this time in the safety of a train. Hogan's next tournament appearance was at the Seminole Pro-Am in Palm Beach, Florida, March 13–15.

The 54-hole Seminole wasn't considered an official event by the PGA, but carried a good-sized purse ($10,000) for forty invited pros on the outstanding Donald Ross-designed Seminole Country Club course. Hogan opened with a dismal 79 and ended up tied for 24th despite a decent 71–70 finish.

Speaking to *Golf World* at Seminole, Hogan chalked up his Los Angeles Open performance to inspiration. "I was enthusiastic about playing again," he said. "My friends inspired me. They all wanted me to do well. I wanted to make a showing. I was inspired at the Los Angeles Open."

But he hadn't come close to duplicating that experience in the three tourneys since. Asked when he was going to get his top game back, Hogan replied, "I'm trying to get my health back, not my golf."

Hogan remained at Seminole until just before the Masters in what would become an annual spring ritual of preparation for Augusta. Perhaps the break from tournament competition would help his physical condition, while allowing him enough work on the practice range to get his game back.

Meanwhile, Snead had stolen the thunder of Hogan's Los Angeles comeback not only by winning the playoff at Riviera, but by tearing up the PGA tour afterwards. Entering the Masters, Snead had made nine starts with five victories, two seconds, a fourth, and a sixth. Snead was the consensus Masters favorite going in, with the only qualification being that he came to Augusta complaining about an aching back. With Hogan still fighting his physical problems and Lloyd Mangrum having just returned to action two weeks earlier following his shoulder surgery, there was a "watch out for the invalids" theme to the Masters previews.

Augusta National was playing particularly tough in 1950. There hadn't been much rain and the greens were like concrete, making approach shots difficult to control. They were also lightning fast, requiring a delicate putting touch.

Rookie Robert "Skee" Riegel, the 1947 U.S. Amateur champion, shot the only score in the 60s in the first round, a 69, but eventually slipped back to finish 21st. There were two sub-70 scores in the second round, a 67 by Jim Ferrier and a 68 by Hogan, scores good enough to earn them the top two spots in the tournament, Ferrier claiming a healthy four-stroke lead at 137.

The Associated Press came up with a new catch phrase for Hogan in its second-round report: "golf's interesting invalid." Mercifully, that one did not catch on. Ben's second round was certainly interesting, though, spiced by four straight birdies starting at the sixth hole, coming on putts of between six and 25 feet. Hogan's four-under 32 matched the course record for the front nine. His round stalled a bit when his second shot found a creek on the par-five 13th, leading to a bogey, but he cleared the water with a bold second shot on the par-five 15th for a two-putt birdie.

The six-foot-four, 215-pound Ferrier was a long hitter, and also one of the best putters in the game. Those strengths made him particularly well suited to Augusta National, where he had finished fourth, sixth, and fourth from 1946 to '48.

Ferrier arrived in the United States with his wife, Norma, from his native Australia in March 1940 for a six-month visit that turned into a lifetime stay. As an amateur, he financed his travels by writing about golf for a couple of Australian newspapers. The winner of four Australian Amateurs and the 1938 and 1939 Australian Opens, he competed in the Masters and a variety of amateur and open events in America in 1940. But that August, a couple of weeks before he expected to compete in the U.S. Amateur, he was informed by the United States Golf Association that it considered him a professional because he had written a golf instruction book.

Ferrier tried to claim that the book only told how *he* played, not how *to* play. (He had an unorthodox swing, with a pronounced dip, because of a knee injury he had suffered as a child that prevented him from straightening his left leg on the follow-through.) It was a pretty weak argument, further undercut by the fact that he addressed instructional topics in some of his newspaper articles. He had passed muster with Australian and British authorities, but the USGA took a stricter stance on instructional writing and amateur status.

As late as December 1940, Ferrier was quoted as saying that he intended to remain an amateur, even though the USGA had already ruled he wasn't one. (In that same article in the *St. Petersburg Times*, he predicted that Ben Hogan, then coming off his first big year, would have "a brilliant but short career in the limelight because he concentrates too hard and practices too much for one of such slight stature.")

When Ferrier decided to accept a contract from Wilson Sporting Goods in 1941 and also take a job as a club pro in Elmhurst, Illinois, he wrote his father—and didn't hear back for several months. "It was something my father had to think about before he accepted it . . . Of course, when I won the PGA Championship in 1947 he was very happy," Ferrier told Al Barkow in *Gettin' to the Dance Floor.*

Ferrier could just as well have been called a Scotsman as an Australian. His father was from Carnoustie, Scotland; his great grandfather was one of the founders of Carnoustie Golf Club. The family pub served as an unofficial clubhouse on what is still Ferrier Street in that Scottish town. But there were no golf pros in the family. "The old caste system was in existence then," Ferrier said.

His father, J.B., was an accountant who got a job in Shanghai, where he married an Australian woman. The couple went to Australia in 1913 and stayed for six years, during which time Jim was born in 1915. He spent the first four years of his life in Australia, then lived in Shanghai until he was eleven. At that point, J.B., an excellent amateur golfer, returned to Australia for good, and took a job as secretary of Manly Golf Club near Sydney.

His father's position afforded Jim with the run of the club, and soon he was beating all comers. Club champion at fifteen, Ferrier came within a whisker of winning the Australian Open at sixteen. In 1936, at twenty-one, he ventured to Scotland and was runner-up in the British Amateur. He traveled back home via the United States, and that experience, on top of a 1934 exhibition by American pros he had seen in Australia, convinced him that America was the place to be for the best competition.

Ferrier played the tour part-time in 1941 and '42, with mixed success. In 1943, he was drafted into the Army even though he wasn't a citizen. "Well, we wanted to become citizens, because we figured we were going to live here and play golf here. It was our new home, the United States," he told Barkow. "We liked it, everything was fun, and joining the Army to become a citizen was a cinch."

Because his bad knee swelled up during basic training, Ferrier ended up in the quartermaster corps and was stationed at the Presidio in San Francisco. During a leave, he scored his first PGA tour victory at the Oakland Open in 1944.

After the war, he elected to play the tour full-time, financed in part by representing Wilson. The Ferriers didn't have a real home in the late 1940s and early 1950s, essentially living out of their car. It was a grand adventure Jim shared with Norma, both on and off the course. Norma was a fine golfer herself, and she was well-known for walking the course with Jim, watching every shot he played.

After the 1950 U.S. Open, Earl Eby wrote in the *Philadelphia Bulletin*, "Those who were in the Jim Ferrier gallery in the Open still retain the picture of the faithful Mrs. Ferrier who followed her husband through the 72-hole grind, rising and falling with him. Thursday and Friday when the heat was at its greatest, Mrs. Ferrier would open a hunt stick, one of those portable leather seats, and make Jim sit on it while he waited for others to putt. She would wipe his face and neck with a towel."

After a round, Ferrier never hung around with the boys, Instead, he would leave with Norma to go wherever they were staying and review his play stroke by stroke, analyzing what he could do to improve.

"She could look at me and tell when my pace was quicker or my movements were different, and that was all I needed," Ferrier later recalled.

Norma was instrumental in Jim winning the 1947 PGA Championship, which was his second tour victory. A week earlier, he had finished sixth at the U.S. Open, poor putting keeping him from having a good chance at victory. When he arrived at Plum Hollow outside Detroit for the PGA, Norma told him to spend his entire practice time working on his putting. It paid off, as he rolled to victory, beating local favorite Chick Harbert in the final. By the time of the 1950 Masters, he owned seven tour wins.

Ferrier slipped to a 73 in the third round, but that wasn't too bad since he had a cushion and the course wasn't yielding any low scores. Hogan had a chance to tie for the lead with a birdie on the 18th hole, but found himself a victim to the tough conditions, his approach shot bounding past the hole and leading to a three-putt bogey.

"That second shot of mine was as fine a shot as I've ever made," said a disgruntled Hogan in the locker room. "And then I come up there and find myself 25 feet away—and with the toughest downhill putt over a fast surface." Hogan knocked the first one five feet past, and missed coming back, to finish the round with a 71 despite making six birdies.

Only five players entered the final round with a chance to win: Ferrier at 210, Hogan at 212, Nelson and Demaret at 214, and Snead at 215. The course had taken a toll on the rest of the field, as nobody else shot better than 218.

Ferrier was being chased by a star-studded group. The trio of Hogan, Nelson, and Snead had dominated the game since the late 1930s, although Nelson was now just a twice-a-year player after retiring to his ranch four years earlier. The thirty-nine-year-old Demaret wasn't far behind them in golf's pecking order, with twenty-three career victories entering the 1950 Masters.

Demaret was known as much for his colorful attire and gregarious personality as his game. But while he now hung out with celebrity pals like Bing Crosby and Bob Hope, Demaret's background was every bit as humble as most pros of the era. He was another Texan, having grown up in Houston in a family of nine children. His father was a carpenter, house painter, and general handyman, but with so many mouths to feed the children all had to work. Just like Hogan, Demaret switched from selling newspapers to caddying (in Jimmy's case, at the age of eight) primarily as a way to make money, but fell in love with the game.

In his early teen years Demaret got a job repairing and making clubs at a municipal course, and at sixteen became an assistant at River Oaks Country Club to the pro, Jack Burke. The job sometimes included babysitting toddler Jack Jr.

Always a life-of-the-party sort, Demaret was a pretty fair singer. While working as a club pro in Galveston, Texas, in the early 1930s, he used to hang out at a local club that brought in some of the country's top big bands, and club owner Sam Maceo sometimes let him fill in on vocals. Jimmy got to know bandleader Ben Bernie, who happened to be a golfer. Demaret gave Bernie golf lessons, and Bernie let him sing with his band. When Bernie asked him why he didn't try the tour, Jimmy responded, "That takes dough." Bernie and Maceo quickly decided to give Demaret a stake to try the 1935 winter tour.

Demaret's personality also helped to land him his first equipment contract. MacGregor's tour representative, Toney Penna, took his boss to see Demaret sing at a local nightclub during a tournament in 1937.

"Toney, I don't know if this boy can play golf or not, that's your department, but as far as a goodwill ambassador is concerned, sign him up because he's worth every penny of it," the boss said.

Demaret won his first tournament in 1938, but wasn't able to make a full run at the circuit until 1940, the year he turned thirty. That was a breakthrough campaign for him, as he won six tournaments, including the Masters.

In an era of drab attire, Demaret attracted attention with the vivid colors of his clothing. It was very much a conscious effort on his part. Along about the time of his first win, he said, "I got the notion that championship golf needed dressing up. To me, the contrast between the beautiful scenery of a golf links, with its bright greens and forest-bordered fairways, and the dull, dingy clothes worn by its contestants, was shocking . . . I began buying the loudest slacks, shirts, and hats I could find."

Grantland Rice wrote that when Demaret steps on the tee "the rainbow ducks behind a cloud and hides its face in shame."

Demaret was conscious of his role as an entertainer on the golf course, and he often bantered with the galleries while smiling his way through a round. Away from the course, Jimmy was known to keep late hours. Many said that he could have won more tournaments if he had taken the game more seriously. But, at his core, Demaret was a people person. "I never met one person who said they didn't like Jimmy Demaret," Snead said.

Make no mistake, though, Demaret could play. He was one of the game's great shot-makers, able to work the ball in either direction, high or low (especially low—he was also one of the game's greatest wind players), soft or hard (he once won a bet by hitting the green on a par three with every club in his bag, from the driver to the putter). After a stateside stint in the Navy during the war, he was the tour's leading money winner in 1947, claiming six victories including his second Masters title.

He slumped a bit in 1949, going winless after his playoff victory over Hogan in Phoenix in January. But the two-time Masters champion was a dangerous threat to Ferrier at Augusta National, especially in the windy conditions that were prevailing.

As was usually the case, golf writers reported on what Demaret was wearing. An Associated Press report gave this wrap-up on his attire for the first three rounds: Thursday, chartreuse pants and a stunning salmon-pink sweater; Friday, purple pants, purple and red shoes, white golf shirt with red piping around formfitting sleeves and neckline; Saturday, rose pants and a nearly matching rose and white shirt featuring a high neckline circling above a dickey.

On Sunday, Demaret came out decked in three shades of green, described in the *Augusta Chronicle* as "looking like an Easter egg" on that Easter Sunday. Would he add a fourth shade at the green jacket ceremony for the winner?

Popular as Demaret was, he drew relatively small galleries that day, as most opted to follow Hogan or Ferrier, who teed off later and appeared to be the most likely winners. Demaret gave the leaders something to think about with a fine 69 in the final round, including a birdie on the 13th hole, which he played six under for the week (two eagles and two birdies).

Hogan, described by the *Chronicle* as "spraying his tee shots all over the course," struggled to a 76 in the final round and a tie for fourth with the rusty Nelson, who shot a 74. Walking the hills of Augusta National for four days appeared to have taken its toll on Hogan. Meanwhile, the third member of America's great triumvirate, Snead, shot a 72 and finished third.

In the end, it came down to Ferrier trying to beat the 283 total posted by Demaret. To do that, he needed an even-par 72 or better, and he was in good shape at two-under for the day through 12 holes. If Ferrier could play the last six holes in no worse than two-over, he would be the champion.

Things began to unravel on the 13th hole, where the big Aussie hooked his tee shot into a creek and made a bogey. Another bogey followed on the 14th, where he left his approach a long way from the hole and three-putted. The 15th was considered a birdie hole, but Ferrier managed only a par.

The firm greens claimed Ferrier as a victim on the par-three 16th, where his tee shot bounced over the putting surface. He chipped to eight feet, but missed the putt. Now he needed two pars just to tie Demaret.

Jimmy was keeping abreast of the action from the radio tower overlooking the 18th green, wearing a set of headphones. Meanwhile, he was bantering with a handful of players and reporters. "If he ties me, I'll beat him tomorrow," Demaret said with a smile after Ferrier's bogey on 16.

Then Ferrier came up short with his approach on the par-four 17th, landing in a bunker, and made yet another bogey. "He's mine, boys!" Demaret exclaimed.

The death march to the clubhouse concluded for Ferrier with a three-putt bogey on the 18th hole, where he needed a birdie to tie. Five bogeys on the last six holes left him with a 41 on the back nine for a final round 75. He lost seven strokes to Demaret on those six holes, which Jimmy played in two under with birdies on 13 and 16.

"Now I know what they say about golf is true. It isn't over until you finish," Ferrier said afterward.

Demaret became the first player to win the Masters three times, and declared, "I'm going to adopt that 13th hole and take it home with me."

Demaret's victory wasn't the only news that week. There was also a showdown in the battle for control of the tour between tour pros and the PGA, which was run largely by club professionals. The week before the Masters, tournament manager George Schneiter announced that a committee of tour players had been formed, with plans of taking over complete control of the tour, either within the PGA or outside it if necessary. All of the game's top players were on the committee, including Hogan, Snead, Demaret, Mangrum, and Cary Middlecoff.

With more players making their living as strictly tour professionals, they chafed at being under the control of an organization of club pros. However, they ran into some harsh realities, and lost this round of what would be a long fight.

The cold, hard fact was that most of the money for operating the tournament bureau of the PGA was provided by the golf-equipment manufacturers. The equipment companies sold their wares through pro shops operated by club pros, and thus tended to take the PGA's side in disputes. With limited sources of other funds (television revenues were still a thing of the future), Schneiter's plan was doomed to failure.

A PGA meeting was called for the Monday of Masters week in Chicago, and Schneiter was summarily fired as tournament manager. However, the tour players' concerns weren't dismissed entirely. In the hours after Demaret's Masters victory, there was another meeting of PGA officials, this time in Augusta. The next day they announced that the players would be given four spots on a tournament committee, joined by three PGA officers. It represented a compromise. Ultimate control still resided in the PGA, but the tour players were inching toward autonomy. They wouldn't achieve it until 1968, when the PGA Tour split away from the PGA of America.

Hogan's next tournament appearance came four weeks later at the Greenbrier Pro-Am, an unofficial event hosted by Snead, who represented the West Virginia resort. It featured twenty-five pros and a collection of high-society folks among the amateur field and spectators, the latter group including England's Duke of Windsor. A well-rested Hogan looked better than he had since Los Angeles, cruising around the relatively short Greenbrier course for a 72-hole total of 21-under 259 and a ten-stroke victory over Snead.

Hogan was originally scheduled to play two weeks later at the Western Open, but thought better of it. The Western at that time moved around the country, and in 1950 it made for a troublesome travel sequence from West Virginia to Los Angeles (with a week off in between), and then on to Fort Worth. As much as Hogan liked

Los Angeles, he knew he would be playing in his hometown event in Fort Worth the following week, with the U.S. Open two weeks after that. He didn't want to over-schedule himself again.

Snead played the Western Open only because he was essentially forced to by his equipment sponsor, Wilson. He won it, then turned the tables on Hogan's Greenbrier victory by winning on Ben's home turf at Colonial. That made it seven wins in the first five months of the year for the red-hot Snead.

Hogan finished a respectable third at Colonial, but the jury was still out on him. He had stunned everyone with his showing at the Los Angeles Open and shot an impressive score at the Greenbrier. But he looked tired in the final round of the Masters, and some of his other showings were lackluster.

Pros observing Hogan's swing opined that he was using a little less leg action and correspondingly more hand action. It was felt that he had lost a little bit of distance, but since he was a longer-than-average hitter that probably wouldn't hurt him.

Mentally, Mangrum felt that Hogan might have an edge, equating it to his own experience of coming back from his Army injuries.

"After I got out of that Jeep smash-up alive, I knew that everything from there in was for free," he said. "Some of the boys worry themselves sick about losing a tournament by a few shots, but I get well immediately by realizing I was lucky to be able to play at all."

But veteran writer Joe Williams of the *New York Herald Tribune* thought that attitude might take away from Hogan's killer instinct and hurt his performance.

The bigger questions, though, were about his physical condition.

In the June issue of *Esquire*, Herb Graffis wrote an article titled "Is Hogan Hogan Again?" With the U.S. Open and its two-round final day looming, Graffis wrote, "At this writing, we don't see Hogan going 36 holes a day, for several years at least. Above all, a golfer needs legs, and Hogan's concentration from here on in must be centered, mainly, about the circulation in those 'drivers.' They may be good enough for 18 holes a day, but the 36-hole final day of the National Open, as well as the killing week-long grind of the PGA match-play championships, would involve strains and risks that aren't advisable."

Hogan's opinion was the one that mattered, though. The PGA, yes, was out of the question with its multiple 36-hole matches. But for the U.S. Open, those strains and risks, he felt, were worth it. The day after the Colonial, he boarded a train for Philadelphia to start preparing for the U.S. Open at Merion.

12

U.S. OPEN QUALIFYING/
LOCAL GUY

JIMMY DEMARET AND Jim Ferrier finished one-two in the Masters in April, but as the U.S. Open approached they were just hoping to make the field.

In 1950, the only players exempt from U.S. Open qualifying were the top twenty finishers from the previous year's championship, the current PGA, U.S. Amateur, and British Amateur champions, all past U.S. Open champions, and the host professional. (Forty-four-year-old Merion head pro Fred Austin turned down that spot, and the *Philadelphia Bulletin* reported after the Open that assistant pro Bob DeHaven was still lamenting that the USGA didn't allow him to take it.) The USGA gave special exemptions to two Americans competing in the British Amateur, James McHale and Bill Campbell, because they were unable to make it back to the U.S. in time for qualifying.

There were no provisions for the top players on the current or previous year's tour. Demaret ranked second and Ferrier third on the 1950 money list through the Colonial, but neither had a guaranteed place in the Open.

So, the day after the Colonial Invitational ended, they headed back out onto the Colonial course for 36-hole U.S. Open qualifying. It was one of 29 sectional qualifying sites around the country, with 1,362 players vying for 133 available spots in the field of 165.

Fifteen of those spots would be awarded at Fort Worth, where many top pros were entered (since the Colonial was an invitational with a field of just 35 players, other touring pros were scattered at other qualifiers). Ferrier shot 71–67 and his 138 total enabled him to make it easily as he finished third in the qualifier. Demaret played his way into Merion, too, though he cut it closer with rounds of 70–71. His 141 total was just two strokes ahead of a playoff for the last spot.

In that playoff, Porky Oliver added to his legacy of being perhaps the hardest-luck player ever to vie for the U.S. Open, losing the final qualifying spot to forty-two-year-old Henry Picard. Oliver had just finished fifth at the Colonial, and would finish the year 12th on the money list despite playing only a partial schedule.

It was the second straight year Oliver just missed qualifying and became an alternate. The previous year, he had headed to Medinah in case a spot opened up. He set a course record in a practice round, and tried to persuade the USGA that they should let him into the field. His lobbying effort wasn't successful. Again in 1950, Oliver would be left wondering what might have been, especially after he finished second in the tour event at Fort Wayne the week before the Open.

Oliver did have some experience playing in the U.S. Open, but that had produced a hard-luck story to top them all. In 1940, Oliver was one of six players to be disqualified in one of the strangest rules violations ever, and it kept him from making a playoff at Canterbury near Cleveland. The first two threesomes to finish the morning round of the 36-hole final day decided to tee off earlier than their scheduled afternoon tee times due to an impending storm.

Those six players were disqualified in a fair, if controversial, decision based on the potential for gaining an advantage on the rest of the field by playing in better weather, as well as the fact that the rules state that the players must start at the time assigned by the committee. The players finished their fourth rounds, pending an appeal, and Oliver shot a 71 for a 287 total, which would have earned him a first place tie with Lawson Little and Gene Sarazen (Little won the playoff the next day).

When the final verdict was delivered, Oliver sat with his head down in the locker room and lamented, "It's not just the honor of having a chance to win the Open. I need the money, and I need it badly."

Oliver was just twenty-three years old at the time. He would go on to win eight tournaments and play on three Ryder Cup teams, but he never won a major championship.

Besides Oliver, the other top American missing out on an Open berth was Virginia pro Chandler Harper, 13th on the money list. Two weeks after sitting out the U.S. Open, he would win the PGA Championship.

Also absent from the U.S. Open field was South Africa's Bobby Locke, who was exempt from qualifying after finishing fourth in the event in 1948 and 1949. Told the previous fall that he needed to write an apology for failing to show at Inverness and the Western Open for his PGA suspension to be lifted (he could have played in the Masters and U.S. Open, in any case), he first wrote a letter merely stating his plans to arrive in the United States in March and stay for three months. After the PGA said that wasn't good enough, he followed with a letter that the organization deemed satisfactorily apologetic, giving him clearance to play. But then Locke, without offering a reason, didn't come to America at all in 1950 except to play in George S. May's big-money All-American Open and World Championship in August, winning the former.

The leading qualifier at Colonial, with rounds of 68–67, was Australia's Norman Von Nida, who played mostly in his native land and in Europe but was making one of his occasional forays onto the American circuit, spending a couple of months in the States after having been invited to the Masters. Von Nida was the only foreign-based player in the U.S. Open field, though Ferrier also had an Australian heritage.

For the third straight year, an African-American qualified for the Open. After Ted Rhodes made it in 1948 and 1949, this time it was Howard Wheeler, who shot 75–69 to tie for fourth in the Philadelphia sectional qualifier and make it by two strokes.

Wheeler was a thirty-nine-year-old who played cross-handed and was probably the best African-American player of the 1930s and 1940s, though he was starting to be challenged by Rhodes at the end of the latter decade. By 1950, Wheeler had claimed five national championships of the United Golf Association, which ran a tour primarily for African-Americans, and he would ultimately finish with six.

Born and raised in Atlanta, Wheeler eventually settled in Phila-delphia. He was a regular at Cobbs Creek, a public course that was the only layout designed by Hugh Wilson other than Merion's East and West courses (and incorporates the same creek that runs through Merion). In 1942, Wheeler was one of eight African-American pros invited to George S. May's Tam O'Shanter Open in Chicago, making them the first black golfers ever to play in an event on the PGA tour. (John Shippen had played in six U.S. Opens between 1896 and 1913, before the formation of the PGA.)

Wheeler was a hit with the Tam O'Shanter galleries because of his unorthodox style and prodigious drives, attracting a big gallery during the practice rounds. Wheeler finished out of the money in the tournament, but at the awards ceremony May presented Wheeler with $200 as the tournament's "most glamorous" player.

On the UGA Tour, Wheeler was known as the "Clown Prince of Golf" and often teed the ball on a matchbox (he would even do this in the U.S. Open) or sometimes a Coca-Cola bottle. His PGA appearances were very limited, but he played at Tam O'Shanter several more times and also competed at the Philadelphia Inquirer Open in 1947, '48, and '49, never managing to finish in the money.

Meanwhile, Wheeler mentored a younger African-American golfer, Charlie Sifford, at Cobbs Creek. Sifford had moved to Philadelphia from Charlotte, North Carolina, 11 years earlier at the age of seventeen, primarily in order to be able to have a place to play regularly.

With pioneers such as Wheeler, Rhodes, and Bill Spiller too old to take advantage by the time they had pushed open the doors to the PGA tour, a gradual process that didn't come to full fruition until the early 1960s, Sifford would become the first African-American to play full-time on the tour. Even Sifford got off to a late start—he was already twenty-eight in 1950 but did not qualify for the Open that year.

It was Wheeler who would make the short drive to play at the exclusive Merion Golf Club, just four miles from the public facility at Cobbs Creek but a world away.

John H. Kennedy writes in *A Course Of Their Own: A History Of African American Golfers* that Wheeler had trouble finding anyone with whom to play a practice round at Merion. He stepped to the first tee alone, as a number of Merion members gathered to watch from the veranda. "As Wheeler's drive whistled straight down the middle of the fairway like a projectile, the club members broke into a spontaneous volley of applause that compensated big Howard for all the rebuffs he had suffered," a sportswriter noted at the time.

For another qualifier from the Philadelphia sectional, Merion also represented a different world than the one he had grown up in not far away, though by now he was comfortable in that world.

George Fazio was the child of working-class Italian immigrants in Norristown, Pennsylvania. His parents spoke Italian almost exclusively, and his father signed his name with an X.

George was one of eight children, including six boys, and was introduced to golf by one of his older brothers. His parents knew nothing about the game, but his mother figured the fresh air would be good for George's health, so she encouraged him to play.

"From the time I was nine until I was about twelve you just couldn't get me off the golf course," Fazio told Al Barkow in *Gettin' to the Dance Floor*. "I got there at daybreak and always went home in the dark. I was one of those wacky kids that, when he likes something, he can't get enough of it."

In those days, the children in large families often went to work, and in Norristown it was permitted for them to go to school only one day a week after age fourteen. Fazio got a job repairing clubs at the Valley Forge Club, where he also caddied.

Born in 1912 (the same year as Hogan, Snead, and Nelson), Fazio had some trouble breaking into the assistant pro ranks in his late teen years as the Depression hit. He became caddie master at the Plymouth Country Club in Norristown, then managed to land an assistant pro job at a new public course nearby in Jeffersonville, in 1932.

Fazio, head pro Bud Lewis, and another man hit upon a lucrative side business by building and operating a driving range at Jeffersonville. It was so successful that they built two more ranges.

That was the beginning of an entrepreneurial life for Fazio. In fact, at the time of the 1950 Open he was involved with a scrap metal business in Conshohocken that he had started a year earlier with his five brothers.

George's nephew Tom Fazio says, "Jack Burke would tell the story of driving from one tour stop to another with George and Jimmy Demaret. One day George was telling them all the ideas he had, when Demaret suddenly interrupted. 'Hey, I see a bank over there,' he said. 'We'd better pull over quick and deposit the money George just made for us before somebody robs us.'"

Through his association with various clubs, Fazio developed some connections with the rich and famous that helped him in his ventures. "He was an engaging personality, and he made a lot of friends," says Tom.

In the early 1940s, Fazio talked his way into the pro position at Pine Valley, one of the most exclusive clubs in the country, across the Delaware River in New Jersey. Later, he was the pro at Hillcrest Country Club in Los Angeles, where the membership roll was dotted with celebrities.

Friends he made along the way included comedian Bob Hope, singer Perry Como, and auto executive William Clay Ford, who would help set George up with a Ford dealership in Norristown later in the 1950s. Local connections with land developers would get Fazio into the golf architecture business in the 1960s. (He brought his young nephew Tom into the business, and Tom would go on to become one of the most prominent architects in the game from the 1980s onward.)

Fazio played on the tour occasionally in the late 1930s and early 1940s, making an extended effort only in 1941. He entered the Navy in February 1944, but was discharged later that same year and in January 1945 took over as pro at Hillcrest.

He stayed there for a year, until a law regarding returning veterans forced him to leave when former Hillcrest pro Stan Kertes returned from the service. Fazio landed on his feet thanks to one of his many connections. A Hillcrest member ran the Schenley company, and set up Fazio and Jimmy Demaret with a $25,000 deal to endorse its rum on tour in 1946.

At the age of thirty-three, Fazio was finally making a full-fledged run at the tour, and he was doing so without financial concerns. He won the California Open in 1945, and in 1946 took his first PGA tour event at the Canadian Open, where he skulled a bunker shot into an unplayable lie on the last hole of an 18-hole playoff but holed a 15-foot putt for the victory. He shared the Bing Crosby title in 1947 (there was no playoff) and never won again after that.

Fazio continued to play the tour pretty close to full time through 1950, while taking club jobs that didn't require heavy commitments (in the spring of 1950, he landed a position at Woodmont near Washington, D.C.), and also starting the scrap metal business. Fazio did finish second seven times in his career and hovered around 20th on the money list each year through 1950, so he was a sound player. Still, his heart wasn't completely in it, and he later admitted he was no Hogan when it came to practice.

"I got tired of (the tour)," he said in *Gettin' to the Dance Floor*. "What are you going to do, hit golf balls for the rest of your life? I'm not saying it's wrong, but for me it was boring. I don't think anybody should take more than five years to do anything. You should do six or eight or 20 things in a lifetime."

Fazio not only did that, he was doing several of them at once in 1950.

Merion members had reason to be pleased with the results of the Philadelphia qualifier—one of their own, Jacques Houdry, qualified to play in the Open on his home course. The twenty-five-year-old Houdry had been captain of the golf team at Princeton, just like Merion designer Hugh Wilson had been many years earlier. Houdry was the reigning Merion club champion, having won the title in 1948 and '49 (he would go on to win the club championship three more times).

His father, Eugene Houdry, was an engineer who came to America from France in 1930 at the age of thirty-eight to pursue his promising research developing a method for producing high-octane gasoline. First used by the Sun Oil Co. (now Sunoco) at its Marcus Hook, Pennsylvania, refinery, Houdry's invention was crucial to the Allied aviation effort in World War II.

Houdry, who hailed from a well-to-do family in France, did well financially from his work and was able to join Merion. His son, Jacques, who was five when the family moved to America, served for the United States during World War II before heading to Princeton. Jacques dropped out of Princeton after three years in order to go to work for his father.

"My father didn't really encourage me to play golf," Jacques said in a 2009 interview. "After that 1950 U.S. Open I became a weekend golfer, and my game went downhill."

The younger Houdry shot a 63 on the East Course just a few weeks before the U.S. Open. The club still has the scorecard today, but since the score came in match play (in an interclub competition) it is not considered the course record. In everyday rounds, he had shot as low as 65. Of course, it was a much different course in U.S. Open conditions and under national championship pressure.

The Merion member with the Princeton background would be paired in the first two rounds with a driving-range pro whose alma mater was the school of hard knocks. His name: Tommy Bolt. Bolt qualified in North Carolina, listing his affiliation as the Par-Way Driving Range in Durham. In fact, the thirty-two-year-old had landed there just two months earlier, lucking into that job when his second attempt at making it as a tour pro came to an abrupt halt after he ran out of money and his car broke down after he played the Greensboro Open.

Bolt grew up in Shreveport, Louisiana, and worked as a carpenter both before and after service in World War II. Late in 1946, a group of friends gave him $1,000 to try the tour. He lasted only eight tournaments.

Bolt went back to hammering nails, this time in Houston. He did that for three years before a friend gave him $800 for another try at the tour, beginning in December 1949. He reached the end of his rope, and the end of his bankroll, in March 1950 in Greensboro. Determined never to be a carpenter again, he headed for

Chapel Hill, where he had heard about an assistant pro job that was open, but his 1941 Nash broke down a couple miles outside of town. Calling a friend who lived nearby to ask for money to fix the car, Bolt found out about the driving-range job in Durham.

It was a fortuitous call. The range owner not only hired Bolt but agreed to sponsor him on tour. In June, Bolt was back on the circuit, and in 1951 he would score his first victory.

There would be no *Tin Cup* moment for Bolt at Merion. But eight years later, he would win the U.S. Open at Southern Hills, the highlight of a career that included 15 wins despite his late start. The *Tin Cup* role at Merion—though it lasted for only one day—would be played by Lee Mackey, an unattached pro from Birmingham, Alabama, who sometimes gave lessons at his local driving range. No one noticed when he shot 74–75—149 at the Country Club of Birmingham to squeak into the Open field, earning the last of four available spots at that site on the third hole of a sudden-death playoff.

13

MERION

THE STAGE FOR the 1950 U.S. Open was the East Course of Merion Golf Club in Ardmore, Pennsylvania, a Main Line suburb just eight miles outside of Philadelphia. It was the second U.S. Open for the club, but Merion's claim to fame wasn't the 1934 Open. The club also hosted the 1930 U.S. Amateur, where Bobby Jones completed the Grand Slam with an eight-and-seven whipping of Eugene Homans in the match play final. Perhaps no championship in the first half of the twentieth century received more attention, and it brought Merion into the limelight.

The East Course was worthy of acclaim in its own right, not merely as the site of an historic moment. Like several other great courses constructed in the early twentieth century, it was the product of an amateur architect, in this case Hugh Wilson, a member whose innate gift for design was revealed when the club was looking to replace its existing course with a better one.

Merion's roots extended back to the founding of Merion Cricket Club in 1865. Golf entered the scene in 1896 with the lease of some land about three-quarters of a mile north of the club's location in the town of Haverford. A nine-hole course was built and expanded to eighteen holes four years later.

Unfortunately, the layout became outdated soon after it opened. The rubber-cored Haskell ball, which flew much farther, was introduced around the turn of the century, and Merion realized it needed a longer course. Unable to acquire any neighboring land, golfers at the club formed the Merion Cricket Club Golf Association and in 1910 found an L-shaped, 120-acre tract about two miles to the southwest in Ardmore.

The land's history included a period as a farm. It had not recently been used for that purpose, but an 1824 farmhouse and barn on the property were renovated to serve as the clubhouse. Part of the property at one time had been used as a quarry, furnishing stones for local construction.

Wilson, who graduated from Princeton in 1902 and was in the insurance business, took the leading role on a five-man committee of members that would be responsible for the design and construction of the course. For outside advice, the club turned to Charles B. Macdonald, who founded and designed Chicago Golf Club in the 1890s. He had moved east and was in the process of building the ambitious National Golf Links of America on Long Island, which opened in 1911.

Macdonald visited the Merion site on one occasion along with his son-in-law H.J. Whigham, a U.S. Amateur champion who dabbled in design himself. They made some suggestions to the committee, which then went to work. Wilson came up with five different plans, and the committee headed up to Long Island to consult again with Macdonald and Whigham, who helped them select the winning plan.

Through the years, the story was told that Wilson made a trip to England and Scotland to give him ideas, and that he designed the layout on his return. Recent research, however, has shown that Wilson went overseas in 1912—after the course was built and seeded in 1911. (While debunking one tale, it lends credence to another: Wilson family lore says that Hugh was originally booked to return on the Titanic before a fortunate change in plans.)

The trip did play a role in the East Course's design, however, when you consider that design includes the placement of bunkers. The course as originally built had very few bunkers; many more were added over the years. The placement of the bunkers was influenced both by what Wilson saw overseas and by observing play on the course.

The East Course evolved gradually over a 22-year period, culminating with the 1934 U.S. Open. Unfortunately, Wilson died of pneumonia in 1925 at the age of forty-five.

Luckily, William Flynn was on hand to see things through. Flynn joined the construction crew at some point when either the East or West Course (opened on another tract of land about a mile away in 1914) was being built. He was the brother-in-law of Frederick Pickering, who had led construction on a number of courses around the country before being hired to do the same at Merion.

Flynn finished up construction of the West Course after Pickering was fired, and it's possible that he helped Wilson with the design of the West. He became the greenkeeper at Merion, while also getting into golf architecture himself, designing two courses in eastern Pennsylvania in 1916. Flynn went into design full-time around 1918, along with partner Howard Toomey. They were responsible for a number of fine courses, including three that have hosted the U.S. Open: Philadelphia Country Club's Spring Mill Course, Cherry Hills in Denver, and Shinnecock Hills in New York. Flynn was very involved along with Wilson in the evolution of the East Course, and it was Flynn who did all of the architectural plans from 1916 through the course's essential completion in 1934 (he called himself a "consulting architect" at Merion.)

In a sense, the ongoing design work at the East Course was like putting the finishing touches on the Mona Lisa, because the course was considered a potential masterpiece from the outset. Another

Philadelphia golf architect, A.W. Tillinghast, wrote an enthusiastic piece for *American Cricketer* shortly after the East Course opened. Tillinghast, who was in the early stages of his own career, noted that while there weren't many bunkers as yet, "I believe that Merion will have a real championship course, and Philadelphia has been crying out for one for many years."

The USGA agreed, bringing the U.S. Amateur to Merion in 1916. That event became known for the sensation created by a fourteen-year-old amateur named Bobby Jones, who reached the quarterfinals. The Amateur championship returned to Merion in 1924, and this time Jones won it by a whopping nine-and-eight margin in the final over George Von Elm. Then came Jones's Grand Slam triumph in 1930 in which he closed out Homans on the 11th green, a green that did not exist when he first competed at Merion fourteen years earlier.

Of the changes to the East Course, the most significant was the redesign of the 10th through 13th holes in 1922. Originally, the 10th, 11th, and 12th all crossed Ardmore Avenue. A decade later, traffic was becoming heavier and this road "hazard" was becoming an annoyance, not to mention potentially dangerous.

The club was able to purchase seven acres so it could extend the 11th and 12th fairways to a new green and tee, respectively, while moving the 11th tee and 12th green to the same side of Ardmore Avenue. It was a fortuitous purchase, because the new green site of the 11th hole was a perfect setting on the other side of Cobbs Creek, creating one of the East Course's greatest holes.

On the other hand, the course lost what had been the only long par four in the middle holes, the 12th, and lost a creekside setting for the short par-three 13th when the latter half of the original 12th disappeared. A new par-three of about 125 yards playing to a green near the clubhouse was created as a replacement 13th. The 10th hole was shortened to about 310 yards and turned into a sharp dogleg left by turning the fairway at the point it reached the road.

New bunkers were being added all along during that 1912–1934 period. The story goes that in the early days, Joe Valentine (a foreman on the construction crew who ended up being the club's green keeper from 1918 to 1962) would spread a sheet on the ground and Wilson and Flynn would go back down the fairway to see how a bunker would look at that spot. Merion's architects both preferred that bunkers be visible, not hidden, so they would be in the player's mind when he planned and executed the shot. The bunkers made such an impression on Chick Evans, who won the 1916 U.S. Amateur on the East Course, that he dubbed them the "white faces of Merion."

Merion was fortunate in its greenkeepers. Flynn got the course off to a good start in its conditioning, and when he moved into architecture he was replaced by Valentine, who became a legend while remaining in that role for more than four decades.

Joe Valentine was born in Italy in 1886 as Giuseppi Valentini. He immigrated to the United States on his own at the age of 18 after receiving a letter from a friend extolling the virtues of America. Several years later, he landed at Merion, and he ended up being named foreman for construction of the East Course largely because he was able to translate instructions to the mostly Italian workers. He had learned English growing up as part of his education in a Catholic monastery, where he was being groomed for the priesthood.

Named greenkeeper in 1918, Valentine always wore a business suit to work and kept his office in the main clubhouse so that he was accessible to members. He even would give them advice on their lawns if they asked.

In 1936, Valentine noticed a particularly hearty patch of grass near the 17th tee, discovering a strain of bluegrass that eventually became the most popular strain in the country, known as Merion bluegrass. Valentine sent plugs of this grass to the USGA green section for research, and it was tested along with numerous other bluegrasses at the Arlington Turf Gardens in Virginia. The testing was slowed by World War II, but finally after showing promise the Merion strain was sent to several sod farms in Oregon in the late 1940s and by the time of the 1950 U.S. Open, seeds of Merion bluegrass were starting to become available.

The advantage of this grass was that it spread out quickly and crowded out weeds with its vigorous growth. In January 1950, a story appeared in the *New York Herald Tribune* describing Merion bluegrass as a strain that would "lick the crabgrass problem" in the northern states. Two decades later, it had become the foundation of the cultivated sod industry, described as the "Cadillac of bluegrasses," though it has since been mostly supplanted by newer strains.

The first four USGA championships held at the East Course were for amateurs (the 1926 U.S. Women's Amateur in addition to the three men's amateurs). There was some doubt about whether the club should host a professional event, but in the end it was decided that the "wholesale presence of professional golfers and their attendants at Golf House (the clubhouse) would not be objectionable." The club invited the USGA to hold the 1934 U.S. Open at Merion, and the invitation was accepted.

That event was won by Olin Dutra, a six-foot-three, 230-pound Californian who had picked up a case of amoebic dysentery on the train ride east. Eating very little and bothered by stomach pains, Dutra nonetheless shot 71–72 on the 36-hole final day to come from eight strokes behind and win the title with a 13-over 293.

The other two main contenders were both knocked out by the 11th hole, only 378 yards but full of trouble. In Bobby Cruickshank's case the "knockout" was almost literal. The second-round leader was struggling but barely clinging to the lead when he came to the 11th hole in the third round. His approach shot plunged into Cobbs Creek (known on this hole as the "Baffling Brook") short of the green, but miraculously hit a rock and bounced onto the putting surface. Overjoyed, Cruickshank tossed his club into the air and exclaimed, "Thank you, Lord!" Unfortunately, he didn't keep his eye on the club, which landed on his head and knocked him down. Shaken up, he finished the third round with a 77 and with a 76 in the final round he tied for third, two strokes back.

Gene Sarazen moved in front of Cruickshank through three rounds and was still the leader heading to the 11th hole of the final round. There "the Squire" hooked his two-iron tee shot into Cobbs Creek, which runs to the left of the fairway before crossing in front of the green. Blocked by trees from shooting at the green after the penalty stroke, he punched out, hit his fourth shot into a greenside bunker, and ended up with a triple bogey seven. Sarazen's closing 76 left him one behind Dutra.

The host for the 1934 Open was the Merion Cricket Club, but in 1950 it was the Merion Golf Club. The original club split into two parts in 1942 when, beset by financial difficulties, it was decided this move represented the best chance for survival.

The Merion Golf Club attracted 238 members at its founding, but the timing wasn't the best. World War II was about to bring gas rationing and limits on golf-ball manufacturing that made it hard to draw members to the club. The golf club survived the war thanks only to the understanding and favorable terms of its mortgage holder, the Provident Life Insurance Company; otherwise, the club would have been in default.

The financial situation brightened considerably after the war, as it did in the country as a whole. In 1947, Provident asked for a considerable payment on the principal, but then the club was in a position to raise a sufficient amount in second mortgage bonds from its members.

The club had not only survived, it was ready to thrive, selected to host the 1949 U.S. Women's Amateur and then another U.S. Open in 1950. (Merion Cricket Club survived, too, and is still at its Haverford location.)

The East Course was a short layout to host a U.S. Open. Officially, it was listed at 6,694 yards. That wasn't an accurate measurement. When the Open returned to Merion in 1971, the total was listed at 6,544 yards. The course hadn't been shortened, just remeasured more precisely. In the interim, two holes were lengthened by about 20 yards each, so the true measurement for 1950 would have been right around 6,500 yards.

During the 1940s, the average U.S. Open course played at 6,885 yards. But the East Course was no pushover. Far from it.

Wrote no less an authority than Bobby Jones about Merion East, "It keeps the pressure on the tournament golfer all the way to the home hole . . . Its variety of fairway contours, the angles of its green surfaces, its contiguous 'White Faces,' and the intelligence of its routing have made for a course that age has not withered nor custom staled."

Accuracy and strategy are paramount on the East Course, particularly in a U.S. Open. The greens are of a reasonable size, but are kept very firm. Approaching them from deep Open rough or even from the wrong side of the fairway (thus having to hit over a greenside bunker) is a recipe for trouble. The putting surfaces aren't wildly contoured, but when the speed is ramped up for the Open they become exceedingly difficult to putt because of their subtle rolls.

The genius of the design is that it often calls for a player to take a more risky line if he wants to be rewarded with an easier next shot or a reasonable chance at a birdie. The par-four fifth is a good example. A creek runs down the left, but the left side of the fairway is also the flattest. That's a much better place from which to approach a right-to-left sloping green than from the right side of the fairway, where you are standing on a side slope that encourages a pull and hitting at an angle where the green is sloping away from you. The shorter par-four seventh is not as difficult a hole, but the best chance to hit your second shot close and make a birdie is from the right side of the fairway—close to out of bounds.

The need for precision and the number of relatively short holes mean that pulling the driver out on every par four and par five is not the play for the pros at Merion East. In fact, they may use driver less than half the time. And there is a long stretch in the middle of the course when they might not use it at all.

The pacing of the round is unusual at Merion in that it starts with six moderate holes (and includes the only two par fives on the layout), follows with seven short holes that offer birdie chances (but plenty of trouble, too), and finishes with five difficult holes capped by a very long par three and a very long par four that in 1950 required approaches with fairway woods or long irons.

It can be tough to wield the driver confidently during that finishing stretch after going so long without hitting the big club. And if you haven't made the requisite birdies during the middle stretch, the finishing gauntlet seems even tougher.

Merion East is very much a lay-of-the-land course; little earth was moved in its creation. There were already some nice features to work with. The topography includes a range of slopes, from gentle to moderate to severe, and not much flat land. Cobbs Creek is put to good use on the 11th hole, as is another creek on the fourth and fifth holes. And the incorporation of an abandoned quarry on the last three holes enables the course to apply the coup de grace at the finish. (The last known use of the quarry was to supply stones for the construction of the Ardmore Avenue School in 1880.)

The 16th, 17th, and 18th holes all cross that quarry, filled with scrub and unkempt bunkers. The long carries off the 17th and 18th tees are only an occasional difficulty for U.S. Open competitors (they can be a nightmare for amateurs), but the second shot over the no-man's-land on the 430-yard, par-four 16th is something everyone must reckon with.

The 16th made a big impression on A.W. Tillinghast. "It is a real gem," he wrote in his *American Cricketer* article. "If your drive is a good one, before you stretches the old quarry, its cliff-like sides frowning forbiddingly. Just beyond, and sparkling like an emerald, is the green, calling for a shot that is brave and true. It seems almost like a coy but flirtatious maiden with mocking eyes flashing at you from over her fan."

The analogy might as well apply to the whole course. Perhaps the legendary Walter Hagen said it best at the 1934 Open, where the winning score was 13-over-par 293.

"This is the type of course where you feel after every round you play that you can break 70 on your next start," said the 1914 and 1919 Open champion. "You are sure of it. But somehow you don't. You are even surer the next time. But something always happens that you weren't looking for."

Sixteen years later, with advances in equipment and a breed of players that included the likes of Ben Hogan, Sam Snead, and Jimmy Demaret, scoring was bound to be lower. But the unexpected still lurked around every corner at Merion East.

14

PREPARATION

THE USGA BEGAN preparing for the 1950 U.S. Open in the summer of 1949, when Richard S. Tufts and Joe Dey visited Merion to make suggestions for how the course would be set up. Tufts and Dey represented the two sides of the power structure at the USGA. On the one hand, it's an organization of volunteers, with its officers and board of directors filled by men giving their time to the game; on the other hand, there is a salaried staff that works full time and runs the organization from day to day.

Tufts was a giant on the volunteer side. His grandfather, James W. Tufts, founded Pinehurst Resort in the sand hills of North Carolina in 1895. Ownership of Pinehurst stayed in the family, ultimately passing to Richard and his two brothers.

Tufts started a two-year stint as secretary of the USGA in 1950, then served four years as vice president, and two years as president. As chairman of the USGA's championship committee in the late 1940s, Tufts took the lead role in defining and standardizing the philosophy of course setup for U.S. Opens. The championship had long been known for difficulty, but when it resumed after the war, the 1946, 1947, and 1948 Opens (at Canterbury, St. Louis, and Riviera, respectively) were not quite as rigorous as they had been before.

Tufts was responsible for an improved effort in clarifying to clubs what was expected, and working with them in order to carry it out. Medinah in 1949 marked a turning point, but Tufts continued to refine the USGA's thinking and revise the championship manual that served as a guide to host clubs.

In a September 1949 letter to Dey, for example, Tufts wrote that "in revising the manual it might be well to emphasize a little more the results we desire to obtain than to set up arbitrary specifications. Take for example the question of the rough. If this is all cut to the same length as required in the manual it will be too long where the rough is heavy and too short where the rough is light."

When he wrote his October 7 memo to Merion on preparation of the course, Tufts incorporated this change. "No specific length is suggested for cutting the rough as the length of the cut depends greatly on the character of the rough itself," he wrote. "Where thin, a cut of six to eight inches would be ample; but where heavy and matted, as is likely where present fairways are allowed to grow up into rough, a cut of even four inches might not be sufficient."

He explained the desired difficulty of playing out of the rough thusly: "The rough should not be so deep as to make recovery impossible or to increase greatly the prospect of lost balls, but it should not be so thin that a wood or long iron can be played from it without difficulty."

While it didn't seem so extreme when stated this way, Merion in fact proved to be a turning point in returning long rough to the Open. It was a development praised by Herb Graffis, then the editor of *Golfing* magazine, in his post-mortem of the championship.

"One stayed on the fairways at Merion or didn't score," he wrote. "That's what fairways are for . . . The pros don't want a course that tough. But they'll be getting that tough rough again . . . after the Merion demonstration of the value of requiring that shots be played as a champion ought to be able to play them."

Tufts's prescription for Merion included narrowing the fairways. He wrote that the narrowing should be gradual, starting at about 220 yards off the tee and reaching the smallest width of 35 to 40 yards at about 280 yards from the tee, a distance that represented a very long drive in those days. It's interesting that Tufts's scheme of gradual narrowing meant the long hitters had a smaller target than the short ones. It's also interesting to note how much wider fairways generally were in 1950, both at the Open and at courses in general.

These days U.S. Open fairways have a width of 25–35 yards. Mike Davis, the USGA official currently in charge of Open setups, has halted the ever-narrowing trend since taking over in 2006 but says don't look for a return to 40-yard-wide fairways because equipment allows today's players to hit the ball straighter as well as farther.

The U.S. Open is known for its rough around the greens, and for this you can credit (or curse) Tufts. "Around the greens the rough should be drawn in close," he wrote to the club. "The greens at Merion are large and present an ample target in themselves for any shot to them, provided no previous error has been made. Therefore, if a player fails to hold the green, he should be penalized."

On nearly every hole at Merion, the rough was brought closer to the green than it had been.

Tufts's specifications for the greens called for them to be firm, but not rock-hard. "They should not hold easily for a poorly played approach shot or for a long iron or wood following a missed drive on a short par four hole," he wrote. "Short irons and chip shots firmly played with good backspin should, however, hold reasonably well. The greens should not be rolled to a point where a ball could gain speed in putting down all but the severest slope."

In 1951, Tufts would bring the North and South Open at Pinehurst to a halt, angered that several top American pros did not stick around for the tournament a week after playing the Ryder Cup in Pinehurst (the North and South had the lowest purse of any 72-hole event on tour). He was old-school, even for the 1950s, a big believer in the virtues of amateur golf and firmly against the commercialization of the game.

When the U.S. Open went to Pinehurst for the first time in 1999, Frank Hannigan, former USGA executive director and later a journalist, asked Richard's son, Peter, what his father would make of the championship coming to the club with corporate hospitality tents and the Pinehurst logo being sold on everything imaginable. "Are you kidding?" Peter replied, "Dad would hate it."

Dey, while also considered a traditionalist, would go on to become the first commissioner of the PGA Tour after its split from the rest of the PGA in 1968. Until then, he was the face of the USGA for more than three decades after his hiring as executive secretary in 1934. While he had some administrative help, Dey essentially *was* the USGA staff in 1950 on substantive matters. He not only directed the day-to-day operations of the organization, he was the hands-on director of the U.S. Open and other championships, too, and became well known for it.

Still, Dey took a backseat to Tufts on Merion preparations and communications with the club, and sent Tufts a memo congratulating him on his letter to the club. He did disagree with Tufts on one point, however. On the par-five fourth hole, Tufts suggested growing a strip of rough short of the creek fronting the green to hold second shots that might run into the creek. "I'd let (the second shots) run—rather, I'd emphasize placement," Dey wrote.

The biggest suggestion made by Tufts was adding several new bunkers on the right side of the short par-four 10th. The existing bunkers on that side weren't far enough from the tee to be much of a factor; the proposed new bunkers would not only tighten the landing area for the tee shot, but also would serve to keep wild shots from going through the dogleg and onto the 11th tee. The club went to work quickly and added bunkers (two instead of several, but they were large) in the place indicated.

Those were the only bunkers suggested by Tufts. Otherwise, his suggestions were mostly about where to grow rough, except for raising the possibility of cutting down a tree close to the 15th tee and lengthening the 14th hole by moving the tee back to a practice area that wouldn't be used for the Open (the latter was not carried out). The only instance where Tufts suggested that existing rough be trimmed to fairway height was at the entrance to the fifth hole, a difficult par four.

Some fairways did not need narrowing to reach the 35-to-40-yard standard, but on those that did Tufts specified whether it was to be done from the left, from the right, or from both sides. Of the five holes where the suggested narrowing was 10 yards or more, three came in the closing stretch: the 15th was to be brought in by 10 yards on the left, the 16th by 15 yards on the right, and the 18th by 15–20 yards on the right. Added to the challenge of the long par-three 17th, Tufts's tightening meant that the players would get no breaks on what was already a demanding finish.

Among other matters discussed by the USGA were Merion's distinctive flagsticks, properly called "standards" because they were (and still are) topped by wicker baskets instead of flags. These standards were probably inspired by those used at one of the courses that Hugh Wilson visited in England or Scotland, but it's not known which one. Merion's other architect, William Flynn, patented this type of standard and sold them to a few other courses in the United States, but all except for Merion eventually switched back to flags.

Tufts wrote to Dey that "I think we also ought to consider the matter of the baskets on the flagsticks. Do we want to use these again or request that they be replaced with flags? Simply because they are different I think there will be some criticism if the baskets are used."

Dey wrote back, "As for Merion's baskets, I'd use them. I think they make a better target than flags . . . I believe Merion is rather wedded to the baskets, and I see no harm in them (despite Dot Kirby's bad break, which might well have been a good one)."

The reference must be to Dorothy Kirby, one of the nation's top amateurs, having a shot bounce off a basket and into a bad place during the 1949 U.S. Women's Amateur at Merion.

Ultimately, Tufts's doubts about the baskets prevailed and the USGA decided to have them replaced with flags for the 1950 U.S. Open. To this date, it is still the only time in 18 USGA events at Merion that flags were used instead of baskets.

Course preparation was in the hands of superintendent Joe Valentine and his crew. In February, he told the suburban *Main Line Times* that he had 13 men on his staff. "They're no youngsters. Some of them have been working out here all their lives," he said. "But they're good workers; not one of them, regardless of age, could be replaced by a younger fellow. If they get tired, they take a short rest under a tree." Valentine said that within the past twelve months, forty tons of fertilizer and 2,500 pounds of pesticides had been used, and the bunkers were filled with 600 tons of sand.

On May 14, Fred Byrod reported in the *Philadelphia Inquirer* that the back tees were closed and fenced off with chicken wire. "A couple of weeks ago, the Merion people were a little apprehensive about the rough," he wrote. "They were afraid it wouldn't come up enough. Those fears seemed groundless to the press and radio men who were club guests last week."

Merion was built on 127 acres (the original 120 plus the later seven-acre purchase), which didn't make for a lot of extra room. It was adequate for the scale of the U.S. Open at the time—television compounds, corporate hospitality, merchandise tents, and daily crowds of 40,000 were still things of the future—yet it was not ideal.

The club didn't have a practice range on either the East or West course. At the East, members would use an area behind the 14th tee or another area next to the 18th fairway and hit practice balls (shagged by their caddies) into either the first or 14th fairway when no one was playing those holes. During the Open, competitors would have to go on their own to the West course, a mile away, and hit shag balls down one of the fairways. At the East Course, the original 12th and 13th greens were maintained in the area east of the clubhouse, so that was a potential place for short-game practice. There was also a practice putting green adjacent to the clubhouse.

Later in the 1950s, an area adjacent to the 16th hole was purchased from Haverford College (whose campus is just to the east, across Haverford Road) and became a practice range for the club. Merion did secure use of this land in 1950 for use as a parking lot for the Open. A fee was charged for using the lot.

In the Scottish tradition, the East Course was situated next to a rail line, the Philadelphia and Western, with a station just about 100 yards from the club entrance, providing an optional way for spectators to get to the course. (The line is now part of the regional SEPTA system.)

A tournament ticket, good for admission all week, cost $7.50. Approximately 2,800 were sold in advance, a figure which rose to a total of 3,685 counting people who bought them during tournament week. Daily tickets cost $1.50 for the practice rounds, $2.50 for Thursday's first round, $3.00 for Friday's second round, $3.50 for Saturday's third and fourth rounds, and $3.00 for Sunday's playoff. Tickets with clubhouse admission cost an additional $3.60 for the week or $1.20 each day. (Adjusting for inflation, regular grounds tickets cost $67.50 for the week and $31.50 for the final round in 2010 dollars, compared to $425 and $110 at the 2010 U.S. Open.)

Gate receipts and net profits on the program were split with the USGA, but the club retained all profits from the sale of food and beverages. It also kept the fees from parking and the sale of ad rights on tickets, but the latter went for only $300. Sales of ads in the tournament program did bring in a nice $23,299.68, however.

In the clubhouse, the members didn't give up their locker room for the Open competitors. Instead, the competitors used a secondary locker room with wire lockers on the second floor of the old barn that made up part of the clubhouse facilities (the pro shop was on the first floor). Since the barn is connected to the main building, this was actually just down the hall from the members' locker room. Open competitors were able to use the bathroom facilities of the members' locker room, but a sheet was put up to close off the main part of that locker room.

The secondary facility had been used in past competitions at Merion. In fact, it became a tradition that the locker Bobby Jones used when he won the U.S. Amateur in 1930 be given to the highest-profile competitor at a given event. At the 1934 U.S. Open, it was Walter Hagen's locker. In 1950, it went to Ben Hogan.

There was a wall dividing the second floor of the barn into two sections. During World War II the second portion had been turned into a badminton court, devised as a lure to draw people to the club at a time when the restrictions on golf equipment might have prevented them from hitting the course. For the 1950 Open, that area was used as the press facility, accommodating about a hundred reporters.

Shoehorned into the space between the 18th green and the clubhouse were facilities for radio broadcasters and a television wagon. This was the second year the U.S. Open was broadcast on television by NBC, after debuting at Medinah in 1949 (there was a local broadcast by a St. Louis station in 1947).

It wouldn't be accurate to call the 1949 and 1950 telecasts national. In those days, network television was limited by the reach of coaxial telephone cable, which meant that it only went as far west as St. Louis, and also did not reach the Southeast. Less than ten percent of the households in the country even owned a television set, though that percentage was larger in the major cities of the East and Midwest where the Open was shown.

The coverage was rudimentary, with one camera on a platform behind the 18th green and the broadcast time limited to one hour (5 to 6 p.m. for the final round on Saturday).

There was no network broadcast of the U.S. Open from 1951 to 1953. But it was back for good in 1954, and by then it was truly national. The medium was rapidly expanding, with about half of American households owning a set by 1954, and U.S. Open coverage was extended to four holes.

Another feature of a modern U.S. Open that first made an appearance in 1949 at Medinah was grandstands at the 18th hole, but they were not brought back for 1950. They interfered with play more often than was expected, and the USGA wasn't happy. "It is doubtful that stands ever will be permitted again," wrote Rules of Golf Committee chairman Isaac Grainger in *USGA Journal*, greatly underestimating the growth of the tournament.

About 15,000 feet of rope was deployed to keep the galleries a healthy distance from greens and tees, but the fairways were not roped off—that wouldn't happen until 1954 at Baltusrol in New Jersey. The name players and leaders would be followed by roving marshals carrying ropes to keep spectators from getting too close on their shots from the fairway and rough. Two hundred marshals were required to man the course at any given time.

The club's newsletter in May offered an apology to members for the hassle of hosting the championship. "We don't think you are going to be as comfortable [in the clubhouse] as you normally are but, if you will bear with us for the duration of the tournament, we will try to make it up to you June 11 and every day thereafter."

Inconvenienced the members might have been, but for most of them the chance to see history made on their golf course—again—was well worth it.

15

PRACTICE ROUNDS

BEN HOGAN SPENT a few days at Merion the week before the Open checking out the East Course after arriving in Philadelphia by train. On that Thursday he told a newspaper reporter he shot "about par" while playing in a foursome with 1927 champion Tommy Armour, local pro Lou Galby, and Merion member Frank Sullivan.

"It doesn't do you any good playing a practice round now," Hogan said. "With the back tees closed and the place as wet as it is now, it's an entirely different golf course from what we'll get next week."

Nonetheless, there was some serious reconnaissance going on. At Merion the story is told that on the eighth hole, a short par four, Hogan found a flat spot on the fairway where he intended to lay up with his tee shot, an area well short of where other players would hit to. Supposedly, in a practice round he told his caddie to "carefully replace the divot, son, because I plan to be here every round."

It was also during these rounds that Hogan began to think about which 14 clubs he would carry. As he revealed to golf writer Charles Price a couple of weeks after the Open, he ultimately made the unconventional move of taking the seven-iron out of his bag and replacing it with a one-iron. "There are no seven-iron shots at Merion," he said.

On Friday, a reporter found Hogan talking to Merion President Arthur E. Billings next to the practice green. Billings asked Hogan how he liked the course.

"It's a fine course and in good condition," he replied, "but I don't think it plays as long as the yardage given on the scorecard."

This was in the days before players or caddies paced the yardage. Players used only their eyes to decide on club selection and Hogan was renowned as an especially good judge of distance. Remarkably, Hogan was correct. When Merion remeasured the East Course about a decade later, it was found to be nearly 200 yards shorter than the scorecard yardage.

Hogan was heading that evening for Washington, D.C., taking time out from his Open preparation to play in the National Celebrities Golf Tournament. He told a reporter that he wouldn't play the East Course again until the day before the Open started.

"I think anybody who plays this course before Wednesday is crazy," he said. "I'll be back Monday, but I won't play this East Course until the day before the U.S. Open starts."

Why?

"Well, because the course may be altogether different Monday and Tuesday from what it will be when the tournament starts Thursday. I think it's best to become accustomed to the way it will play on the big days."

Oddly, Hogan didn't stick to that plan. After his return, he played on Tuesday and then played only the last five holes on Wednesday, spending the rest of his time hitting balls on the West Course.

Hogan wasn't the only top player getting a look at Merion the week before the Open. Immediately after winning the Colonial, Sam Snead headed to Philadelphia instead of the tour's next stop in Fort Wayne, Indiana. On Tuesday, Snead played a practice round on the East Course. His advance prep work was a sign that Snead was doing everything he could to figure out a way to finally capture that elusive first Open title.

The back tees were roped off, but Snead said he shot a 69 playing from as far back as the ropes would allow. After another round on Wednesday, Snead left town to play in a minor tournament in Allentown. But on Thursday he spoke by telephone to Laurence Leonard of the *Richmond News Leader* in Virginia and made a bold statement in a story that was picked up by the Associated Press.

"The man who wins it will have to beat me," said Snead of the Open. "I'm not playing sensationally but I'm playing well."

Snead was wary of Hogan, saying, "I actually think Hogan is the man who might make some trouble. He's the man I've got to beat."

As for the defending champion, Snead remarked that he didn't think Cary Middlecoff "will putt those greens well enough" to keep the title. Of course, putting had never been considered Snead's strong suit, but apparently he was confident on the greens based on his play thus far in 1950.

"My idea is that an even greater premium than usual will be placed on putting," he said. "The course definitely puts a premium on good, accurate driving. It isn't a long-iron course. A drive and medium iron appears to be enough on most holes. And remember, the greens are large, fast, and well undulated."

Another early arrival was Frank Stranahan, getting to Merion on the Thursday before the Open straight from his victory at the British Amateur. In a rare case of good fortune involving air travel and weather, Stranahan's flight from across the Atlantic couldn't land as scheduled in New York, which was fogged in, so it touched down in Philadelphia instead.

The twenty-seven-year-old Stranahan was the one amateur who had showed he was a threat to win an event against the pros, though he hadn't yet managed to capture one. Was it an omen that after winning the first leg of the old-style Grand Slam, Stranahan was heading to Merion, where Bobby Jones had completed his?

"I haven't any visions of duplicating Bobby Jones's Grand Slam," Stranahan demurred on arriving in Philadelphia, saying that he was hoping for "just a good showing" in the Open.

Those players practicing in that preliminary week were hindered by rain and wet conditions. The greens were certainly softer than would be expected at a U.S. Open, but Stranahan was hoping they didn't firm up too much.

"I hope the course is a little soft for the tournament," he said. "Those greens are tough to hold under ordinary circumstances."

A great amateur of another era withdrew from the Open on the Friday before the championship. At fifty-nine years old, Chick Evans, exempt from qualifying thanks to his victory in the 1916 U.S. Open, would have been the oldest man in the field. He also had just competed at the British Amateur, but found on his return that the "press of business," as he told the USGA, forced him to withdraw, and not return to the site of his 1916 U.S. Amateur victory (he and Jones are the only two players to win the U.S. Amateur and Open in the same year).

Evans wasn't the only player to pull out. The pairings were officially released on the Sunday before the Open, but on the very next day it was announced that eleven players on that list had withdrawn.

This seems like an extraordinarily high number. But it must be considered that air travel was prohibitively expensive for many qualifiers and road trips were more difficult in 1950. Also, there were virtually no hotels in the immediate vicinity of Merion. For most, that would mean finding lodging in downtown Philadelphia. Many stayed at the Bellevue-Stratford, the official in-town headquarters of the championship. Merion was able to place some contestants in private homes. Others stayed with friends. Lloyd Mangrum, Cary Middlecoff, and amateur Bill Campbell stayed with James McHale, a Philadelphia amateur who was playing in the Open himself.

The majority of the qualifiers were not tour players. With a field of 165 and the expectation of only the top thirty places being paid (based on the 1949 Open), their chances of earning a check were very small. Thirty-six of the qualifiers were amateurs.

So perhaps it's not quite so surprising that, faced with the reality of actually making the trip to Philadelphia to play on a brutally tough golf course and have their heads handed to them by tour pros, a number of players decided not to bother. (One does have to wonder why, if that's the case, they tried to qualify in the first place.)

The withdrawals were all no-names, replaced by other no-names from the same sectional qualifier. Thus, the spate of withdrawals did Porky Oliver no good, since no one from the Fort Worth qualifier withdrew. It was the same story for several more withdrawals before the start of the championship, leaving Oliver on the sidelines. The number of amateurs was ultimately pared down to twenty-seven starters.

Hogan had what seems like an odd interlude of "silly" golf at the National Celebrities in Washington the weekend before the Open, but perhaps it served to refresh him for the difficult week ahead.

Participants in the event, where proceeds went toward recreational equipment for the children of Washington, included Bob Hope, Danny Kaye, Milton Berle, Arthur Godfrey, Frank Sinatra (only as a walking scorer), and Jim Thorpe. There were various senators, congressmen, and military leaders, including General Anthony "Nuts" McAuliffe of Battle of the Bulge fame. The eleven men pros included Hogan, Gene Sarazen, Henry Picard, and George Fazio; there were also 10 women pros on hand, led by Babe Zaharias.

Hogan cruised to first place by six strokes with a 65 on the Army-Navy Country Club on Saturday followed by a 34 for nine holes on a rain-shortened Sunday. On the first tee, Hogan received a citation from Attorney General J. Howard McGrath for having completed "the most courageous comeback in sports" during the past year.

Returning to Merion and the start of official practice rounds, three topics dominated the media build-up to the championship: Ben Hogan and his comeback, Sam Snead and his continuing U.S. Open quest, and how well the pros would be able to handle Merion.

Then, as now, speculation on who would win was a big part of the pre-championship story. But whereas today it's usually the media that does the opinionating, in 1950 the writers asked others, especially players, who *they* thought would win. It's frankly a bit of an awkward question for a player to answer, which is no doubt why somewhere along the line they decided to stop answering it altogether.

It's striking how heavily favored Snead and Hogan were. Or maybe we should just say Snead. The *Bulletin* polled 25 competitors and local pros and reported that 85 percent of them picked Snead to win. You would think that they would have been given pause by his past U.S. Open travails, but they must have been swayed by his performances up to that point in 1950. Snead was on a record pace in scoring average at 68.96, his $20,728 in earnings topped second-place Demaret by more than $7,000, and he had already won seven times, including the last two times he had teed it up.

Hogan did have some backers, though. Fazio, for one, picked him to win and to break par for 72 holes. The *Inquirer* asked three veteran Merion employees—superintendent Joe Valentine (at the club for 43 years), caddie master Joe Markey (41 years), and locker room supervisor Joe Taylor (27 years)—and they all picked Hogan. Taylor hedged his selection by saying "if . . . and it's a big if . . . he can play the 36 holes on Saturday without getting tired."

That was the crux of the issue. Hogan hadn't been required to play 36 holes in one day since coming back from his accident, and there was a big question whether his legs would hold up to the strain well enough to enable him to win.

The forty-eight-year-old Sarazen, winner in 1922 and 1932, put it best when he said, "If they were going to play it without walking—just hitting the shots—I would pick Ben without a moment's hesitation. But, unfortunately, he will have to walk."

To another writer, he said, "Ben just can't do it. Thirty-six holes in one day will kill him."

Hogan returned to Philadelphia on Monday, but didn't play. It was reported that he drew more attention sitting on the clubhouse porch than most of the golfers did while on the course.

On Tuesday, Hogan shot a 71 while playing with Demaret, who declared, "Ben is playing well and he's practically a cinch to win." The next day, Hogan limited himself to five holes, perhaps to conserve his strength and gird himself for battle. He also talked to columnist John Webster of the *Inquirer*. While his words were not particularly optimistic (Webster even called them "gloomy"), the writer noted a determination in Hogan's eyes that might have been a truer indication of his readiness.

"No, I'm not steamed up for this one," Hogan said. Asked if he was steamed up for Riviera when he won in 1948, he responded, "Yes, I was steamed up that time, all right . . . When I'm steamed up, that's the best. The worst thing that can happen to me is for me to take it as a matter of course, like I'm playing a practice round."

Regarding his physical condition, Hogan said, "I feel better than I ever did," but conceded that playing 36 holes on Saturday would be a grueling test.

"Yes, I expect that'll really wear me down—if I'm still there by Saturday. That's a tough grind . . . the gallery, getting under or over ropes. Yes, I'll be tired, all right."

Hogan also noted that his relative lack of play "will prove a hindrance" to him. "Nowadays, you've got to compete with these fellows. If you don't, you are bound to be handicapped."

Washington Post sports columnist Shirley Povich noted a more positive development.

"I'm more relaxed than I ever was in my life," Hogan told him at the National Celebrities tournament, "and now I'm enjoying the game more than I ever did."

He would have more support from the galleries than ever, too.

Wrote Webster, "If the next three days should take a storybook course to see the tight-lipped Texan crowned the champion in the cool of a Saturday evening, his comeback would be the greatest of all time . . . and the most popular."

Despite being the favorite, the vibes for Snead at Merion were not all positive. For one thing, he was returning for the first Open held in the Philadelphia area since 1939 at Philadelphia Country Club's Spring Mill Course, the site of his most notorious blow-up.

"So, here I am in Philadelphia again," he said, sitting in the locker room after his arrival on Tuesday. "Golf writers here gave me a bad time in 1940 at Torresdale-Frankford. I won that tournament but because I took a 74 on one round, headlines in the papers read: 'Snead blows it again.' Those boys couldn't forget that eight I took at Spring Mill in the 1939 Open . . . Why don't you forget that awful round?"

Looking back at that disaster, when he made a triple bogey eight on the 18th hole of the final round and finished two shots out of a playoff, Snead said, "Gosh, those reporters came rushing up to me to ask me what happened. That's just exactly what I was trying to figure out. It's all in the business, I guess."

The *Bulletin's* Ed Pollock summed up the fascination of following Snead by writing, "In one moment, he seems super-human and in the next he's proving he isn't."

Snead shot a 71 in his final practice round before the championship, the same as Hogan.

Practice round scores were dutifully recorded by reporters as an indication of players' form heading into a tournament, and players willingly gave the information. Today, no reporter would think to ask a player his score in a practice round. The change is not so much a difference in reporting as a difference in the way players view practice for a major championship. In 1950, they generally prepared by playing a regular round and keeping score, often with wagers riding amongst themselves.

Today, players are more concerned with preparing for what they will face in the championship than with playing the course as they find it in the practice round. Upon reaching the green, instead of putting toward the position of the hole that day they will often hit a number of practice putts toward the various points where they expect the hole to be located during the championship. Also, they might pick up a tee shot in the rough and toss it back into the fairway.

It is, in a sense, a more relaxed approach, but also more serious in its preparation for the tournament. Being unconcerned with score also alleviates the potential frustration associated with playing really well in a practice round. After all, why waste such a good score when it doesn't even count?

Predictions of the winning score are a part of championship preview coverage today, but in 1950 they practically bordered on an obsession. These questions sometimes frustrated the players.

"How do I know whether par will be broken this time?" Snead asked the day before the championship proper began.

Olin Dutra's winning score in 1934 of 13-over par 293 would certainly be bettered this time, but speculation that par might be broken for 72 holes was swatted down by most players. The poll of 25 players predicting the winner also asked whether they thought the winner would break par 280—only two did.

That poll came before practice got underway in earnest. After getting a good look at the course, Demaret was the only well-known player predicting a 280 score, while Paul Runyan said 283, Sarazen 284, Middlecoff 285, and Armour 286.

Snead and Hogan for the most part didn't allow themselves to be drawn into the discussion, though Hogan told Webster, "A man could do 280 or better, depending on where they put the pins. If they're out there where you can shoot at them, it's not so tough. But when the pins are around the corners—where they will be on this course—it's tough."

An *Inquirer* reporter wrote that "there is a strong suspicion in the Merion locker room that the big-name pros are simply building up the course in order to make themselves look good when they tear it down."

Pat Abbott, a club pro from Memphis and two-time runner-up in the U.S. Amateur, thought the course was vulnerable to the top players—not himself—because of its relative lack of length.

"A long belter such as Snead will be hitting a lot of seven-, eight-, and nine-irons for his second shot to the green. And that means birdies in this league," he said. "Of course, the USGA undoubtedly will pick out some choice locations for the pins, but that won't be anything new to the players either. From what I've seen the course plays short and is right down the top pros' alley."

It turned out that the big-name pros knew what they were talking about. In fact, Merion was even tougher than they thought it would be, with a score of 287 reaching a playoff (though a winning score in the low 280s looked likely at the halfway point until course conditions became more severe for Saturday's double round).

What made Merion so tough? First, there was the nature of its design, where in order to get a reward, players had to take risks. Then there was its fearsome finish, with a trio of challenging closing holes that took a backseat to no course. There was the fact that even its "birdie holes" were not as vulnerable as they might appear. There were its greens, which were difficult to read and tough to putt. Add in U.S. Open conditions, with narrowed fairways, thick rough, and firmed-up greens, and breaking par in any round, let alone for 72 holes, was a tall order.

Mother Nature lent a helping hand to the USGA in making the course as challenging as possible. A wet May—there were 20 days of rain in the month—made the rough sprout up and thicken into an intimidating tangle. But the weather turned dry during tournament week, allowing the greens to firm up.

The rough was certainly a topic of discussion among the players. Demaret said that Merion "demands more accuracy than any course I've ever seen." Lloyd Mangrum said, "I'd like to have the hay-baling concession here."

P. J. Boatwright Jr. was then a twenty-two-year-old amateur playing in his first and only U.S. Open. "On seeing Merion for the first time, I was amazed by the rough. It must have been 10 inches high in places," Boatwright wrote 21 years later when the Open returned to Merion—at which time he was executive director of the USGA and had replaced Dey as the organization's main setup man for the Open.

Old-timers hailed the return of long rough, which had been mostly absent in previous post-war Opens, and practically mocked the current crop of players who were having difficulty handling it.

But, intimidating as it may have looked at the beginning of the week, the tall grass wasn't the biggest factor as the days wore on. Because the entire course wasn't roped off, the rough got trampled down during the week by the galleries. In fact, when the USGA began roping off courses in the 1954 U.S. Open at Baltusrol, following the suggestion of architect Robert Trent Jones, it was more for the purpose of being able to preserve the rough than it was for gallery control.

The scoring difficulty was more a function of the firmness of the greens, their billiard table qualities making them much harder to hit and hold, and also tougher to putt.

"The greens are awfully fast and call for expert, not just good, putting," said Merion head pro Fred Austin.

Fortunately for Hogan, the putting woes that he became infamous for late in his career had not popped up yet. In fact, Povich wrote that "nobody in the pro ranks outputts Hogan."

The only player to receive any significant mention as a favorite, besides Snead and Hogan, was Demaret. Gayle Talbot of the Associated Press called him the second most popular choice, but that was only because the question mark of Hogan's physical condition.

Hogan, in fact, picked Demaret to win, and while this could be ascribed to Hogan simply thinking it improper to pick himself, his reasoning reveals what qualities he felt were important at Merion East.

- He's fine on the tee shots.
- Ditto the No. 3 and No. 4 woods.
- He's great on the shots from the high grass around the greens.
- He's a very good approach putter.

Demaret, by the way, caused a controversy the previous week at Fort Wayne, where he was the biggest "name" player but withdrew after a first-round 75 complaining of a sprained wrist. "I wonder about that," said tournament chairman Al Kwatnez. "To me and other Jaycee officials his appearance looked like a token one. I saw him use what looked like a No. 5 iron for his putts on two or three greens. That seemed to characterize his attitude."

Sarazen, in a bylined story for the International News Service, rated Snead, Hogan, and Demaret, in that order as the "first flight" for the Open. The second flight in his estimation consisted of defending champ Middlecoff, Mangrum, Jack Burke Jr., and Norman Von Nida. Burke had just joined the tour full-time in 1950 at the age of twenty-seven, and made quite a splash with three wins in the first three months of the year. Australia's Von Nida had performed impressively in Europe and his native country in the late 1940s, and had threatened in a couple of American tournaments in the spring of 1950. In Sarazen's third flight were Jim Ferrier, Clayton

Heafner, Johnny Palmer, 1947 Open champion Lew Worsham, Jim Turnesa, Skip Alexander, and amateur Stranahan.

Nobody seemed to be picking Middlecoff at Merion. Even though he finished second on the money list in 1949 and had won twice thus far in 1950, he was not yet recognized as one of the game's elite. There was also the thought that defending an Open championship was difficult, with back-to-back wins last having been accomplished by Ralph Guldahl in 1937–38.

"The so-called hex surrounding the defending champion won't bother me," said the Memphis dentist. "I'll play my regular game and if I'm lucky, who knows?" Middlecoff, by the way, was assigned the caddie who worked for the winner, Dutra, in 1934.

Some observers didn't have much confidence in Middlecoff's putting, and he didn't seem so sure about it himself. He switched putters after his first practice round, going to a lighter putter that he felt was better suited to fast greens.

Despite his 1946 U.S. Open title and the fact that he was one of the game's top players throughout the late 1940s, Mangrum hardly received a mention in the pre-championship buildup. Perhaps it was because of his absence for the opening part of the 1950 season, or maybe because his game was never as impressive to look at as Snead's or Hogan's. But he was one of the game's best putters, and that should have earned him some consideration at Merion, as should have his victory the week before at Fort Wayne.

Another prominent player receiving little attention was Ferrier, though it was noted that he shot a 68 in his final tune-up. The practice-round sensation was Doug Ford, a pro for exactly one year, who shot a 66 and a 67 in his last two warm-up rounds. Ford would go on to be known as one of the game's fastest players, so unlike Middlecoff he wouldn't have been worried about the notice handed to every player upon registration warning against slow play. The notice stressed that the snail's pace of some players was costing the game popularity, so the Open competitors were instructed to "be observant, reach your decision quickly, and execute your shots with promptness and dispatch."

The USGA's Dey said, "The time has come when we simply must act if the game is not to be seriously injured. The thing is getting completely out of hand."

Dey noted that the starting field had been cut from 171 players to 165 in order to get everybody around before sunset. He presented figures that in the first round the previous year at Medinah the first threesome took three hours and 27 minutes to complete eighteen holes, and the last group four hours and 16 minutes. In the second round, the last group was even slower at four hours and 21 minutes.

"That is just awful, and it doesn't make sense," said Dey. "It hasn't been so long since three hours was considered adequate for a round. This is murder on spectators as well as on players who wish to play at a reasonable speed."

Of course, today's spectators and the few pros who actually play quickly would love to play a round at the pace they played in 1950. You can add about an hour to those times for a round in the Open today, with threesomes taking more than five hours to get around in the first two rounds. The field is now 156 players, with intervals of eleven minutes between tee times compared to eight minutes in 1950.

Dey said that dawdlers would face the possibility of a two-stroke penalty, or even disqualification for a repeat offense. If a player or group of players appeared to be holding up play, the USGA would first investigate to make certain that the gallery wasn't responsible.

"We won't, of course, do anything precipitately," Dey said, noting that a warning would probably be issued before any penalties.

In the end, no penalties were issued, even though the pace of play did not improve in the opening rounds. The pace in Saturday's double round was helped by the cut and a switch from threesomes to twosomes.

Another USGA notice, this one issued the day before the championship, was more pleasant for the players: It was announced that the purse would be increased from about $10,000 to about $15,000, with everybody who made the cut now being paid.

The purse had been $6,000 in the last pre-war Open in 1941, then $8,000 in 1946, and $10,000 in the following three years. The jump to $15,000 in 1950 was announced as for one year only, but it stayed at that level through 1953, and continued to rise after that. In 1960, it was $60,000; in 1970, $195,000; in 1980, $340,000; in 1990, $1.2 million; in 2000, $4.5 million; and in 2010, $7.5 million.

16

FIRST ROUND

BEN AND VALERIE Hogan's home away from home during their stay in Philadelphia was the downtown Barclay Hotel. A stately edifice overlooking Rittenhouse Square, the Barclay was home to Frank Sullivan, the Merion member with whom Hogan played one of his practice rounds in the previous week.

Sullivan was a lawyer who worked for Lippincott, publishers of Hogan's 1948 book *Power Golf.* He was well-known in state and local political circles (he represented Pennsylvania's Democratic Party) and also played a key role in the survival of Merion Golf Club after its separation from the cricket club in 1942. His legal expertise not only helped guide the golf club in the details of the separation, he helped persuade the authorities that a law requiring a club to be in existence for a year before obtaining a liquor license didn't apply in such a case.

This week, Sullivan's role was host and chauffeur for the most prominent player at the Open. The most prominent player was also the most fragile. Hogan's routine at Merion revealed the extent of his leg problems, as he was forced to go to extraordinary lengths just to be able to compete. Upon waking, Hogan would immediately soak for an hour in a tub of hot water and Epsom salts.

He then would painstakingly wrap each leg from crotch to ankle in elastic bandages to minimize swelling. For a painkiller, he took aspirin.

Hogan was assigned tee times in the half of the field that started in the afternoon on Thursday and the morning on Friday. This meant a shorter turnaround between the first and second rounds, but, on the plus side, a longer time to recover on Friday and to prepare for Saturday's double round. He was not given a particularly early tee time on Friday (10:08 a.m.), so his morning ritual did not have to start in the pre-dawn hours.

The first tee time Thursday was 8 a.m., and the first player off the tee was Dick Mayer, a promising twenty-five-year-old from Greenwich, Connecticut, who had turned pro the previous year and was one of the few pros of the era to come out of the country club set. Seven years later, he would win the Open; on this day he shot a respectable 73.

The next group included a hardscrabble pro from Davenport, Iowa, named Jack Fleck. At twenty-eight, he was still two years away from joining the tour, and was playing in his first Open. Five years later, he would beat Hogan in a Open playoff at San Francisco's Olympic Club in one of the game's greatest upsets; on this day he shot a 79.

The story of the first round was twenty-six-year-old Lee Mackey, the aforementioned unattached pro from Birmingham, Alabama, whose 64 was a stunning round in many respects. Nobody had ever shot a 64 in the Open before. The championship record of 65 was set three years earlier by amateur James McHale at St. Louis Country Club, but that round came in a year when scoring was relatively low, which wouldn't prove to be the case at Merion. The 64 wouldn't be matched for another 14 years, nor broken for 23. It still has been bettered only four times.

If anyone was going to shoot 64, Mackey was hardly a likely candidate. His only victories to that point had come in the Birmingham city amateur and the Michigan assistant pros' championship. He was not a tour player. The lowest round he had ever shot *anywhere*, including casual rounds on undemanding courses, was a 65.

Mackey and fellow Alabaman Harold Williams were given spots in the field at the tour's Fort Wayne stop based on having qualified for the Open, so they headed off for a two-week road trip. Mackey had to borrow money from his father before hitting the road. He finished well out of the money against a relatively weak field at Fort Wayne, shooting 77-76-71-73.

Staying in downtown Philadelphia, Mackey and Williams went to a show the night before the first round, getting in bed at around eleven o'clock. At 10:16 the next morning, Mackey, a crew-cut, 165-pounder, was on the first tee. In his practice rounds, he had decided that the East Course was "a place where you wanted to avoid trouble, a course where it paid to keep the ball where you wanted it," he wrote in 1952 for the magazine *Golfing Alabama*.

Mackey avoided trouble all right. After hitting his drive on the first hole into a bunker, he never missed another fairway from the tee. He visited the rough only once, that coming on his second shot on the par-five fourth. Mackey did miss four greens, but got up and down on each occasion, and rode a hot putter, finishing the round with just 26 putts.

On the first hole, Mackey went from the fairway bunker to a deep greenside bunker, but blasted out to within six inches of the hole to save par. After routine pars at the second and third, he recovered beautifully from his only trip to the rough, getting a birdie out of it when he hit his third shot on the long fourth hole to within five feet and made the putt.

"I was now one under but still not thinking about a particularly hot round as I knew of troublesome holes ahead," Mackey wrote.

He missed the green on the fifth, but had an easy chip and saved par with a two-foot putt. After a routine par on the sixth, he took advantage of the relatively short par-four seventh and eighth for a pair of birdies. He hit both approach shots to within six feet of the pin, making a putt with a big break on the first one and an easier flat putt on the second.

Mackey hit his five-iron tee shot on the par-three ninth into a bunker, but, just as he did on the first hole, hit a recovery to within inches.

"Some lady was standing over in the shade near the green watching the folks go by and I remember her 'oohing' and saying that the ball ought to have gone in the cup," Mackey wrote. "'What a shame,' she said but I told her I was mighty thankful for a three."

Mackey, of course, did not start out with a walking gallery and played the front nine in solitude. There wasn't a big crowd on Thursday morning anyway, and many of the folks on hand were watching the group of Cary Middlecoff, Tommy Armour, and Horton Smith playing directly in front of Mackey.

Not wanting word of his round to spread too fast, Mackey asked the walking scorer in his group to tell any inquiring spectators that he was two over par, not three under.

She agreed, but had to tell the truth when she telephoned Mackey's nine-hole score to the press room and the big scoreboard near the clubhouse. Word would soon filter out. A number of fans headed to the 13th green, which was close to the clubhouse, to await Mackey's arrival. Others rushed to the early holes of the back nine.

Mackey made par on the 10th and decided to play safe on the tricky 11th. He hit a three-wood from the tee and steered his nine-iron approach shot to the center of the green rather than going for the flag located close to the creek. Lo and behold, he sank a 30-foot putt to go to four under.

Mackey parred the 12th hole, but considered it a key to his round. He got a bad break when his approach shot spun back off the front of the green, and his chip left him a tough downhill putt of eight feet. He made it to keep his momentum going.

The gallery was waiting on the short par-three 13th, and Mackey hit a nine-iron to within two feet and birdied to go five under. If he parred in, he would tie the Open record of 65. (He said later he wasn't aware of the record, nor did he hear it mentioned by the growing gallery.)

The 14th was a difficult par four, but Mackey emerged unscathed with a par. The 15th was a repeat of the 11th. Mackey aimed for the center of the green with his approach shot, this time to avoid a bunker, and ended up 40 feet from the hole. It was a putt with a big break, but somehow it fell.

"The gallery really came to life but still nobody said anything to me," Mackey wrote. "I still didn't feel particularly nervous. I knew I was six under par, though."

He came within an eyelash of getting to seven-under on the 16th. A well-struck six-iron shot left Mackey with a six-foot birdie putt, which caught the lip of the hole but spun out.

Now two pars would give Mackey the record, but they would have to be hard earned on a pair of brutish holes. Mackey called the 17th a "gruesome looking thing," a long par three playing over the quarry. Mackey hit a one-iron off the tee and felt like he hit it perfectly. The ball carried a few feet too far, though, landing on the back tier of the green instead of hitting into the upslope. It bounded all the way to the back of the green, leaving a putt of at least 50 feet. He left it four feet short, then left his second putt an inch short and took a bogey.

His magic wand had finally let him down. Oh, well, a par on the 18th would still give him a 65. That was no sure thing on the 458-yard par four that would ultimately rank as the toughest hole in the Open.

Playing partner Robert Roos, who wrote a blow-by-blow account of Mackey's round for the July 1950 issue of *The Golfer* magazine, observed that Mackey's drive on the 18th wasn't too well hit, actually flicking the ground on the front part of the tee before taking off on its flight. It just barely made the 210-yard carry over the quarry, but rolled into a reasonably good position.

Mackey needed a three-wood to reach the green, and had to bounce it onto the putting surface at that. But what a shot it was, a deadly accurate blow from such a long distance that rolled to within 10 feet of the hole.

"More experienced and greater 'name' golfers than Mackey would have taken endless time trying to figure out just where to putt the ball," Roos wrote, "but Mackey . . . stepped up without hesitation, as though putting for practice on his living room rug, and stroked the ball into the center of the hole for an unbelievable 64."

Mackey told it this way: "Everybody was quiet as death as I placed my ball again. I didn't take too much time lining it up. I must have figured it true. The ball never faltered after I hit it, it was in all the way. The gallery really let go then."

Throughout what should have been a pressure-packed back nine for an unknown playing in front of a gallery that grew to the biggest crowd he had ever encountered, Roos wrote that Mackey "played very calmly, did not seem disturbed." Mackey was described in newspaper accounts as "phlegmatic," and it was written that he didn't even crack a smile when he holed the putt on the 18th.

Mackey wrote that "except for a little nervousness on the first tee I don't remember feeling too shaky" and he "felt no particular pressure" coming down the stretch. He might have been more nervous to face the media crowd that greeted him walking off the 18th.

"A posse of photographers beset him—for the first time in his life he had become photogenic!" wrote *Philadelphia Inquirer* columnist John Webster. "He gulped at the request, then busied himself and willingly answered a flood of questioners while the picture men fumed and fretted."

Mackey was so flustered by having to face the reporters that he first told them he was twenty-eight years old, and moments later had to correct himself, saying, "I plumb forgot my right age."

The young Alabaman not only had to go over his round for the waiting scribes who had never heard of him, he had to fill them in on his life story.

Mackey had gone straight from high school to a three-year stint as an Army private, serving wartime duty in Australia. Upon his return, he became a protégé of Sam Byrd, an Alabaman who had played major league baseball for the New York Yankees and Cincinnati Reds before switching to pro golf, where he won six tournaments between 1942 and 1946.

Byrd lived about ten blocks away from Mackey in Birmingham, took an interest in the youngster, and in 1947 got him a job as an assistant at Plum Hollow Country Club near Detroit, where he was the head pro. "You can't say enough about Sam Byrd," Mackey told the reporters. "I owe everything in my swing to him."

Byrd, incidentally, was playing at Merion, too, and shot an 80 in the first round.

Mackey didn't explain why he left Michigan, but he returned to Alabama after three years and now wasn't affiliated with any club. Ray Kelly's *Bulletin* story said that he "teaches on a driving range when he can get work . . . This is his first Open and he needs a job. He's a cinch to get one now."

The headline read: JOBLESS UNKNOWN SHOOTS RECORD 64 TO LEAD STARS IN NATIONAL OPEN GOLF.

Eventually, Mackey, wearing a plaid, button-down shirt (which is perhaps why Webster described him as "by no means a golf fashion plate"), obliged the photographers with some posed shots.

P. J. Boatwright, the amateur who later became USGA executive secretary, recalled in 1971 that after his round he rode back to the Bellevue-Stratford Hotel with a few pros, including Mackey.

"Mackey was quiet, very subdued," Boatwright remembered. "He certainly gave no indication of being aware of his fantastic achievement. In fact, he seemed a little dazed."

Mackey's traveling buddy, Williams, had a fine round himself, shooting a 69, and the two went out for a celebratory dinner. "I had to buy it," Mackey recalled. "Harold told me if he ever shot a 64 he'd buy mine."

The star of the day had to return to Merion that evening for a radio interview. Then it was off with Williams to another show downtown.

Mackey would crash to earth with an 81 in the second round, and finish tied for 25th after following with rounds of 75 and 77. His 64 is all the more mind-boggling when you consider his career ledger in the U.S. Open. Mackey would qualify for the championship only two more times. In 1951, at Oakland Hills, he shot an 84 in the first round and withdrew. In 1958, at Southern Hills, he opened with an 86 and again withdrew. So for his other five U.S. Open rounds besides the 64, he had a scoring average of 80.6.

Mackey stole the headlines from Hogan, who shot a 72 that left him in a tie for 18th place, by no means out of the running. There's an expression that says you can't win a tournament the first day, but you can certainly lose it, and at least Hogan didn't do that. Things didn't look very good after the first nine holes, on which he shot a three-over 39, but he rebounded with a one-under 33 on the back nine.

Reports on Hogan's round were very sketchy. The *Bulletin* sent out a reporter who watched his first four holes and wrote about them in detail. The story wrapped up with a couple of quick quotes from Hogan, with nary a word about the rest of his round.

Hogan, playing with Johnny Palmer and veteran Jimmy Hines, struck the ball nicely on the first two holes, missing birdie putts of 12 and 15 feet. He then hit an uncharacteristically wild iron shot on the par-three third, his ball hitting a tree near the green. It dropped into a reasonable position, from which he pitched to four feet, but he missed the putt and took a bogey. He made a routine par five on the fourth.

After that, the scorecard showed bogeys on the sixth and seventh, both par fours. We don't know how he got them, but the *Inquirer* reported that Hogan had 19 putts on the front nine and 16 on the back. If that was accurate, he must have hit 15 greens in regulation and one of those front-nine bogeys must have been a three-putt.

According to the *Inquirer*, Hogan wasn't getting his approaches within birdie range. That fits with what he later said was his strategic approach for the week of aiming toward the center of the greens instead of the flagsticks. He got himself back into decent position on the scoreboard with a pair of birdies on the back nine, holing a long putt on the 12th hole (reported at 30 feet in one publication and 45 feet in another) and a 15-foot putt at the 16th. He made a bogey on the 15th.

The *Bulletin* quoted Hogan saying his game was "pretty sharp" and that his chances hinged on his condition. "I seem to tire the last four holes of every round."

Hogan's 72 was nothing for his backers to worry about when you considered that the other primary threats to win the championship were in the same ballpark. Defending champion Middlecoff and Masters runner-up Jim Ferrier were at 71, Jimmy Demaret and Lloyd Mangrum at 72, and Sam Snead a stroke back at 73.

Six players broke par on Thursday, but only one of them—Skip Alexander—was a player with the credentials to have a realistic chance to hold on through four rounds. Al Brosch had second place at 67, followed by Alexander and rookie Julius Boros at 68. An unheralded pair of players named Williams were at 69—Alabama's Harold and local pro Henry Jr.

"The boys around the press tent who know the players were saying tonight the winner will come from the 72–73 groups—not from the quarter horses who have taken an early lead, but never have demonstrated they can go the distance in this event," wrote Bus Ham in the *Washington Post*.

Brosch came in with his 67 just three groups behind Mackey, giving photographers an opportunity to shoot the two leaders together. Brosch was a thirty-eight-year-old who even today is still acknowledged as the best-ever pro to make Long Island his permanent home. In 1950, he was about halfway to his career totals of 10 victories in the Long Island Open and nine in the Long Island PGA.

One of the few players of the day to wear eyeglasses, Brosch was a regular on the winter circuit but never became a full-year tour pro. Brosch never won on the PGA tour, but he had the ability to shoot a great round or two on occasion. Just a year earlier at Medinah, he led the U.S. Open through two rounds before fading to 13th place. In 1951, he would become the first player to shoot a 60 on the PGA tour, doing so at the Texas Open. He spiced his first round at Merion by holing a two-iron second shot for an eagle on the uphill sixth.

Alexander, another of those rare eyeglass wearers, finished a couple of hours earlier, in the fifth group of the day. He also came to the 18th at three under with just one bogey on the card, but had an adventure on the finishing hole. After a good tee shot, he hit a three-wood for his second but hooked it badly. There being few spectators on hand at that point, his shot was free to bound unchecked long and left of the green, coming to rest on a flap of the starter's tent by the first tee.

USGA Rules of Golf committee chairman Isaac Grainger wrote about the situation in the association's publication *Golf Journal.* A gust of wind blew the ball off the flap, but since wind is not an outside agency the ball was in play where it lay—now sitting on a paved path and up against some radio cables. The cables and a tent rope both interfered with Alexander's swing, and as obstructions were moved without penalty.

He didn't get relief from the concrete path, though. In fact, the possibility is not even discussed in Grainger's write-up. In 1950, there were no such thing as cart paths, because there were no such thing as golf carts, and players did not get relief from pavement. Only after cart paths became a common part of courses did they get written into the rules as immovable obstructions. The path Alexander's ball had ended up on was a walkway near the clubhouse, and he now faced a shot over a bunker intervening between himself and the green.

The possibility of a double bogey loomed large, but Alexander produced a magnificent shot, picking the ball off the concrete, just carrying the bunker, and watching the ball stop just 12 feet from the hole. He missed the putt, but couldn't feel too badly about the bogey.

The thirty-one-year-old Alexander was born in Philadelphia, but he hardly considered the Open a homecoming—his family had moved to Durham, North Carolina, when he was an infant. He learned the game with left-handed clubs given to him by a local pro, switching to playing right-handed in high school.

He wasn't necessarily pro material when he entered Duke University, but he was by the time he graduated in 1941. "When I went to Duke, I was a 77 shooter," Alexander later recalled. "By necessity, I quickly learned how to shoot 72."

What was the necessity? "The other kids on the golf team liked to play for money," he said. "In fact, none of them would give me a chance to play for anything else—like fun, for example. Money was scarce in those days, especially for me. Heck, a dollar Nassau amounted to a fortune."

Alexander couldn't play without betting. He didn't have enough money to keep losing matches. The only way around it was to get better. By the time he graduated, he won the Southern Conference championship twice and finished 15th in the Greensboro Open as an amateur. On the national scene, he was medalist in the 1941 U.S. Amateur and won the North and South Amateur.

Next came four-and-a-half years in the Army in World War II, first in the infantry and then in transportation in the Pacific. Like so many of his generation, his life plans had been put on hold for the war, but in 1946 Alexander turned pro and hit the circuit. In 1947, he won three times in "satellite" events where the top players didn't compete. He got his first official win in Tucson in 1948 when he shot a final-round 62, including a 29 on the front nine and an eagle on the 18th hole. A big man and long hitter, Alexander reached the par-five 18th with an eight-iron for his second shot.

He finished fifth on the 1948 money list with $18,173, adding a second win at the Capital City Open. Alexander was an ironman, teeing it up in 36 tournaments as he traveled the country that year, rarely taking a week off. He slumped a bit in 1949, falling to 16th on the money list. That doesn't sound so bad until you realize that he made just $5,398 for the year.

Alexander began to get his game back together early in 1950, finishing second at the Rio Grande Open. He also finished second at Colonial two weeks before the U.S. Open, and was cheered greatly by the $2,000 check he earned for it.

"Man!" he exclaimed. "I feel like I won this tournament. Two thousand dollars is first place money in the winter tournaments."

Alexander entered the Open 12th on the money list. But could he hold up in a major championship? His best finish so far in a big one was 11th at the 1948 U.S. Open.

At 2:08 in the afternoon, Boros commenced what was essentially his first round as a tour professional, and what an auspicious start it was. For most of his round, the thirty-year-old from Connecticut was burning up the course at the same pace Mackey had done earlier. Was another 64 from a virtual unknown in the offing? As it turned out, no.

Just as Mackey had been described in newspaper accounts, the word phlegmatic often would be attached to Boros in what turned out to be an exceptionally long career. *Golf Digest* editor Jerry Tarde wrote on Boros's death in 1994 that he was called "Phlegmatic Julius Boros" so often by the wire services that it might as well have been his first name. On this day, however, Boros appeared to have some trouble with his nerves down the stretch, as he let the round slip away from him.

Boros went Mackey one better with a four-under 32 on the front nine and went to five under with a birdie on the 11th. He stayed there through the 15th, having navigated through the minefield of the East Course without a bogey to that point. The first chink in his armor came when he missed the green and made a five on the par-four 16th. Then he pushed his drive well to the right on the 18th hole, near a tree, and ended up making a double bogey that dropped him to a two-under 68.

Still, it was an impressive start for a player who had turned pro at the end of November 1949 and just finished his six-month waiting period before being able to collect prize money under PGA rules. (The only tournament he played in during that time was the Masters, an event not run by the PGA where he would have been eligible to get a check, but finished out of the money.)

Another shot back at 69 was Henry Williams Jr., the pro at Tully-Secane Country Club in Secane, Pennsylvania, just eight miles from the front gate of Merion Golf Club. The son of an Allentown professional, Williams was the current Philadelphia PGA champion. He had played the winter tour for the first time in 1950, but earned just $92 for his efforts. On the other hand, the thirty-three-year-old Williams had reached the quarterfinals of the PGA Championship in 1949, so perhaps he shouldn't have been dismissed out of hand as a contender.

In fact, an Associated Press pre-tournament story pegged Williams as one of two local pros who could stage a Sam Parks-style upset (the unheralded Parks was a Pittsburgh pro who won the 1935 U.S. Open in his backyard at Oakmont), the other being George Fazio's cohort, Bud Lewis. And on Monday, Williams had shot a 69 to beat Sam Snead at a small tournament in Allentown.

Harold Williams was even more of a long shot, but he didn't seem to be bothered by the pressure on Thursday. In fact he was enjoying himself. The *Bulletin*'s Ed Pollack, observing play on the 17th hole for a column, heard Williams exclaim after driving from the adjacent 18th tee, "Dog gone it, I hate to think that's the last time I get to hit the ball with my driver in this round."

While six players broke par, none shot even-par 70. There were 11 players at 71, including Middlecoff, Ferrier, 1949 Philadelphia Inquirer Open winner Joe Kirkwood Jr., tour rookie Al Besselink who grew up nearby in New Jersey, veterans Henry Picard and Denny Shute, and Pat Abbott, the Memphis pro who thought Merion would yield low scores.

Middlecoff made a stunning gaffe on the par-five second hole, where he missed a putt from eight inches and made a double bogey seven. "I got careless or lazy," he said after the round. "That shocked me back into concentration." Like Hogan, the defending champion rallied with a 33 on the back nine.

Demaret was decked out in what the *Bulletin* described as "a cherise jersey, chartreuse slacks, and green suede shoes." His 72 would have been better if not for a double bogey on one of the easier holes on the course, the short par-three 13th. He hit his tee shot into a bunker, didn't escape with his first attempt, came out to within 15 inches, and then missed that short putt.

In reading tournament reports of the era, it seems that missing putts from inside two feet was more common than it is today. In general, this might have been due to the greens not being in particularly good condition at many tour stops. At Merion, however, the reason is likely that the greens were very slick, and the players weren't used to putting on such speedy surfaces.

It was a common practice in those days to let the ball die into the hole rather than hitting short putts firmly. On fast greens like Merion's, that meant even short putts would have some break. Instead of rapping the ball firmly to take the break out, the players became so tentative on the slick surfaces that they even left some putts in the three-foot range short, which would be unheard of on tour today.

Tournament favorite Snead was a shot further back at 73 and really struggled on the greens. He was quoted as moaning after the round, in his hillbilly style, "Ah putted like mah arms was broke." The worst example was on the fifth hole, where Snead had a birdie chance but three-putted from 12 feet to make a bogey instead.

In truth, Snead was also a little bit wild off the tee, and that helped to account for going three over on the first 11 holes. He steadied himself after that, but finished the day with just one birdie, that coming on the fourth hole.

Merion's own Jacques Houdry got off to a rough start on the first six holes and finished with a 77, a far cry from the scores he had been shooting just a month earlier on the East Course. Looking back on it in 2009, Houdry didn't recall feeling any particular pressure playing the Open at his club—he just didn't happen to play well.

While he couldn't remember much about his own round, Houdry remembered the antics of his playing partner Tommy Bolt very well. Bolt was just starting out on the tour, but he would later develop such a reputation for his temper that he would become known as "Terrible Tom." If anything, the young Bolt was worse.

"He threw his clubs a number of times. He was a madman on the golf course," said Houdry. "As soon as we got off the golf course, he was all right, pleasant to talk to."

On the first hole of the first round, Bolt hit a short-iron approach with a right-to-left draw, which Houdry noted was a mistake on a green that sloped away from the player and right to left. The ball landed on the putting surface and bounced over the green.

"He went crazy, but really what happened is he hit the wrong shot. To hold the green, he should have faded the ball," Houdry said. "He got back onto the green and holed about a 30-foot putt for a par. You would have thought he would be happy, but instead he was swearing up and down, saying what kind of a terrible course is this, going on and on."

Bolt had earned a note in that morning's newspaper by making a hole-in-one on the ninth hole in Wednesday's final practice round, but his first-round score was an apoplexy-inducing 79.

A player already well-known for his temper in 1950 was Clayton Heafner. The story is told that the fiery North Carolinian once withdrew from a tournament in a huff because the starter mispronounced his name on the first tee. Another Heafner story, related by famed newspaper columnist Red Smith, was told about the 1939 U.S. Open at Philadelphia Country Club. Heafner shot a spectacular 66 in the third round to move within a stroke of the lead, then finished with a horrific 80 and only three clubs in his bag because he had broken the rest.

This Philadelphia experience was shorter, but with another frustrating ending for Heafner. The 1949 U.S. Open runner-up withdrew at Merion after shooting a 44 on the front nine. No reason was recorded, but it's probably not wrong to assume that it was in a fit of anger. (It's also possible he played more than nine holes, since the ninth isn't very close to the clubhouse. He could have walked off more easily after the 13th, or maybe the 10th, but only his nine-hole score was recorded.)

A man named Bernie Hren of Tacoma, Washington, had a sadder story. He flew across the country on Wednesday as a late replacement for Eddie Hogan (no relation to Ben) of Portland, Oregon, who withdrew at the eleventh hour and opened up a spot for an alternate from the Northwest sectional qualifier. Hren shot an 88 on Thursday and quickly flew back to Tacoma on Friday without playing in the second round.

Jack Stewart of Phoenix was another who got in as an alternate, though he had more notice and was able to arrive a couple of days earlier. An auto dealer, Stewart had recently been given a gift by his employees of a new set of golf clubs. He used them at Merion, and somehow contrived to shoot a 96 with them, including a 50 on the back nine. There has been only one U.S. Open round higher since 1910, a 100 in 1941 by Brazilian amateur Walter Ratto, who really should not have been in the field but was given an exemption when he and another player from Brazil arrived in the country too late for sectional qualifying.

There were forty scores of 80 or higher at Merion, including an 81 by 1949 first round leader Les Kennedy and an 83 by 1947 Ryder Cup team member Herman Barron.

The USGA's campaign against slow play was thwarted by the organization's own course setup, as rounds were, if anything, taking even longer. "The pace lagged while players paid unusual attention to the tricky rolls and fast turf," the *Bulletin* reported. No penalties were assessed, as it wasn't a matter of a couple of groups holding up the rest but most of the field playing at the same relatively slow pace.

The crowd for the opening round was reported in the press as 7,000. According to ticket sales it wasn't quite that high, but it was pretty close as estimates go. If a good proportion of those with weekly tickets attended, there might have been more than 6,000 spectators.

The only sour note was that many of those spectators apparently didn't know where to park, or else they didn't want to pay to park in the official lot. The next morning's *Inquirer* reported that parking "was a big problem" and that Merion announced that a public parking lot adjacent to the 16th hole had a capacity of 5,000 cars.

17

SECOND ROUND

THE TEMPERATURE ON the Friday of the U.S. Open soared to 95 degrees. According to the next morning's *Bulletin*, the baking sun hit hard, "chasing most of the gallery to shade under trees and making all look a bedraggled, sorry lot, including a lot of lovely gals."

There were no reported sunstroke casualties, but the *Inquirer* did turn up this anecdote. "With a torrid sun beating down all day, it was only natural to suppose that the gentleman stretched out near a tree on the 18th fairway was a victim of the heat. An SOS for a doctor was sent out and Dr. Thomas Costello approached the man, who—surprised at the furor—said, 'I'm OK. Just taking a nap.'"

Upstairs in the "barn" portion of Merion's clubhouse, the writers in the press room on one side of the wall and players in the locker room on the other side were both sweltering. With so many people packed in a space without air conditioning or a lot of ventilation, it must have felt like a sauna by mid-afternoon. Really feeling the heat that day was first-round hero Lee Mackey. He got the brunt of it, with a 2 p.m. tee time. And there was the figurative heat of being the leader of the national championship.

As one veteran had said about Mackey's calm demeanor the previous day, "He won't get scared until he sees his name in the papers in the morning."

Mackey remained cool on the outside on Friday, keeping his emotions in check. That, apparently, was just his nature. But he didn't bring the same game with him—unfortunate, because he had a big audience.

Lincoln A. Werden wrote in the *New York Times*, "It was a strange sight to see many of the thousands of fans to whom his name was unknown yesterday, offering words of encouragement between strokes as though he were an old friend . . . [The gallery] was extremely partisan and curious. They wanted to get a glimpse of the man who shattered the 50-year championship record and once they saw him, they hoped he would be at the most three or four over par today."

No such luck. Mackey shot an 81, nearly a stroke a hole higher than the day before. (Incidentally, some in the gallery were confused by the fact that in the threesome following Mackey was an amateur named Lee Markey. Those who started out following the wrong guy would have seen a similar brand of golf. Markey also shot an 81, but in his case it was an improvement on his 84 of the first round.)

The first sign of trouble for Mackey came at the par-five second hole, where his drive nearly went out of bounds. From deep rough, he advanced his ball only 50 yards and ended up one-putting for a bogey. On the East Course's other par five, the fourth hole, his second shot found the rough and he dumped his third into the creek in front of the green, ending up with a double bogey.

By the time Mackey reached the turn with a four-over 40 on the front nine, many in the gallery had seen enough and abandoned him. He still led the championship at this point at two under, but they were right in their judgment that it was not worth trudging around in terrible heat to see Mackey on this day. After finishing the ninth hole, Mackey asked an attendant to buy him a bottle of cold soda from the concession stand. On the 10th hole, he made his fifth straight par—and then it really fell apart.

The young Alabaman didn't make another par the rest of the day, sent reeling with five straight bogeys, followed by a double bogey, a brief recovery with a birdie on the 17th, and a closing bogey. On the 14th hole, he hit his tee shot out of bounds and followed it with another tee shot that he thought was out of bounds. While preparing to hit a third time from the tee, officials yelled that his second was in play.

In the locker room, Mackey said that he felt more relaxed on the course than he did the day before. He summed up the difference between his first and second rounds succinctly and accurately, "Yesterday, I couldn't get off the fairway. Today, I couldn't get on."

Playing partner Roos wrote in his *The Golfer* article that Mackey had a few "mental lapses." He elaborated, "When Mackey found the rough the second day it appeared that he tried to get too much distance coming out of the rough in several instances and then, finding himself on the green in over-regulation figures, putted too strongly in an attempt to get his pars."

Looking back later, Mackey admitted to a case of nerves, both before and during the second round.

"I couldn't sleep [Thursday night]," he wrote. "Naturally I played that [first] round over a hundred or so times but I also was trying to play the next day's round. I don't remember what time I finally got to sleep but I do know it wasn't for long.

"That might have had something to do with my 81 the next day, although I think I must have got nervous a little and speeded up my swing."

While Mackey shot himself virtually out of contention on Friday, Hogan shot himself into the thick of it. Neither development was surprising.

Hogan, starting his round at 10:08 a.m., before the heat was at its worst, shot a one-under 69 that could have been even better in two respects.

The first was putting. He had two three-putts, made a third bogey when he missed a six-foot par putt, and failed to convert birdie tries of eight, nine, and twelve feet. The second disappointment was his finish—three under for the day with three holes to play, he made bogeys on the 16th and 17th.

Hogan's iron play was excellent, though, and that was a good sign heading into Saturday's 36 holes. A fairly detailed account of his round in the *Bulletin*, plus the statement in the *Inquirer* that he had 34 putts, leads to the conclusion that Hogan hit 17 greens in regulation, missing only the long par-three 17th. It's not clear if he was putting from the fringe on any holes, which would count as a missed green the way official statistics are compiled today (one report said he was "on the edge" on the 11th).

His tee shots in the second round were not quite as precise, as he missed four fairways. One of those came at the eighth hole (so much for hitting his tee shot to the same place all four rounds), but while showing that his game wasn't always perfect it also gave Hogan a chance to show he wasn't always stone-faced in competition. Observing that his ball had come to rest in the vicinity of a vendor's truck, he quipped to the gallery, "Here's where we stop for a soda."

In truth, it was more of a statement than a quip, because he really did stop for a soda. He then proceeded to hit a beautiful shot out of the rough to four feet for a birdie on the short par four.

Hogan's putter wasn't completely cold. He made a couple of putts early in the round, an eight-footer for a birdie on the par-five second (also after an approach from the rough) and a 20-footer for a birdie on the sixth. He cooled off with a three-putt at the seventh, got his birdie from four feet on the eighth, parred the ninth, and needed only an 18-inch putt to birdie the short par-four 10th.

The rest of the round was an exercise in frustration on the greens. He missed from eight feet on the 12th, nine feet on the 13th, and left an 18-foot putt hanging on the front lip on the 14th, all for birdies. He three-putted the 16th and missed a six-foot par putt after chipping to the 17th, but managed to avoid a third straight bogey when he holed a five-footer for a par on the 18th.

Still, it was a good day for Hogan—when the dust settled he ended the second round just two strokes out of the lead with his 141 total.

There were some less encouraging signs on the physical front, especially considering that the 36-hole windup lay just ahead. First, Hogan was stopped in his tracks by cramps in his legs walking from the 11th green to the 12th tee. The *Washington Post* also reported that he was limping approaching the 18th green.

None of the newspaper stories quoted Hogan, so he must have either declined interviews or given only cursory answers. On the drive back to the hotel, he felt nauseous, asked Frank Sullivan to stop the car, opened the passenger door, and threw up on the ground.

The heat, combined with the condition of his legs, had taken its toll on Hogan. Back at the hotel, he soaked his swollen legs in a tub of Epsom salts for an hour. The Hogans had an early dinner with Sullivan, during which Ben admitted to his host that he dreaded the double round coming the next day. Later, he confided to Valerie that he wasn't sure he would even be able to finish. He went to bed early, at around nine o'clock, in order to be ready for an early wake-up call in the morning—and also, perhaps, simply from fatigue.

The most surprising development on Friday was that of the three heavy favorites, two had shot themselves out of contention after only 36 holes. Sam Snead's Open bugaboo continued unabated, the only difference being that this time he blew up early in the championship instead of late. He shot a 75 in the second round for a 148 total, nine strokes off the pace, leaving his supporters wondering how they possibly could have picked him to win. Jimmy Demaret was even worse, with a 77 for a 149 total that barely made the cut.

Snead had an early tee time, 9:04 a.m., and there were only about fifty spectators on hand to watch him start the round. The crowd grew as more fans made their way to Merion, but Snead didn't give them much of a show. He uncorked a couple of wild drives and had no touch on the greens. The putting surfaces were even faster than the day before, and Snead seemed to be spooked by them, being so careful that he left a lot of putts short. When he would adjust and hit the ball harder, he would hit it *too* hard and knock the ball past the hole. The firmness of the greens got him, too. He made bogeys on the fifth and sixth holes in identical fashion: an approach shot that didn't hold and rolled 50 feet past the hole, and three putts from there.

On the 10th hole, Snead contrived to leave a three-foot birdie putt short. The Slammer bogeyed the 14th hole to go three over for the round. Then came the crushing blow, a double bogey on the 15th. For the second time in the round, he uncorked a wild drive to the right. He'd gotten away with it on the second hole, where he drove out of bounds onto Ardmore Avenue. The distance-only penalty then in effect, plus a nicely played hole after his second tee shot, enabled him to escape with a par.

Snead wasn't so fortunate on the 15th, however. His drive settled under a small tree. He had to take a crouching stance and was unable to shoot at the green, finishing in the rough. His third shot went into a bunker. From there it was onto the green and two putts for a six that turned Snead into a sad figure coming home. The championship favorite had 38 putts and didn't make a single birdie on Friday. Indeed, he had now gone 32 holes without one since his lone birdie on the fourth hole of the opening round. His troubles left Snead in his own little world on the course, and not a pleasant one. On the 12th hole, one of Snead's playing partners, Jim Turnesa, holed a 30-foot putt for a miraculous birdie after a drive into a bunker. The other player in the group, Jim Ferrier, called out, "Nice shot, Jim!" when the ball fell into the hole. But Snead, related John Webster in the *Inquirer*, never raised his head.

Demaret was even worse. Maybe he was dressed too warmly: the *Bulletin* reported that along with his azure slacks and purple and gray shoes, he was wearing a navy blue sweater with a white dickey, even though it must have already been pretty hot by his 11:04 tee time. That same article said his gallery of 200 was "considerably on the distaff side."

This was one day when clothes didn't make the golfer. Demaret double bogeyed the first hole after his tee shot ended up in such deep rough that he could only advance the next one only 25 yards. He drove poorly on the second hole, too, hitting it out of bounds; like Snead, he was able to recover for a par. Unfortunately, he also mimicked Snead with back-to-back bogeys on the fifth and sixth—and things didn't get any better from there. Later, Demaret would say, "I need a scythe to play this course."

The leader at the end of the day was Dutch Harrison, the easy-going forty-year-old Arkansas Traveler, who shot a 67 on Friday for a one-under total of 139. This was after not even reporting to Merion until Wednesday, a day after the registration deadline. He was one of seven who arrived late, and it was written in the paper on Wednesday that they "won't be permitted to start unless they give satisfactory explanations for their delay in reporting." Apparently, Harrison's explanation was satisfactory. On Friday, he said that he had been "too tired" during his first-round 72. "I'm still tired, but that wonderful shot I just hit gave me a lift."

The shot he referred to was a pitch from heavy rough next to a bunker on the 18th green to within two feet of the hole to save par. The lie was so bad that Harrison said the ball was "out of sight," and he had to stand in the bunker to play the shot, but no one who had watched Harrison through the years was surprised that he pulled it off. He could hit softer shots around the greens than anyone on tour in those days, and that was an advantage chipping to the firm greens of the East Course.

Harrison didn't give a reason to reporters for his being tired or for his late arrival. But it had been a rough few months for him. On February 15, he filed for divorce from his wife, Emma, and she then filed a counterclaim stating that she "assisted him in the development of his ability as a golfer and that his present situation in the field of professional sports is due in considerable measure to the assistance rendered him."

Dutch had to travel back and forth to Little Rock a number of times for meetings and hearings between January and July, when the divorce became final. That might have been the reason for arriving late at Merion.

At an April hearing, Emma was temporarily awarded $200 a month, while being ordered to turn over tax records and also Dutch's trophy for the 1949 Canadian Open that was in the house where she was now living alone. Harrison needed to bring it with him when he returned to Canada to defend his title in August. After Emma didn't return it within the scheduled time, a sheriff had to go retrieve it.

Meanwhile, during the first half of 1950 the new love of Dutch's life, Hawaii territorial senator Thelma Akana, was in Washington, D.C., lobbying for Hawaiian statehood, and also spending time with Harrison on tour when she was able. The two had met when she was in a traveling party accompanying a group of pros playing the Philippine Open and a subsequent series of exhibitions in the Philippines the previous November and December. Romance blossomed almost immediately between Dutch and the outgoing forty-five-year-old widow with four children, who had assumed her late husband's territorial senate seat.

Through it all, Harrison continued to play well, winning the Wilmington Open in North Carolina that March and entering the U.S. Open sixth on the money list, although he had a bad moment at the Masters where he withdrew during the first round after hitting two balls into the water on the 16th hole.

Harrison's skills as a shot-maker were paying off at Merion, where none of his five birdie putts in the second round were longer than 12 feet. He was one over for his first eight holes, with a birdie and a pair of bogeys, then cruised around the last 10 holes in four under, a birdie on the par-three ninth followed by a three-under 31 on the back nine with birdies on 10, 13, and 16. The latter came after a beautiful six-iron approach over the quarry to within four feet of the cup. "I shot me some golf today," is how he summed it up.

Morris Siegel wrote in the *Washington Post* that Harrison was a breath of fresh air for golf writers. "Weary of hearing players describe their rounds as 'I was lucky' or 'I had the breaks,' they cotton to the drawling Arkansan who says simply: 'I hit a helluva tee shot on No. 5 . . . That four-iron shot on No. 9 was a honey . . . Nobody in the world could have putted better 'n me today.' The guy's got color."

The story-telling Harrison related to reporters that he had started the game playing left-handed, and embellished it by saying that he won the 1929 Arkansas Amateur as a lefty at age nineteen (actually, he had been playing right-handed for a couple of years by then). Coincidentally, Harrison played the first two rounds with Skip Alexander, who also started out as a left-hander. Alexander, after his opening 68, slipped to a birdieless 74 on Friday, but he was only three strokes off the lead at 142.

Even Hogan started out, very briefly, with left-handed clubs. But all had switched, and southpaw swingers on tour were unusual in those days. There was only one in the Open field, Loddie Kempa, a pro from Kansas City who made the 36-hole cut.

Right on Harrison's heels was a pro who *wished* he played left-handed, Johnny Bulla, who shot the low round on Friday, 66, for a 140 total. A natural left-hander, Bulla learned to play right-handed by necessity because left-handed clubs were hard for him to come by and his first golf teacher told him there was no future for left-handed golfers.

At about the age of forty, a few years after the 1950 Open, Bulla began to dabble with playing left-handed. "The first time I played, I shot a 76 left-handed. Within a year's time I was breaking par," he said later. Looking back, Bulla estimated that he could have been 10 to 12 percent better if he had played left-handed, which would have translated into who knows how many more victories (his final career ledger showed just one win, with nine seconds, and ten thirds).

Like his buddy Harrison, Bulla had other things weighing on his mind in 1950. His Arizona Airways venture had not gone well. "We were a little before our time in starting an airline in Phoenix," Bulla said in 2001, noting that other airlines were successful there later as the area grew.

In the spring of 1950, Monarch Airlines, Challenger Airlines, and Arizona Airways agreed to merge to become Frontier Airlines. Monarch was the predominant element in the merger and its executives were the ones who ran the new company. Bulla was out of the airline business. The merger was effective on June 1, just a week before the start of the U.S. Open and a day before Bulla's thirty-sixth birthday.

The financial woes of Arizona Airways must have been the reason Bulla, who had made his living representing first Walgreens and then Sears on tour, took a club job for the first time in a decade in 1949 even while his Sears contract was ongoing. It wasn't one of those sweetheart arrangements that allowed for a lot of tour play; Bulla pretty much dropped off the tour after signing with Westmoreland Country Club near Pittsburgh in the summer of 1949. Still with a home in Phoenix, he played two events on the winter tour in 1950, the Los Angeles Open and the Phoenix Open (renamed the Ben Hogan Open). Bulla didn't tee it up again until the Masters in April, and his next tournament after that was the U.S. Open—just his fourth start of the year.

Bulla hadn't finished better than 15th in his first three efforts, and opened with a 74 at Merion with bogeys on four of his last five holes, but he found something in the second round. His 66 would hold up as the second best round shot all week, and it was the first and only round without a bogey.

Known as an excellent ball-striker who struggled on the greens, Bulla's putting was outstanding on Friday. His total of 29 putts was the lowest of the contenders, as far as anybody could reckon. Wearing a flower-print shirt, Bulla preserved his bogey-free round by getting up and down from a bunker on the 18th hole, sinking a five-foot par putt. The man described by Arthur Daley of the *New York Times* as being big enough to play tackle for the Chicago Bears (this at a time when you could do that at 220 pounds) also saved par from a bunker on the 10th. Bulla's birdies on the back nine came on putts of 20, 10, and 10 feet on Nos. 11, 13, and 14. His three-under 31 on the back nine matched Harrison's second round and Mackey's first round for the best of the week.

Bulla was tied for second at 140 with Ferrier, who shot a 69 on Friday, and Julius Boros, who had a 72. Hogan was alone at 141.

For the second consecutive day, Boros let it slip away at the end, again playing the last three holes in three over. This time it was three bogeys instead of a bogey and a double bogey. Had he parred the last three holes, he would have ended up with a two-stroke lead through 36 holes. The rookie from Connecticut was one over on the front nine, but moved to one under with birdies on 11 and 13. Down the stretch, he missed the green on 16, 17, and 18, failing to convert a three-foot par putt on 17. The *Bulletin* reported that he "missed the chance of a lifetime and showed it while dragging his steps into the locker room." At the time no one was familiar with Boros's ambling gait, so it's quite possible he was moving at his normal pace. Of course, the 90-plus degree temperature might have had something to do with the foot-dragging.

In any case, once he got over whatever frustrations he might have felt about his finish, Boros had to be happy about the first two rounds. In his second tournament where he could earn money, he was in line for a good check, with a chance to do even better than that. And he was probably feeling good about life in general, having just been married the previous month.

His bride was Ann "Buttons" Cosgrove of Southern Pines, North Carolina, daughter of Frank and Maisie Cosgrove, owners of Mid Pines Resort. She was an excellent golfer herself, winner of the Charlotte Open in 1949 and soon to be the winner of the Massachusetts Women's Amateur two weeks after the U.S. Open. She's the one who was mainly responsible for persuading Julius to turn professional on the verge of his turning thirty.

Boros grew up as one of six children born to Hungarian immigrants in Fairfield, Connecticut. His father, a laborer and machinist, made about $20 a week. Julius learned the game as a caddie, and also by sneaking onto a course that was next to their home. Nicknamed "Peanut" because of his small size in his early caddie days, Boros grew rapidly upward and outward in high school and would end up with the nickname "Moose." He was six feet tall and, in 1950, weighed 200 pounds.

Boros served four years during World War II in the Army Air Corps, mostly stationed in Biloxi, Mississippi. It helped to be an excellent golfer even if you weren't a pro; Boros owed his Biloxi posting mostly to a general there who enjoyed playing golf with Julius during off-duty hours.

After using the GI Bill to get an accounting degree, Boros found another patron in wealthy businessman Roger Sherman. With Boros already making a mark in Connecticut amateur golf circles, Sherman hired him as an accountant for his construction firm. He would work on the books in the mornings, and work on his game in the afternoons at Rockledge Country Club in West Hartford, which Sherman owned. Boros would get time off to play in tournaments.

The teaching pro at Rockledge was none other than Tommy Armour, who became a notable instructor after winning the U.S.

Open, British Open, and PGA Championship. He wasn't successful with Boros, though. Armour wasn't enamored of Boros's swing, and asked him to make a few adjustments. Boros tried them—and shanked his first three shots. "I said, 'Tommy don't teach me anymore,' and walked away," Boros later recalled, and the story was backed up by another witness. Later that year, Armour was asked if Boros could make it on the pro tour.

"I don't think so," the famous pro replied. "He has no firm left side. His swing won't hold up for four rounds."

The lesson with Armour was the only one he would ever have, but Boros continued to work on refining his individualistic swing. He could do so year round, because Sherman also owned Southern Pines Country Club in North Carolina, and arranged for Boros to go there in the winter and do the club's books—and, of course, practice and play golf.

It was there that Boros met Cosgrove, then a college student, and a romance blossomed. It was also in North Carolina that Boros finished second to Sam Snead in the 1949 North and South Open at Pinehurst. While the PGA didn't consider the North and South an official tournament that year because of the low prize money, it drew a field with many tour pros, so it was an impressive showing by the amateur.

Snead encouraged Boros that he could make it on tour, and with his bride-to-be also urging him on, Julius turned pro on November 29, 1949. It's a move that his mother had always opposed. Weighing the security of Boros's accounting job against the uncertainty of trying to make a living traveling a pro circuit where the prizes were meager and a large portion of the field came away with nothing each week, her verdict was, "You'll starve. Stick with your accounting," as Julius later recalled.

In fact, though, the backing of the wealthy Cosgrove family, in addition to probable continued support from Sherman, changed the equation. Upon turning pro, Boros was installed as one of the professionals at Mid Pines, giving him a source of extra income. He and Buttons scheduled a wedding for May.

His playing aspirations had to be put on hold for six months because of the PGA probation period for accepting prize money. The U.S. Open was his first tournament as a regular tour player, and he was making quite a statement through 36 holes.

The other player at 140, Ferrier, was trying to make a statement that his Masters disaster hadn't scarred him. He had finished second the very next week in Atlanta, and also in the Western Open in May. That gave him three runner-up finishes thus far in 1950, good for third on the money list, though he was winless for the year to this point.

Ferrier missed only one fairway in his second-round 69, that leading to a bogey on the fifth hole. Normally a reliable putter, Ferrier three-putted the 15th and 16th for bogeys that cost him the lead. But he made four birdies along the way, outplaying and upstaging playing partner Snead.

Ferrier was one of seven players who broke par for the day, including two in the group of six at 142 who were tied for sixth, Skee Riegel and Bob Toski, who each posted a 69.

Riegel spent some time at Merion when he was growing up—trapping turtles and flying model airplanes, not playing golf. Raised in the nearby working-class suburb of Upper Darby, Riegel didn't come from the country club set. In fact, he didn't play golf at all until the age of twenty-three.

"I had no interest in golf because the guys who were interested in golf were a little strange, I thought, a little weird," Riegel said later.

After graduating from Lafayette College, where he was the captain of the football team, Riegel took up the game only on the insistence of his wife, Edith. On their honeymoon, Skee went to a country club in Reno, Nevada, looking for a lesson. The heavyset man behind the counter said he could oblige. Unbeknownst to Riegel, the man was the club's chef.

"I really thought the chef was the pro," Riegel said later. "He came out and watched me try to hit a few balls. I didn't know that the club pro was playing in South America at the time. I guess the chef felt he could make a few bucks, so we took a bucket of balls to the first tee. That's how I started playing."

Incredibly, Riegel qualified for the 1940 U.S. Amateur just two years after picking up a club for the first time. After serving as a flight instructor in the Air Force during World War II, he was medalist in the 1946 U.S. Amateur with a 36-hole qualifying score of 136 and then won the 1947 U.S. Amateur at Pebble Beach.

Playing out of Tulsa, Oklahoma, Riegel continued to be a force on the amateur scene for the next couple of years while also playing in some tour events with a fair degree of success. Known for having the strongest arms in golf this side of Frank Stranahan, Riegel finished 11th at the Miami Open in December 1949, and in January 1950 announced he was turning pro at the age of thirty-five.

Like Boros, Riegel faced a six-month probationary period, but he played some tour events during that time. He had to pass up a check in a couple, would have finished out of the money anyway in some others, and collected $244 for finishing 21st at the non-PGA-run Masters.

Toski was a twenty-two-year-old from Massachusetts in his second year on tour and his first U.S. Open. At five-foot-seven and 120 pounds, he was one of the few tour players smaller than Hogan. His 69 could have been better, as it included bogeys on the 16th and 18th.

By far the most dangerous players at 142 were Lloyd Mangrum, who shot a 70 on Friday, and Cary Middlecoff, who was fortunate to emerge with a second straight 71. The defending champion got a break on the par-three ninth, where his tee shot skipped out of the water hazard and he was able to make par. He also parred the 15th despite hitting a tee shot out of bounds, the distance-only rule helping him there.

The others at 142 were Alexander and forty-two-year-old Henry Picard. The man who had been such a help to both Hogan and Snead early in their careers virtually retired after 1946, but decided to play a little more in 1950, entering the invitationals at Greenbrier and Colonial as well as the Masters, and playing in his first U.S. Open in four years.

Picard was one of eighteen players in the field who had also competed in the 1934 U.S. Open at Merion. The two players who had essentially given away that 1934 championship on the 11th hole and finished second and tied for third, respectively—Gene Sarazen and Bobby Cruickshank—were doing surprisingly well in 1950.

Cruickshank shot a 72 in the first round, then slipped to a 77 on Friday, but it was still an impressive accomplishment to make the cut at the age of fifty-five. The forty-eight-year-old Sarazen, winner of the U.S. Open in 1922 and 1932 and runner-up in 1934 and 1940, was even better, sitting just five strokes off the lead at 144 after a pair of 72s. Sarazen's last victory on tour had come in 1941, but he was still in the news periodically, usually with a comment about how things were better in his day.

Three weeks after the Masters, *Golf World* reported on an exchange at the trophy presentation, where one of the onlookers sympathized with Ferrier blowing the lead down the stretch. Mangrum said, "Second place isn't too hard to take when it's worth $1,500."

"Oh, yes it is," Sarazen replied, "when you get it that way."

"You don't have to feel too bad about a 75 when it's good for second place," Mangrum insisted.

"That's the trouble with you guys," Sarazen said. "You play for the money. In my days we played for the titles."

In late April, Sarazen gave the Associated Press an early assessment of the U.S. Open contenders. He picked South Africa's Bobby Locke (who ultimately didn't enter), in part because "he hasn't been playing the easy, barbered courses of the grapefruit circuit. The touring pros are going to get a jolt when they hit Merion—it's no bonanza."

In the same article, Sarazen said that Demaret wasn't a threat in the Open. "I don't think he won the Masters, I think Jim Ferrier lost it."

A couple of weeks after that, Sarazen criticized Snead for saying he wouldn't go to the British Open because of the cost.

Demaret had heard enough. Two weeks before the U.S. Open, while playing the Colonial, Demaret blasted Sarazen for "forever running the game and its players down" and said that the source of Sarazen's frustration was that he "can't get in the money (on the current tour). There's no reason he shouldn't be winning today if the old timers were so much better, as he persists in saying, than players today."

Sarazen actually wasn't playing the tour much in 1950. Reached at his New York home, he responded, "I can't understand Jimmy's blast. I like him and consider him a friend of mine."

Maybe so, but it's not likely they were getting together for tea at Merion.

Another player who had played Merion in 1934 was Al Brosch, who at the age of twenty-two shot 78–81 to miss the cut. Brosch missed the cut again in 1950 even after his first-round 67, plummeting to earth with an 84 in the second round.

Fred Byrod in the *Inquirer* wrote, "The best explanation for Brosch's collapse is that he practiced for an hour in the blistering sun, then took a cold shower before starting out (for his 2:24 tee time). He was in a state of chill all the way around."

Only the low 50 and ties (52 players, as it worked out) made the cut from the field of 165. Others besides Brosch on the wrong end of the cut line were Armour (150), Australia's Norman Von Nida (150), amateur Bill Campbell (151), hot young pro Jack Burke Jr. (152), Merion member Jacques Houdry (153), rookie pro Doug Ford (154), Tommy Bolt (155), Jack Fleck (161), and local African-American pro Howard Wheeler (162, including an 85 in the first round).

The diminutive Von Nida posted two top-five finishes during the run-up to the Open, but he also had been quoted as saying that he needed a swing adjustment to get the distance he needed to better compete with American pros. "Ben Hogan absolutely amazes me," he said of the Texan's ability to hit the ball a long way despite his small size. "Even after watching and studying him, I still don't see how he does it."

Von Nida would win sweep the Australian Open and Australian PGA later in 1950 at the age of thirty-six, but he never returned to the United States for any extended period.

The twenty-seven-year-old Campbell, who later would serve a stint as president of the USGA and be elected to the World Golf Hall of Fame for his accomplishments as an amateur player and as an administrator, hurt his chances when he didn't prepare properly before the first round. "I didn't feel I had enough time to go to the West Course to warm up," he recalled in 2009. "I paid the penalty." Campbell started out with a triple bogey, bogey, and double bogey on the first three holes, leading to a first-round 78 from which he could not recover.

Burke ranked fifth on the 1950 money list coming into the championship, but was sunk by a 42 on the front nine in the second round. Ford was another young pro who entered with high hopes, but looking back on it thought that shooting a 66 and 67 in his last two practice rounds might have been his undoing. "I thought it was a very easy course," he said, but he found out otherwise when the bell rang.

British Amateur champion Stranahan rallied to make the cut on the number with a 70 in the second round after a 79 in the first round. He was one of three amateurs to make it to Saturday, joined by Philadelphia's James McHale, and young P. J. Boatwright out of South Carolina.

The Williams boys who shot 69 on Thursday both fell back in the second round. Mackey's Alabama traveling companion, Harold Williams, blew to a 40 on the front nine and shot a 75, but his 144 total was one stroke better than Henry Williams Jr., who slid to a 76.

In addition to Boros and Riegel, another rookie pro making a good showing was Al Besselink, who shot 72 and 71 for a 143 total that was just four strokes off the lead. His six-month probationary period ended at the beginning of March, and in that month he picked up $587.50 in three Florida tournaments, including a sixth-place finish in one of his old Miami haunts. He sat out the tour for the next two months, but no doubt he was playing for money somewhere—in gambling games probably involving bigger money than they played for on tour. That point was driven home by the check Besselink received in Fort Wayne the week before the Open. For a three-way tie for 25th, the last money spot, he collected $33.33—gas money for the trip to Philadelphia.

Also at 143 were Johnny Palmer, who played on the U.S. Ryder Cup team in 1949; Henry Ransom, as well known for his 1948 fight with Von Nida as his two victories to that point; and Bill Nary, a long-hitting pro from California.

Nary survived playing the first round in the company of Jack Stewart, who shot a 96. With Stewart's withdrawal, Nary was plugged into Demaret's group for the second round, and thus had reporters following him as he shot a 70. Nary took advantage of his length to reach the par-five second hole in two shots for a two-putt birdie (the hole was listed at 555 yards, but probably played more like its 1971 listed length of 535). He used a one-iron off the tee on many of the par fours.

There wasn't as much of a stigma attached to withdrawing after a bad round in those days. Eleven players didn't show up after the first day, on top of the three who walked off the course during the opening round. It left a lot of players in twosomes for the second round, but with withdrawals in three consecutive threesomes, the USGA turned it into two threesomes (Nary took the empty spot in Demaret's group caused by Clayton Heafner's withdrawal, and James Wernli filled a spot in the group ahead).

Wernli was one player who wasn't going to withdraw. An active Army major stationed in Hawaii, Wernli won the only available spot at the sectional qualifier in Honolulu. He had traveled the farthest to get to Merion, and he was going to make the most of his experience at playing with the game's top players. Like many one-time qualifiers from various walks of life, it gave him tales for a lifetime, and he made a reasonable showing with rounds of 79 and 81.

Another player determined to drink in the Open experience was sixteen-year-old Mason Rudolph. He found it was a little more than he bargained for, especially when he dumped three balls into the brook on the 11th hole in the second round and made a 12, the highest score on any hole by three strokes. It contributed to a second-round 84 on top of an opening 85. (He actually beat two players, Wally Grant finishing at 171 and Robert Harrington at 176.) Not discouraged, Rudolph qualified for the Open again the next year and went on to a productive PGA tour career that included five victories and seventeen U.S. Open appearances, with a best showing of a tie for eighth in 1966.

Two players who received no attention in the first two rounds were George Fazio and Joe Kirkwood Jr., both at 145 (Fazio 73–72 and Kirkwood 71–74). They would bear watching on Saturday—but that was a day when all eyes would be on Hogan.

18

THIRD ROUND

ONE OF THE distinctive aspects of the U.S. Open was its 36-hole conclusion. In explaining its rationale for the double round, USGA executive secretary Joe Dey said, "The ability to play championship golf over 36 holes on the last day is the hallmark of a champion." In other words, the U.S. Open was not the Ozark Open, and the USGA was going to make it as tough a test as possible to determine a national champion.

Dey offered a second reason, which was fairness. By cutting the field to 50 players and sending them off in two rounds on the final day, "the chance for a wide difference in playing conditions is less than a larger field over two days."

All well and good, perhaps, but this policy was making it tough on the championship's marquee player. Early in the week, Grantland Rice wondered whether Ben Hogan would even attempt the 36-hole grind.

Just two strokes off the lead, and holding up reasonably well through the first 36 holes, there was no question Hogan would *try* it. But would he be able to *do* it? And, even if he made it all the way around, would fatigue or leg pain affect his performance to the extent that he wouldn't be able to make a run at the title? Considering that Sam Snead and Jimmy Demaret were out of the picture, a healthy Hogan would have been considered a strong favorite heading into the tournament's final two rounds. Instead, he was a big question mark.

He was also a strong gallery favorite. While the practice of widely spacing the leaders in the final-day pairings was supposed to spread out the galleries, that wouldn't be the case at Merion. For good measure, the USGA paired Hogan with defending champion Cary Middlecoff, spicing up the feature pairing even more.

Hogan was given a 9:30 a.m. tee time. Considering his morning preparatory routine, that meant getting up at about 5:30, but it could have been worse. The third-round times ran from 8:00 to 10:30, with none of the leaders going off after 10:00 (the final five twosomes consisted of players near the bottom of the field). The pairings stayed intact for the fourth round, with tee times four-and-a-half hours after the third-round times. Playing in twosomes, players were expected to take no more than three-and-a-half hours to complete their rounds.

In the first group off the tee at 8:00 were a couple of players who had grown up in the suburbs of Philadelphia, Al Besselink and George Fazio. Besselink was four strokes off the lead at 143, while Fazio, at 145, trailed by six strokes.

Contenders were paired together, but not based directly on scores. The tee times of twosomes containing players with scores of 142 or better were:

8:06 and 12:36	Bob Toski (142) and Joe Thatcher (144)
8:12 and 12:42	Gene Sarazen (144) and Henry Picard (142)
8:30 and 1:00	Johnny Bulla (140) and Lloyd Mangrum (142)
8:42 and 1:12	Skee Riegel (142) and Johnny Palmer (143)

9:00 and 1:30	Dutch Harrison (139) and Julius Boros (140)
9:30 and 2:00	Ben Hogan (141) and Cary Middlecoff (142)
9:42 and 2:12	Skip Alexander (142) and Claude Harmon (145)
10:00 and 2:30	Jim Ferrier (140) and Henry Ransom (143)

Harrison was known as the type of player who was hard to catch once he got in front. Charles Price wrote in *Golf World* in 1948 that Dutch had "the most elusive pair of heels in golf," and quoted a fellow player as saying, "When he's 'right' for a tournament, he'll let you know before it even starts and then go beat your brains in."

"I expect I can hold up as well as the next one," Harrison told reporters after taking the lead in the second round. "I believe a couple of 71s would win for me and I might be able to do it. I'm playing pretty good."

But Harrison's reputation as a front-runner came with an asterisk. None of his 11 victories had come in a major championship, and he had never led in one. This was unfamiliar territory, and it was impossible to say how he might react to the pressure. His best finish in a major was reaching the semifinals of the 1939 PGA Championship, where he was drilled by Byron Nelson. In a stroke play major, he had never done better than seventh, accomplishing that at both the 1941 U.S. Open and 1942 Masters. In both of those tournaments, he was well behind and moved up in the standings with a good final round; he had never been in contention to win.

Only once had Harrison ever entered the final round of a major within five strokes of the lead. That was at the 1940 U.S. Open at Canterbury, where he was five strokes back through 54 holes and was one of the six players disqualified for starting the final round ahead of his scheduled tee time.

Every one of the top five contenders through 36 holes had either demons or question marks to contend with. Ferrier was only two months removed from his epic back-nine collapse at the Masters; how would he handle the pressure cooker this time? Bulla was most of the way through a career that netted him one win out of eighteen top-three finishes; he had been runner-up in three majors and lost the 54-hole lead in the 1939 U.S. Open. Boros hadn't even been able to win the big one at the state level, with a history of frustration at the Connecticut Amateur and Connecticut Open; he was a neophyte at professional golf, and had faltered down the stretch in each of the first two rounds at Merion.

Behind that trio at 140 came Hogan at 141. Even he had let some big ones slip through his grasp before finally breaking through with three major titles in 1946 to '48, though of course the main doubts about him concerned his physical condition.

The pressure at the U.S. Open was unlike that of any other tournament. It wasn't just the prestige of the national championship. Even more than that, it was the money. Whether or not the commonly stated figure of an Open victory being worth $50,000 in ancillary income was true or not, imagine the extra pressure such a perceived bonanza put on a player's shoulders during an era when winning $10,000 in prize money for the entire year put you the top fifteen on the money list. Winning the Open was the difference between making a very good living or scratching and clawing to make a buck. What's more, you had to do it on a course setup that was far and away the most difficult that players faced all year. No wonder scores went soaring.

One player feeling the strain perhaps more than anyone was the young Toski.

"I was too young and immature to handle the pressure," Toski said in a 2009 interview. "I remember standing on the first tee and thinking, 'What am I doing here?' The magnitude of it struck me."

So did the difficulty of a U.S. Open course. "In regular tournaments, fairways were wide and there wasn't much rough," he said. "Then you get to the Open, and all of a sudden it felt like you were walking down an aisle in church."

With a case of nerves, the fairways seemed even narrower, as Toski discovered. He started his third round with three straight bogeys and carded an 80 to plummet from contention.

Harrison was shaky at the start, too. He double bogeyed the first hole when he bunkered his approach, came out onto the green, and then three-putted. His lead was gone. Not that it really meant a lot. With no real-time scoreboards, and the leaders' tee times spread out, there was no minute-by-minute drama to the tournament standings. It was just a matter of playing your round and finding out how you stood at the end, until perhaps the final round when news would spread by word of mouth, slowly and not always accurately.

An unfortunate feature of the 36-hole Saturday was that the third round tended to get lost in the shuffle. Since they turned right around and played the final round, the drama of the conclusion got most of the attention in the newspapers and lingered in the minds of spectators.

The *Bulletin* did file a detailed account of how Hogan and Middlecoff fared in their third rounds, while Lincoln Werden of the *New York Times* delivered a summary of the morning round at the end of his lead story. All we know about Harrison's round is that he struggled to a four-over 40 on the front nine, with bogeys on Nos. 3, 5, and 8 to go along with his double bogey on the first and a birdie on the sixth. But he shot himself right back into the tournament with a one-under 33 on the back nine for a 73, with a birdie on 12 and pars on the other eight holes.

He was paired with Boros, who played with quiet efficiency on the front nine while Harrison was giving strokes away. Boros churned out nine straight pars, pleasing what Werden called "a loyal band of rooters" who came down from Connecticut to watch.

Making the turn, Boros was even par for the tournament and three strokes in front of Harrison. The usual way to assess how players stood at a given point in those days was to do so in retrospect, basing it on how all players fared through a certain hole. Looking at it that way, through 45 holes of the championship Boros and Ferrier shared the lead at even par; they were followed by Middlecoff and Palmer at one over; Hogan at two over; and Harrison, Mangrum, Bulla, and Ransom at three over.

Boros crashed to earth on the back nine, just as he had done in the first two rounds, only this time it was even worse. He disappointed his fans by making four straight fives starting at the 11th hole, a five-over stretch instigated by a pair of three-putts and then a bunkered tee shot on the par-three 13th. Bogeys on 17 and 18 put him at eight-over for the tournament on the closing three-hole stretch and left him with a third-round 77.

Ferrier fell from grace in remarkably similar fashion, also making four straight fives starting at the 11th. His problems were triggered by an approach into the water on the 11th, following the examples of Cruickshank and Sarazen, who both had lost the lead on that famous hole in 1934. The 378-yard 11th had been the fifth most difficult hole that year. The pros found a hole of that length less of a challenge in 1950, when it ranked 12th in difficulty, but it was still capable of taking a toll if you weren't careful.

That's where Mason Rudolph made his 12 the day before, and on this day amateur Frank Stranahan had an adventure that led to a quadruple bogey eight. Like Cruickshank in 1934, his second shot hit a rock and jumped out of the hazard, but it ended up in the rough. From there, his chip skidded over the green and back into the hazard, leading to disaster. The man considered by some to be a contender for the title risked not even ending up as low amateur.

Back to Ferrier, the Australia native righted himself after his bad stretch and hit a wonderful four-wood to within a foot of the hole on the 18th for a birdie that left him with a 74. At 214, he was three strokes out of the lead, still in the running.

As for Hogan, he hardly looked like himself in the third round. Instead of moving to the forefront with his famous brand of precision play, Hogan was spraying the ball all over the East Course, visiting the rough seven times and bunkers three times. He stayed in the game only thanks to some nice scrambling.

Ben started the third round well enough, with pars on the first two holes and a birdie on the par-three third. But on the par-five fourth, he drove into the rough. That set up a long third shot to the green and, ultimately, a three-putt bogey from 50 feet. Hogan missed the green on the fifth, but saved par with a five-foot putt. He made another scrambling par on the par-four sixth, where he drove into the rough and couldn't reach the green with his second shot, saving a stroke by getting up and down from 20 yards short of the green.

He missed a birdie chance at the short par-four seventh, failing to hole a five-footer. Then, an odd incident occurred on the eighth. Facing a longish birdie putt on the sloping green, Hogan, as he had done all week, did not rest his putter on the ground, fearing that the ball would move on the slick greens. Sure enough, this time the ball did move, rolling about four feet closer to the hole. He quickly looked up at a USGA official, who confirmed that there was no penalty. The rule then was the same as now: A player is deemed to have caused the ball to move if it moves after address, incurring a two-stroke penalty, but he has not addressed the ball if he has not touched the ground with the club. In this case, Hogan simply played the ball from its new spot and two-putted for par.

Hogan missed another green on the ninth, hitting into a bunker. He couldn't save par this time, finishing the front nine with a one-over 37. On the next four holes, Hogan made two birdies followed by two bogeys. Birdie putts of 15 and six feet on the 10th and 11th got him to one under on the round. But he drove into the rough and hit his second shot into a bunker to bogey the par-four 12th and three-putted the 13th, missing a three-footer.

Hogan missed another green on the 14th, though not by much, chipped to four feet and made his par. On the 15th, he hit his most errant drive yet, finishing out of bounds by three inches. It only cost him a bogey (there was that distance-only penalty again), and in fact he missed a 10-foot putt for a par.

We will pause here to note that a lot of drives were hit out of bounds in 1950, particularly on the second and 15th holes. There were perhaps four reasons for this. First, the out-of-bounds stakes impinge closely on these holes. It doesn't take a ridiculously wild shot to hit into Ardmore Avenue on the right of the second or Golf House Road on the left of the 15th. Next, the fairways were wider then, and thus the edges of the fairways were closer to the out of bounds. It's more likely a ball would take a big hop on the fairway and bounce out of bounds; in the Merion Opens in 1971 and 1981 the same shot might have been caught in the rough. Third, clubs and balls in those days were not designed to give players help on off-line shots as are today's big-headed drivers and aerodynamically designed dimple patterns. And lastly, players might not have been as inclined to steer away from the out-of-bounds with the milder distance-only penalty in effect instead of stroke-and-distance, under which an OB tee shot means a probable double bogey.

On the 16th, Hogan hit his approach shot a distant 80 feet from the hole, but was able to two-putt from there. Pars on the 17th and 18th holes allowed him to emerge with a 72, a round that could certainly have been worse and which left him only two strokes off the lead, just as he had started.

It wasn't a round that inspired confidence for the finale. If Hogan's shots were uncharacteristically wayward on his morning round, what would happen when fatigue set in and his legs started to ache on the second trip around the East Course? And what if it was more than an ache? Could his swing hold up if its underpinnings were giving way?

Hogan rested between rounds while consuming a bowl of soup on the club's covered terrace with Valerie. Shortly after Hogan headed off to begin the fourth round, a Philadelphia society reporter asked Valerie for her thoughts. "I was terribly worried about his going back out," she said. "I don't think his legs are really up for this."

Middlecoff's 71 was one stroke better than Hogan, and he joined Ben at 213 through 54 holes. It was a round Middlecoff let get away at the end, with bogeys on the last two holes— both coming in strange fashion—costing him a share of the lead.

Middlecoff's round started out in a rather boring mode—a good thing in the U.S. Open, where pars are golden. They were even more valuable than usual on this day, when the greens were getting harder, pin positions were difficult, and scores were soaring. The defending champion birdied the first hole with a 12-foot putt and then reeled off twelve straight pars. Middlecoff, not Hogan, was the one in the pairing playing with precision, hitting every green. He missed birdie chances from inside 10 feet on Nos. 4 and 7.

Things began to get weird on the 12th hole, though. Hogan and Middlecoff were being followed by a large gallery, and a spectator inadvertently kicked Middlecoff's ball from the fairway to the rough after it came to rest. Not having seen it from the tee, Cary was getting ready to play from the rough when some fans who saw the incident alerted the marshals, and officials ruled he could replace the ball where it originally stopped in the fairway.

Middlecoff's first real slip-up came on the short 13th, where his tee shot plunged into a bunker, finishing close to one of the clumps of grass that made Merion's bunkers distinctive—and also annoying if they came into play. His recovery shot narrowly avoided the grass and ended up less than two feet from the hole, an effort so good that he applauded it himself.

He found another bunker on the 14th, and his string of pars ended when he couldn't get up and down, but he got the stroke back with a birdie at the 15th, making him one-under for the round heading to the quarry holes.

Middlecoff made it safely through the 16th, but was wide right with his tee shot on the par-three 17th, the ball bouncing off a spectator and ending up on the 18th tee. He pitched on and made a bogey.

On the 18th, Middlecoff didn't catch his second shot very well, making contact too high on the ball. The semi-topped shot scuttled up onto the green about 60 feet short of the hole. He ended up with a crescent-shaped dent—what amateurs used to call a "smile"—on the soft-covered balata ball, though it was not a happy occasion. He showed a USGA official the ball, saying that he planned to replace it because it was damaged and unfit for play. To his surprise, the official said the ball had only a "slight abrasion," and didn't allow the substitution. An unhappy Middlecoff three-putted for a bogey, and later complained that "the ball was almost cut through." Considering his known temper problems, it's a good thing he had some time to cool off before returning to the course for the final round.

Moving into the lead through 54 holes was Mangrum, the man trying to mount a comeback considerably less glorious than Hogan's following his scuffle with a neighbor the previous November. It had taken Mangrum a while to get back into the swing of things since his return in March from shoulder surgery, and he still wasn't entirely certain about his driving game coming to the U.S. Open. Mangrum experimented with four different drivers on Wednesday before picking one. He must have made the right choice.

Mangrum wasn't a total stranger to Merion, having played the East Course in the 1937 Pennsylvania Open at the age of twenty-two. After shooting an 81 in the rain in the first round, Lloyd finished fifth in that event thanks to scores of 69, 71, and 71 in the last three rounds.

Thirteen years later, Mangrum was one of the best players in the game, playing the East Course for the national, not state, championship. Through 10 holes, he was two over for the round and four over for the championship, but then he caught fire with birdies on 11, 15, and 16 set up by excellent iron shots to within six feet or less of the hole. His two-under 32 on the back nine gave him a 69 for the third round and the 54-hole lead at 211. The 69 would be the only subpar round all day on the 36-hole Saturday as the East Course was slapping the players around. There had been 13 subpar rounds during the first 36 holes; now Merion was getting its revenge.

There was only one 70 in the third round, accomplished by Palmer to quietly move within two of the lead, having opened with a 73 and a 70. The North Carolinian was thirty-one years old, but was thought of as one of the new breed since he hadn't played much on tour before the war.

After a stint in the Air Force, Palmer had a choice of going to work at an aluminum plant in his small hometown of Badin or trying his luck on the tour. Wisely, he chose the tour, and from 1946 to 1949 he won five tournaments. The most important was the World Championship of Golf in 1949, where he snagged the biggest first-place check of the year, $10,000, helping him to third place on the money list in a year when he also was runner-up to Sam Snead in the PGA Championship.

That track record stamped Palmer as a real threat heading into the fourth round. So did his calm demeanor: Snead had nicknamed him "Old Stone" because his face remained the same no matter how he was playing. Palmer did not consider himself a particularly good long-iron player, but that didn't hurt him much at Merion, and he had an outstanding short game. He demonstrated that in the third round by saving par three of the four times he ended up in greenside bunkers.

Through 54 holes, the leaderboard looked like this:

Lloyd Mangrum	72–70–69—211
Dutch Harrison	72–67–73—212
Ben Hogan	72–69–72—213
Cary Middlecoff	71–71–71—213
Johnny Palmer	73–70–70—213
Jim Ferrier	71–69–74—214
Henry Ransom	72–71–73—216
George Fazio	73–72–72—217
Bill Nary	73–70–74—217
Julius Boros	68–72–77—217

Fazio came out of nowhere. His 145 total after two rounds placed him in the middle of the pack, and a 40 on the front nine dropped him further from contention. Suddenly, the current Philadelphia Open champion reeled off five straight threes on his scorecard, pars on the 13th and 17th bracketing three straight birdies, all on 15-foot putts. Even with a bogey on the 18th after a drive into the rough, he shot a two-under 32 on the back nine and shot up the standings, replacing Riegel and Besselink as the local threat.

Just two weeks earlier, Fazio told *Golf World* that he had changed his putting method to a more natural one (letting the clubface open on the backswing and then square up at impact), and it had been saving him three to six strokes a round. The stated amount of stroke savings was instruction-tip hyperbole, but no doubt the new stroke and increased confidence were helping Fazio at Merion.

Among the players going the other direction—fast—was Bulla. Still, he ended up as the subject in a large photo sequence and accompanying story in the next day's *Bulletin* titled "Humid Atmosphere Eased As Boxer Pup 'Steals' Show," with the kicker head, "Dog Days at Merion."

The 14th tee was located across from homes on the other side of Golf House Road, and a Boxer who belonged to one of the homeowners (a Merion member) decided to wander over and see what was going on at the golf course just when Bulla happened to be coming through. "Nobody told [the Boxer] that the golden anniversary U.S. Open tournament was in progress," the *Bulletin* noted. "Perhaps he wouldn't have cared, for who knows how a dog's mind operates?" Just as Bulla was preparing to hit his drive, the dog ran up, grabbed the ball in its mouth, and darted away.

"Thanks, pup. Maybe I would have hooked that one out of bounds," said Bulla, who pulled out another ball, knocked it down the fairway, and made a par. Playing with eventual 54-hole leader Mangrum, Bulla was tied with Lloyd to that point. Then it all fell apart. Bulla made a triple bogey on the 15th and played the last four holes in five over, losing seven strokes over that stretch to the fast finish of Mangrum.

Talking to Al Abrams of the *Pittsburgh Post-Gazette* a day later, Bulla said it wasn't the dog that turned him in the wrong direction, calling that "the funniest thing." His biggest problem, he said, was putting.

"I missed one of the greatest opportunities ever offered to a golfer to win the Open. I just couldn't make it. I putted miserably—three putted four greens and took four on another." Bulla's third-round tally was a 78.

Veterans Sarazen and Picard, playing together, couldn't maintain their pace of the first 36 holes, Sarazen blowing all the way to an 82 and Picard a 79. Also saying good-bye to their chances in the third round were Riegel (79), Alexander (77), and Besselink (76).

It was a rough round for the three amateurs who made the cut: McHale (78), Stranahan (79), and Boatwright (79), who all ended up at 228. Boatwright was only two over for the round when, like Bulla, his fortunes turned for the worse on 14th tee, after an unusual scene resulted in his ball being knocked off the tee.

Playing fifty-four minutes behind Hogan, Boatwright found himself on the 14th tee while the main attraction was coming up the adjacent 18th hole. "We were nearly trampled as 'Hogan's Herd,' precursor of 'Arnie's Army,' thundered across the tee," Boatwright wrote in 1971. "I felt as though I was bucking traffic during the rush hour in Grand Central Terminal. I know the 14th tee must have been roped, but the rope didn't restrain the gallery, which kicked my ball right off the tee."

Boatwright said his problems arose not from the commotion, but from having looked at the scoreboard behind the 14th tee and seen that Stranahan and McHale both finished at 228, while if he could par in he would be at 221. Armed with that information, he promptly went five-six-seven on the next three holes, all par fours.

Snead still attracted a few fans even while he was essentially playing out the string. On the 15th hole, he heard a camera click as he was lining up a putt, stepped back, and said, "That kind of stuff would be all right if I were winning this tournament. But I'm not even close."

With nothing really to lose, Snead uncorked two big shots and reached the 595-yard downhill par-five fourth in two shots, the only player to do so all week. Needing a score in the 60s to have any chance at all, Snead shot a 72; it moved him up the field, but not enough to put him in contention. Snead's quest for a first Open would have to wait. But Hogan's quest for an Open win for the ages was still very much alive.

19

FOURTH ROUND (EARLY ACTION)

THE WEATHER WAS hot on Saturday afternoon, but not as hot as it had been the day before. That was good news for the players, who had to play 36 holes, and also for the fans. There weren't any grandstands, so a large portion of the gallery walked the course rather than stationing themselves at one green and watching everyone come through. They all knew who they were going to follow this afternoon.

Estimates of the crowd in various newspapers ranged from 12,500 to 18,000. A final accounting of ticket sales shows that the tally was 9,773. Since members and other volunteer marshals had to pay for their tickets, and there weren't a lot of ancillary people on the site in those days, there probably weren't a whole lot more than that—unless some people managed to sneak in.

Other than slowing down the Ben Hogan–Cary Middlecoff pairing, which had to wait for the gallery to get settled before they could play each shot, there were no major problems with the crowds, even without gallery ropes. Ray Kelly in the *Bulletin* quoted marshals who said they never saw such a large throng so easily managed. "Present at all times was the politeness that goes with the game of golf," Kelly wrote.

In the middle of Hogan's gallery was a La Salle University student named Jim Finegan, who would go on to become a golf writer of note. Looking back on the round in 2009, he remembered the spectators being orderly even while scrambling to get a view.

The strange thing about watching golf in person, of course, is that you miss the action on most of the course. In 1950, you couldn't even watch it vicariously via leaderboards. Hogan's faithful just had to trust that things were going their man's way. They couldn't even get an idea of what was happening on other parts of the course by listening for gallery roars—with so many following Hogan, the rest of the field was playing in near isolation. And with the leaders spread out, rather than playing in consecutive groups, word-of-mouth reports were hard to come by.

In fact, things *were* going Hogan's way. It was a strange afternoon, when a difficult course, U.S. Open pressure, and perhaps just a sheer coincidence of all the leaders happening to play poorly at the same time led to an astonishing backing up of the field. From a lead of one over at the start of the round, a seven-over total ended up making a playoff.

Fred Byrod in the *Inquirer* wrote that the Open was seemingly a hot potato that no one could quite handle. Arthur Daley in the *New York Times* wrote that the championship had "all the characteristics of a cake of soap in a bathtub, being slippery, elusive, and then tantalizingly lost altogether."

Another way to put it would be that the players were choking their guts out.

These were the front nine scores of the players who, besides Hogan, began the third round at the top of the field: Lloyd Mangrum, 41; Dutch Harrison, 40; Johnny Palmer, 41; Middlecoff, 39; Jim Ferrier, 40; Henry Ransom, 39. With a one-over 37, Hogan "surged" into the lead. Incredibly, Mangrum started out with bogeys on six of his first seven holes, a birdie on the other one providing only a small amount of relief.

"I got started out bad and fouled up one hole after another," Mangrum said after the round. "I made four or five bogeys I had no business making." These included a trio of three-putts on the early holes.

Ferrier pretty much threw away his chances at the very first hole. The big Aussie drove into the rough, then rocketed his approach long and left and watched it go out of bounds over the green. He dropped a ball and hit a poor third shot that ended up under a tree. Unable to reach the green from there with a restricted swing, he punched out, pitched on, and two-putted for a triple bogey seven.

"It was apparent that both Jim and (his ever-present wife) Norma were crushed by the turn of events, but neither made any big show of it," the *Bulletin* reported.

Harrison didn't wait much longer to implode, making double bogeys at the third and fourth holes. Palmer showed he wasn't ready to win a major after all, playing the first six holes in five over including a double bogey on the fifth.

Bulla was almost out of contention coming into the fourth round, but put the final nail in his own coffin on the second hole of the afternoon when he four-putted for a triple bogey eight. It was pure carelessness, leaving a 10-foot putt a foot short, leaving the next one on the lip, and then stubbing the ground behind the ball without making contact (counted as a stroke), before finally tapping in.

Hogan was unaware of this foolishness all around him, but he did have a bird's-eye view of Middlecoff, who was hardly doing any better at the outset. "Doc" bogeyed both par fives, the second and fourth, and followed with a double bogey on the fifth to go four over for the round at that point. A drive out of bounds was the culprit on the second hole, where Middlecoff had to one-putt to escape with a bogey. A second shot into a bunker cost him at the fourth. On the fifth, he hit into the creek that runs down the left side of the hole.

Hogan began his round playing rather cautiously, perhaps because of his wildness in the morning, aiming for the center of the greens. He two-putted for pars from 50 and 20 feet on the first two holes, but three-putted for a bogey from 30 feet on the third. The good news was that his ball-striking looked to be under more control; the precision Hogan was back. He gave himself a birdie chance on the par-five fourth, but missed from six feet.

We don't have details on Hogan's play from the fifth through the ninth; the *Bulletin* reporter must have taken a break on those holes. But Finegan remembers that Hogan hit every green in that stretch. "He could not have been hitting more precisely, shot after shot," Finegan said of Hogan's entire round.

Lincoln Werden in the *New York Times* wrote that during the front nine "word came to (Hogan) that some of the others were 'blowing up.' His expression did not change. It seemed a bit grim and determined as he holed par after par."

Well ahead of Hogan, among the early starters, came the only two forward moves of the day, both from players starting well behind. George Fazio, starting at seven over, was even par through six holes and said after the round, "I got the idea maybe I had a chance, and I began to grind. Maybe that's why I three-putted the seventh. I only had a seven-footer, and I went for it, but it was downhill and the ball slipped a couple feet past."

The scrap metal dealer made the turn with a one-over 37 and set about making as strong a showing as he could on the final nine, not knowing what kind of placing it could earn him. He parred the first three holes on the back nine, made a four-foot birdie putt on the 13th, gave it back with a bogey on the next hole, and moved back to even par for the round with a nine-foot birdie putt on the 15th.

"On the 16th, my drive was a couple of feet off the fairway and in a deep divot hole," he recounted to writer Joe Greenday for an article in the 1971 U.S. Open program. "I was 170 yards from the green with the quarry staring me in the face. Trying to get home from there, nine times out of ten I would put it in the quarry. Under any other circumstances, I would have played it safe. This time, however, I decided it was all or nothing. I took a four-iron, dug it deep, and hit it as hard as I could. I knew it was a good shot but when I walked up to the green and saw the ball four feet from the hole I thought this is like catching lightning in a bottle." Alas, Fazio missed the birdie putt. With pars at the difficult 17th and 18th, Fazio wrapped up a round of even-par 70 and posted a 287 total. As Al Laney wrote in the *New York Herald Tribune*, "It seemed ridiculous at the time that 287 would not be bettered, but as Fazio sat in the clubhouse hour after hour he began to see that he might win with it."

Joe Kirkwood Jr. started the final round eight strokes behind after rounds of 71, 74, and 74. Yet, in a year during which he starred as Joe Palooka in three movies, Kirkwood almost stepped out of a supporting role at Merion and had a real chance of winning the U.S. Open.

One of those movies, *Joe Palooka in Humphrey Takes a Chance*, had just been released on June 4, the Sunday before the start of the Open. It was presumably shot during the period from mid-January to mid-March when Kirkwood was absent from the tour, as Joe managed to get in a good amount of tour golf heading into the Open. He tied for third with Middlecoff (behind Harrison and Fazio) at the Wilmington Open in North Carolina on the first weekend of April and tied for 14th at the Masters the next week. He came into the U.S. Open with earnings of $1,887.50 in nine starts on the year.

Playing in the fourth group off the tee, Kirkwood shot a two-under 34 on the opening nine, which would hold up as the best front nine of the afternoon and gain him five to seven strokes on all of the leaders except Hogan and Fazio. He made his fourth birdie of the round on the 10th hole, getting him to three under for the round and six over for the championship.

Three more pars brought him to the fairly long walk past the clubhouse from the 13th green to the 14th tee. Nobody knew it at the time, but as it turned out Kirkwood could have won the Open by playing the last five holes at even par. Easier said than done, of course, especially when you consider that would have meant shooting a 67 in a round where the scoring average of the field was 75.9 (and that by players who had made the cut).

Kirkwood was derailed by a strange and unfortunate incident. *Golf World,* in its story about the Open, reported that Joe was upset when a spectator consoled him on the death of his father, who was actually very much alive. The report said the spectator had read an article in a Philadelphia newspaper that identified Joe Jr. as the son of the trick-shot artist but erroneously reported that Joe Sr. had died a couple of months earlier in an auto accident. On receiving the spectator's consolation, Joe Jr. assumed that his father had just died. He immediately bogeyed three straight holes and finished with a 70 for a 289 total that was two strokes higher than what Fazio had posted.

The story had Kirkwood bogeying 15, 16, and 17, with the incident occurring on the 15th tee. Actually, Kirkwood bogeyed 14, 15, and 16, and the 14th tee is a more likely place for the incident as it is close to the clubhouse where a lot of spectators were gathered. Another difficulty is that a search of Philadelphia newspapers turned up no articles during the week with any reference to the elder Kirkwood having died. Perhaps the newspaper wasn't the source of the confusion. It happened that Kirkwood Sr. resigned as pro at Huntingdon Valley in the Philadelphia area two months earlier, so that departure might have contributed to the mix-up somehow. Maybe Kirkwood misunderstood what the spectator said.

Anyway, Kirkwood's bid for what would have been the greatest final-round comeback in U.S. Open history (the record is held by Arnold Palmer, who won from seven strokes behind in 1960) was derailed. Other than the *Golf World* report, which came out a few days after the tournament, it passed virtually unnoticed. Without real-time scoring or wire-to-wire television coverage, Kirkwood's bid for the title stayed under the radar. The only thing that was noted in the papers the next day was that the 70s shot by Fazio and Kirkwood were the low scores of the final round.

One other player who teed off ahead of Hogan was briefly in the picture. Bill Nary began the final round at seven over and had a nice front nine in which he shot even par. The six-foot-three Nary hadn't won on tour, but he was good enough to post some high finishes and was able to supplement his relatively meager income with prizes from long-drive contests. He won even more in money games at Los Angeles country clubs with Babe Zaharias as his partner, later recalling that they never lost a match. ("She was a hell of a good woman, the best woman you would ever want to meet," he told the *San Diego Union-Tribune* in 2003. "And oh my gosh, she was one of the best competitors I ever saw.")

Nary made *Ripley's Believe It or Not* in 1949 for missing a one-inch putt at the Rio Grande Valley Open—not by whiffing a hasty attempt, as sometimes happens, but by hitting it too hard and having it pop out on the far lip. In 1952, he would set a positive "believe-it-or-not" kind of putting record (broken only in 2002) by taking only seven putts in nine holes while shooting a 60 at the El Paso Open. At Merion, Nary came to the last two holes at eight over, needing a birdie to tie for first. Instead, he made two bogeys and finished at 290.

Here is how the leaders stood with nine holes remaining, passing through the ninth hole at various times: Hogan four over; Mangrum and Middlecoff six over; Harrison, Kirkwood, and Nary seven over; Fazio, Ferrier, and Palmer eight over; and Ransom nine over.

Mangrum was playing near the front of the field, in the sixth pairing off the tee. He managed to steady himself after his terrible start, making eight pars on the back nine along with a bogey on the 15th. The 35 on the back gave him a 76 and a 287 total that matched Fazio, but he didn't think it would hold up. Sitting in the locker room, a downcast Mangrum said, "I think if it's your turn, you're gonna win. Don't you think so? I really thought I was gonna take it today, but it looks like it's just [Hogan's] turn . . ."

Mangrum nodded to the window, looking out over where Hogan was now proceeding up the 14th fairway. After a short, bitter laugh, Mangrum said, "I was always a strong finisher. That was my game. But the way I played today—it's embarrassing."

A couple of groups later, Palmer stumbled in with a 79 and an eventual tie for 10th at 292. Next came Harrison, who matched Mangrum's 41–35—76 but started out a stroke behind him and so finished that way at 288. Like Mangrum, he had eight pars and a bogey (on the 12th) on the back nine, but the details weren't chronicled anywhere so we don't know exactly what missed opportunities or squandered strokes Dutch was left to ponder as he fell just short in his bid for a first major victory. Harrison was paired with Julius Boros, who for the first time all week parred the 16th, 17th, and 18th holes. It was too late, though, as he shot a 74 for a 291 total which earned him a ninth-place finish. His first tour paycheck was for $300.

20

FOURTH ROUND (THE FINISH)

ALL THE ATTENTION was focused on Ben Hogan and Cary Middlecoff as they reached the back nine, for it seemed that the winner would almost certainly come from this feature pairing. They were followed by an ever-growing crowd that "swarmed over Merion's hills and through Merion's valleys almost like some natural migration of insects when seen from afar," wrote Al Laney in the *New York Herald Tribune*.

The 10th hole was pivotal in their private duel. With Hogan two strokes ahead of Middlecoff at that point, both players hit their tee shots into the same fairway bunker—one of the bunkers installed at the USGA's suggestion. On Saturday, the par-four 10th was the easiest hole on the course, playing to a 4.01 average; no other hole played less than .15 over par.

The hole was listed at 335 yards on the scorecard, but in 1971 without any changes its official yardage was given as 312, due partly to more accurate measuring and also perhaps to using a different point as the turn of the dogleg. The green, or the vicinity of it, was in range of longer hitters from the tee even in 1950 because the hole played shorter if you could cut the dogleg. But due to the sharp turn of the fairway and the fact that the tee was back in a chute of trees, you would need to hit a right-to-left shot to have a go at it. Also, the USGA had drawn in the rough on the left to discourage that route, so most players just played down the fairway with a long iron or fairway wood and still were left with only a short wedge to the green.

Hogan and Middlecoff managed to turn a birdie hole into a testing one with their tee shots, which ended up just two feet apart in the bunker, about 60 yards from the flag. Hogan played his ball first and hit a decent shot, reaching the green but finishing 50 feet from the hole. Then came the defending champion, whose shot flew too low, catching the lip of the trap and falling back into the sand. Middlecoff's next attempt came up 20 yards short of the green, setting up a double bogey that left him four behind his playing partner after Hogan two-putted for a par.

Middlecoff had been tripped up by his Achilles heel. As Jim Moriarty wrote in *Golf World* in 2005, Middlecoff "may well have been the worst bunker player of any great champion since the days of the rut iron."

The 11th was another layup hole off the tee, and then a short iron over the brook to the green. This time, it wasn't pivotal. Middlecoff drove into the rough, but made a par. Hogan found the fairway and hit a nice second shot—described in different accounts as stopping seven or twelve feet from the hole—but missed the birdie putt.

It was at this point in the second round that Hogan's legs had cramped up, and that was just an 18-hole day. This time, he would endure a greater physical setback. After hitting his drive on the 12th hole, Hogan was seen to stagger and almost fall, grabbing onto someone for support.

Hogan told writer Jim Trinkle in 1971, "My legs locked. Harry Radix (an acquaintance and sponsor of the prize given out for the Vardon Trophy) was there. I told him, 'Let me hang onto you for a little bit.' I started moving my foot real slow. I told Harry, 'My God, I don't think I can finish.' My legs had turned to stone."

Middlecoff walked up the fairway, alone, while Hogan tried to gather himself. "I saw Doc looking back, wondering what was wrong," Hogan said.

Speculation from those on hand was that Hogan had twisted a knee. More likely, though, it was the effects of extreme swelling caused by the poor circulation in his legs.

An Associated Press story noted that from that point onward, either Hogan's or Middlecoff's caddie picked Hogan's ball out of the hole and Middlecoff, in a sporting gesture, marked his fellow competitor's ball on the greens so that Hogan didn't have to bend his legs. (Players were not allowed to lift and clean their ball on the green in 1950, but in stroke play they lifted it if it might interfere with or help another player, which in practical terms meant any time it was within a few feet of the hole as well as when it was directly on another player's line.)

Hogan managed to get enough feeling back into his legs to make his way down the 12th fairway.

Richard Tufts was the USGA official assigned to Hogan's pairing. "I had naturally watched [Hogan] closely for signs of fatigue, as many others had," Tufts later recalled. "He seemed to be experiencing no difficulty until he walked up the hill on the 12th, and after that I could see that every shot was an effort."

Hogan said he "eased off" his second shot on the 12th, perhaps meaning that he didn't catch it as crisply or spin it as much as he wanted, for the result was a shot that took a big bounce on the back of the green and was headed well past the putting surface until it caught a spectator's leg and was stopped on the back fringe. "Must have some friends," Hogan said when he reached the green.

He was able to use a putter from just off the green, but faced a delicate downhill shot and knocked it about six feet past the cup. He missed the six-footer. Now he was two over for the round and needed to play the last six holes in no more than one over to beat Lloyd Mangrum, who had just finished, and George Fazio. Middlecoff, meanwhile, did better from a bunker this time, getting up and down to save par. He was now three behind Hogan. Middlecoff wasn't out of it, but he told USGA executive secretary Dey that he felt like he was.

Dey had left the official tent and walked out onto the course to see how things were going, picking up Hogan and Middlecoff on the 12th hole. On the next hole, Middlecoff confided to Dey, "I just can't do it, Joe. I just can't."

"What do you mean?" Dey asked.

"I can't play my game for thinking about Ben," Middlecoff responded. "Did you see him on that last hole? He almost fell off the tee. Gee, he's making a great go of it. I can't concentrate."

A notorious bundle of nerves even in the best of times, Cary seemed weighed down by the events of the day—the huge crowd, the pressure of defending a title, his own double bogey at the 10th, and Hogan's physical battle.

Hogan crossed Ardmore Avenue to the 133-yard 13th, the last hole of the short middle section of the East Course, still looking for his first birdie of the round. He could get his tee shot no closer than 30 feet, and made a good effort on the birdie putt, which narrowly missed. Middlecoff also made a routine par.

The twosome had now neared the clubhouse. What followed is an incident that has been passed on in Merion lore. Hogan's legs seized up on him again so badly that he felt he just couldn't finish. "I can't make it," Hogan is said to have told his caddie. "Put my bag on the rack, and I'll pay you."

The caddie, the legend goes, responded, "No, Mr. Hogan, I don't work for quitters. I'll see you on the 14th tee, sir."

The tale must have had its origins in the caddie yard. There is no record of the name of Hogan's caddie, and nobody remembers him. It is thought that caddies for the Open were drawn out of a hat (they were all Merion caddies; players were not allowed to bring their own caddies in those days). The recollection is that

Hogan's caddie was one of the younger ones, but that's in a caddie corps that had a lot of grizzled veterans. Young would have meant he was in his twenties, not that he was a snot-nosed kid.

The kicker is that while this story doesn't seem all that credible— a man of Hogan's determination and will abandoning his Open quest when he had the lead with just five holes to play?—it was actually confirmed by Hogan late in his life. Twice. First, Hogan confirmed it to golf writer Charles Price. Later, Merion historian John Capers had a chance to talk to Hogan in his office, and asked him about it.

"He said he didn't know what to do," Capers related. "The caddie was going to the next tee with his clubs, so he just figured he might as well go there himself,"

Of course, we don't know if the caddie really made that cheeky comment, or if that is an embellishment that makes the story even better.

As Hogan limped to the 14th tee, his large gallery grew even larger. The fans who had been trailing him all along were joined by those who had been staying around the clubhouse area. Thousands of people would try to follow him for most or all of the final five-hole loop—just about everybody on the property except for those staking out front-row spots by the 18th green.

Play was proceeding at a snail's pace by 1950 standards. Hogan was walking slowly and the fidgety Middlecoff was one of the slowest players in the game as far as getting ready to hit his shots. But most of all the delay was a matter of having to wait for the large crowd to settle into place before the action could proceed. You can bet that the USGA wouldn't be levying any slow play penalties against this twosome, no matter how far they fell behind.

According to spectator Jim Finegan, it wasn't *that* hard to see all of the shots, though you might not always have the best view. He was keeping a running account of where Hogan's shots ended up. From the standpoint of the gallery, it helped that the fans could fill in behind the players in the fairway to watch the approach shots and in front of the green to see the action there. Also, there weren't nearly as many people gathered around the greens as there are now. Able to walk down the fairways with Hogan, the fans were so close that they could really see what he was going through.

"I think the gallery was truly sensitive to his pain," Finegan said. "He just felt so weary, putting one foot in front of the other. It was taking so much out of him just to get to the ball . . . I can't remember when a man in contention was so physically incapacitated."

The remarkable thing is that Hogan continued to hit the ball so well. "There was no breakdown in the swing," according to Finegan.

The par-four 14th, not an easy hole, was a routine par for Hogan. Middlecoff, clinging to life, also two-putted for par.

Hogan let a precious stroke slip away on the 15th, but it wasn't due to his ball-striking. He hit a perfect drive on the 395-yard par four (realistically, more like the 378 yards it was listed at in 1971) where he had gone out of bounds to the left in the morning. The hole was cut behind a bunker on the right side of the green. Playing it safe, Hogan hit his second shot toward the center of the green, finishing about 25 feet to the left of the hole.

From there, he left his first putt about two-and-a-half feet short. Then, stunningly, he missed that one.

Hogan recalled in 1971 hitting his second shot to eight feet, and other accounts have echoed that. But the reports in the various newspapers the next day said it was 20 or 25 feet; the *Bulletin* reporter who was following Hogan around and providing an eyewitness account had it at 25. (Estimates of his second putt ranged from as 18 inches in the *New York Times* to 30 inches in the *Bulletin*.)

The *Bulletin* used Hogan's 15th hole to lead its detailed final-round account, under the headline BOLD BEN HOGAN GOES TIMID AND 'BLOWS' A CHANCE and subhead, "Safety Play Costs Vital Stroke on 15th Hole of Final Round."

This is an example of hindsight being 20/20. Hogan's play away from the flag was certainly the smart shot with a two-stroke lead. Heck, it probably would have been the smart shot even if he were tied for the lead, considering the difficulty of the hole location and the overall treachery of the East Course on this day. A shot toward the flag that cleared the bunker could easily have bounced over the green. It's not like he played 50 feet away from the flag. Hogan clearly should have been able to two-putt from 25 feet. Leaving the first putt short was also cited by the *Bulletin* as an error of caution. This may be true. Or it might simply have been a lack of putting touch. It's not like Hogan should have been expected to give his 25-footer a strong run at the hole for birdie.

The real gaffe was missing the tiny putt, and Hogan knew it.

"To be sure, there was some break and the surface of the green seemed a bit scuffed up along his line, but the putt was not struck solidly and he clearly missed it," Tufts later recalled. "He seemed quite a bit upset."

Hogan was now six over for the championship, and needed to play even-par golf on perhaps the toughest three-hole finishing stretch in golf to beat Mangrum and Fazio. Middlecoff missed a golden opportunity to move within two strokes of Hogan, as he also bogeyed the 15th to fall to nine over.

The 16th, a par four measured at 445 yards on the scorecard (probably more like the 430 listed in 1971), was not an easy one for the players or the gallery. The down-and-up trek through the old quarry in front of the green was a tough one for Hogan. Not only were his legs aching, playing 36 holes in sweat-soaked bandages on a hot day must have added to his discomfort and fatigue. As for the gallery, a limited number would have been able to follow the players' narrow path through the sand- and scrub-filled quarry, if marshals allowed it. Most would have skirted around the depression. The ones who were in good position around the 16th green were those who skipped the walk down the parallel 15th hole.

Hogan got up close and personal with the gallery on the 16th, and got away with it. After a good drive, he pushed his approach shot to the right. Just as happened on the 12th, his only other inaccurate approach, he got a favorable bounce off a spectator. This time the ball struck a woman in the thigh, dropping into the rough about 10 feet off the green, when it could have ended up in a more unfavorable position. Like Sam Snead at Greensboro, Hogan was reaping the benefits of having a gallery as a backstop.

Hogan was sending that gallery through an emotional wringer as they feared a second straight bogey was in the offing. He chipped nicely to four feet, but that left him a putt that wasn't good for anybody's nerves. This time, though, he made the testing putt. Pars on the last two holes would still bring him victory.

Middlecoff, on the other hand, was out of it. He hit his second shot into the quarry on the 16th. With a rock wall ahead of him and his ball lying in some thick overgrowth, his only shot was to knock the ball sideways into one of the bunkers that dotted the quarry. He ended up with a double bogey that brought his title defense to an inglorious end.

The next hole of the gauntlet for Hogan was the longest par three on the course, the 230-yard 17th (listed at 224 in 1971). It played downhill, and it is likely that Hogan used a two-iron from the tee, though it was not recorded.

Through the eyes of one particular twenty-one-year-old college student on the scene, Hogan looked pleased when he hit his tee shot. "I think he expected it to move a little left to right," Finegan said, "but it never moved. It just hung straight on that line."

The ball landed on the green but bounced into the back left bunker. Had the ball faded, it would have ended up on the narrower back portion of the green in the vicinity of the flag. Had the ball carried a little less far, or if the green had been less firm, it might have stayed on the wider middle portion of the putting surface.

Instead, it was in the bunker, and now Hogan would have to get up and down to preserve his lead.

Don Donaghey of the *Bulletin* wrote that Hogan told reporters afterward in the locker room that he was burned up about what happened on the 17th. "I hit a wonderful tee shot to the left of the green that suited me," he said, "then it hopped into the back bunker."

From there, Hogan hit a pretty good bunker shot that settled six feet from the hole. Thousands of spectators watched from the vicinity of the 17th tee, which was above the green and afforded a good view, while those circling the green got a closer look.

Hogan studied the putt for a long time. "Back and forth went Hogan three times," wrote Werden in the *New York Times*. "He took two practice swings. Finally he took a stance and stroked the ball. It went on almost to the cup and then stopped."

At this crucial moment, Hogan had left a putt short—his lead was completely gone. After watching a dispirited Middlecoff complete a three-putt from 15 feet, Hogan headed to the 18th tee, needing a par just to tie.

The back nine started out as a coronation march. Then it turned into a physical test of survival. Then it became a challenge of handling a tough golf course turning into a beast with hardening conditions at the end of the day. Would it end up as a sad scene, the opposite of what the fans had come to see?

The U.S. Open is a merciless event. In 1920 at Inverness in Ohio, fifty-year-old Harry Vardon, probably the greatest player the game had seen to that point, appeared to be on the brink of a final, glorious triumph. With seven holes to play, the Englishman had a four-stroke lead—then a storm blew in. Battling a strong wind and his own shaky putting, Vardon went seven-over par on the last seven holes, shot a 42 on the back nine, and finished one shot back.

Would a similar tragedy play out for a leg-weary Hogan at Merion? There was a good chance of it. He was already reeling, and the 458-yard 18th (listed at the same yardage in the 1971 measurement, and playing every bit of it) was the toughest hole on the course. The scoring average for the week was 4.65, which meant that chances of a bogey were greater than chances of a par.

The tee shot called for an uphill 210-yard carry over the quarry. P. J. Boatwright admitted that he "had to struggle" to make it over, but he was a short-hitting amateur. Hogan had never worried about the carry. But what if his legs locked up again? Then anything could happen.

It was the length of the hole, combined with the U.S. Open setup, that made the 18th such a challenge. If you drove the ball in the rough, there was no way to reach the green.

Hogan's driver hadn't let him down yet in the final round, and it didn't here. He struck the ball solidly down the fairway and began another slow walk through the quarry.

Others were proceeding much more quickly to Hogan's ball. They included Hy Peskin, a thirty-five-year-old photographer for *Life* magazine. Born in Brooklyn as Hyman Peskowitz, the son of Jewish immigrants from Russia had started as a copy boy at the *New York Daily Mirror* before becoming a photographer for the paper. Shortening his name to look better in photo credits, Peskin by 1950 had earned a reputation as one of the top sports photographers, with a knack for finding an angle that others hadn't thought of. At Merion, he was covering his first golf event.

Peskin had followed Hogan for a few holes, but hadn't yet gotten the shot he wanted. He hung back while Hogan played the 17th, staking out an advanced position next to the 18th fairway at the approximate spot where Hogan's drive would finish. After Hogan and Middlecoff hit their drives, Peskin raced to a spot directly behind Hogan's ball.

Standing very close to Peskin was Bill Campbell, the amateur who had missed the cut and followed Hogan for the entire fourth round. Also standing behind Hogan was another competitor in the championship, young Bob Toski, who finished his final round about two hours earlier and came out to watch his hero Hogan play the 18th. Former PGA promotion man Fred Corcoran was on the scene, and so was Jimmy Hines, who missed the cut after playing the first two rounds with Hogan. Settling into the first row about 25 feet away from Peskin was Finegan.

Hogan approached his ball to consider his options for a shot of more than 200 yards over terrain that plunged downward ahead of him and then rose gently up toward the distant green. Walking alongside him was USGA official Tufts. "Before he reached his tee shot he asked me whether it was true that Fazio was in with 286, and I told him I had been too busy refereeing to pick up any news," Tufts recalled.

Fazio and Mangrum both were finished with 287 when Hogan proceeded past the clubhouse to the 14th tee, the most likely time Ben could have found out about scores that had been posted. But that's the point when Hogan was in such pain he contemplated quitting, so he might have had too much else on his mind. It's also possible that Tufts's memory was a bit off. Hogan might have known that Fazio and Mangrum finished at 287, but wanted to find out if anyone had bettered that score since then.

When he got to the ball, Hogan spotted Hines and asked him, "What's low?"

"Two eighty-six," Hines replied. "Bill Nary, I think." (Nary was just three twosomes ahead of Hogan, and a rumor had spread like wildfire among the gallery that he finished at 286. Actually, while he did come down the stretch with a chance to catch the leaders, he had faltered at the finish and posted a 290.)

Corcoran interrupted. "No," he said. "Two eighty-seven is low."

Hogan glared intensely at Corcoran, who repeated emphatically, "Two eighty-seven is low."

Trusting Corcoran, Hogan knew that a par would tie. A birdie would win, but that was a longshot. There had not been a single birdie posted yet on the 18th in the final round, nor would there be in the groups following Hogan. In the third round earlier on Saturday, there had been only one birdie, accomplished by Jim Ferrier with a pin-seeking four-wood shot.

Out in the 18th fairway, considering perhaps the most important shot of his career, Hogan thought about hitting a four-wood. That's what he would need to reach a flag that was on the back right of the green, protected by a front right bunker. The required shot would be a fade to avoid the bunker. It's a shot that a maestro like Hogan was certainly capable of pulling off, but he elected not to try it.

"The green rolls away from you back there and then drops off altogether," Hogan later told Price. "I didn't want to leave myself a pitch if I went over. So I decided to hit the one-iron, hoping to keep it on the front of the putting surface."

Conservative play had gotten Hogan to the 72nd hole tied for the lead at the minefield called Merion, and he wasn't going to change now. Not that pinning his hopes on an 18-hole playoff the next day was any sure thing. There was no way Hogan could know how his legs would respond to being asked to play a fifth round in four days. For that reason, there must have been some temptation to shoot for the pin and try to get it over with. But the risk-reward ratio was simply weighted too heavily toward risk, with a very small chance of being rewarded with a birdie.

He selected the one-iron[1], the club he had put in the bag at the start of the week instead of the seven-iron. Price wrote that this was the only time in the entire championship that Hogan used the one-iron. If that's true, it's a bit of an indictment of Hogan's decision about his set make-up. If carrying a one-iron was so important on the East Course, wouldn't he have needed it before the 72nd hole? Wouldn't he have used it off the tee on some of the short par fours? Perhaps what was meant was this was the first time he used it from the fairway. Or maybe Hogan was so prescient that he put the club in the bag because knew he might need it on the 18th hole when it mattered most.

Hogan hit the shot, and it came off just like he pictured it, landing short of the green and bouncing onto the putting surface, rolling to a stop some 40 feet to the left and short of the hole.

Peskin's photographic shot came off just like he pictured it, too, and it became perhaps the most famous golf photo of all time. It graces the cover of this book.

"I knew as I shot it I had something really terrific," he told Bob Cullen for a 1998 article in *Golf Digest*.

Peskin's Speed Graphic camera was primitive by today's standards. After every shot, he had to replace a four-by-five-inch sheet of film, which meant he had only one chance on an action shot. He had to focus by estimating the distance between himself and his subject, not by looking through the lens. There were no ultrafast shutter speeds in those days.

Such equipment limitations were the norm. (An exception was the series of shots of Johnny Bulla and the dog on the 14th tee from that morning, shot by what is referred to in the *Bulletin* photo credit as a "machine gun camera.") The action shots that made the papers were usually planned well in advance by the photographer, rather than by hustling into position and adjusting camera settings on the fly.

Peskin's shot was not only special for its time, it is nearly unique historically. The ability to shoot from directly behind the player was lost when fairways began to be roped off just four years after the 1950 U.S. Open. With photographers limited to standing an arm's length inside the gallery ropes, they can get the behind-the-player view on a shot to the green only on par-three holes, eliminating the chance for such a dramatic 18th-hole shot (it's rare for a course to finish on a par three). These days, the photographers camp around the green on the finishing hole, while television cameramen are the only ones permitted directly behind the player.

Peskin's shot catches Hogan at the moment of his follow-through. His back is to the camera, but he is instantly recognizable because of his distinctive white cap. He has come up onto his toes on his right foot, and you can see the extra spike he put into his shoes for improved traction. He is not wearing a glove. The gallery lines the way to the green, five- to 10-deep all the way, following the curve of the fairway. Around the green, the crowd is even greater as they have massed to see the championship's denouement. To the left of the fairway, not in play but visually arresting, is one of Merion's bunkers with its distinctive tufts of grass. Up ahead, to the right of the green, is the bunker that Hogan is trying to avoid with his shot.

Behind the green rises a tall flagpole with an American flag, and the tops of a couple of tents behind the gallery. There are no grandstands. There is no television tower. Somewhere there is a platform with a television camera, but it is hard to pick out from such a distance. This momentous event is being seen by a lucky few with television sets in certain parts of the country, but for the most part it's a drama shared only by those on the grounds at that moment.

Hogan's shot to the 18th green has gone on to be thought of as one of the greatest shots in the history of the game. This is no doubt in part because of Peskin's perfect image, which has been reprinted countless times and stamped into the brains of all avid golfers and golf fans. But Hogan later told *Sports Illustrated* writer Dan Jenkins that the shot wasn't that great. "I was 40 feet from the pin," he said. "I probably should have hit a four-wood."

That's a fair point. But Hogan was being at least a bit disingenuous, as he was known to be from time to time. He did hit the shot very close to where he wanted, though it would have been nice if it had flown a little bit farther. He did it under crushing pressure, using the club in the bag that was most difficult to hit.

Most amateurs dare not hit a one-iron; they would be unable to get the ball airborne with the low-lofted club. Even the pros find it difficult. Lee Trevino once joked that in a lightning storm, you should hold a one-iron in the air because "even God can't hit a one-iron." Today, few pros try to hit a one-iron; the club, called "the knife," has largely disappeared from tour bags, replaced by hybrids and five-woods that are much more player-friendly.

Hogan told sports writer Galyn Wilkins in 1969 that he chose the iron because, "I wasn't a very good four-wood player at that time," and he later said the same thing to Hogan Company vice president Doug McGrath. No doubt exaggerated humility, because Hogan was one of the better ball-strikers with any club in the bag. But perhaps true in the sense that Hogan might have felt he wasn't hitting his fairway woods quite up to his own high standard at the time.

The greatness of the shot lay not in the brilliance of the result—it lay in the determination of the man swinging the club. The determination of a man who had overcome near-fatal injuries to return to the highest level of golf when such a return didn't seem possible. The determination of a man who could keep alive the dream of a storybook victory in the game's most important championship, if only he could find it within himself to execute a sound swing under intense pressure on legs that were aching badly. The determination of a man who practiced more than anyone, just so he knew he had a swing he could rely on. When the chips were down, on the 72nd hole of the 1950 U.S. Open, Hogan executed the swing.

In truth, all the result of the shot really amounted to was stopping the bleeding. But sometimes stopping the bleeding is vitally important in championship golf. If Ferrier had been able to stop the bleeding at the Masters, he would have worn the green jacket. Hogan, just when he was in danger of throwing the U.S. Open away, had righted himself at the moment of truth.

But he didn't have a spot in a playoff locked up yet. There was a not-so-small matter of getting down in two putts from 40 feet on an afternoon when the greens were like lightning and Hogan's putting touch was anything but sure. Already, he had three-putted three times in the final round.

The gallery let out a big cheer when Hogan's approach shot found the green. They applauded their appreciation as he slowly made his way up the fairway, a "pathetic but somehow gallant little figure," as Laney described him in his report.

By the time Hogan reached the green, the tension returned and the crowd fell silent. Many of them couldn't see much of what was happening. Some carried cardboard periscopes with mirrors that helped them to see over those in front of them. Most would settle for a fleeting glimpse of Hogan, or of the ball as it rolled toward the hole, and rely on the audible response of the front part of the gallery to tell them the result.

Hogan surveyed the putt and judged that it would break slightly to the right. He took his stance, and the gallery held its collective breath. Hogan struck the putt a little too hard. "In view of the break back of the hole, he was very bold with his long putt, even for Hogan," Tufts later wrote, "and I remember being afraid it would go too far the moment he struck it."

The same downslope on the back portion of the green that Hogan feared would send his second shot over the green was now sending the ball past the hole on his third shot. What's more, he had misread the putt, and it actually broke to the left. The ball came to a stop four feet past the hole, creating a murmur from the crowd that left those without a view uncertain of the precise outcome—they only knew Ben hadn't holed it, nor had he left himself a tap-in.

Now Hogan faced a four-footer with his tournament life on the line. It was the fourth time in the last four holes that he faced a putt in the knee-knocking range of two to six feet. How much could a man's nerves take?

"I didn't think he would make it coming back," said Toski.

After taking a lot of time with his putt on the 17th, which he missed, Hogan went to the opposite extreme on the closing hole.

He played quickly, just giving the putt a cursory look, standing over it, and pulling the trigger before anyone expected him to. The ball found the hole.

Twenty-one years later, Hogan explained that he hit it so fast because he was disgusted at having given the outright victory away and just wanted to get off the golf course. "I thought, 'The devil with it.' I didn't take any time with the putt," he said. "I didn't rush, understand, but I put my putter behind the ball and hit it. It went right into the middle of the cup. I could care less. I was so discouraged at losing those three shots. I had it won easy." At another time, he told Price, "I was as surprised as anyone else when it went in."

The crowd let out a roar that "rocked the surrounding county," according to Ray Kelly in the *Bulletin*.

It was a roar of relief that Hogan had not blown the championship, a roar that released the pent-up tension and emotions of a long day, a roar that let Hogan know how much the people appreciated his supreme effort in dragging himself around the course in pursuit of the title, a roar of tragedy averted. But it wasn't a roar of joy. Hogan hadn't won anything, he had just lived to fight another day.

"There was a deflating quality about the finish," Finegan said. "Yes, Hogan had hit terrific shots on 18 and gotten safely into the cup, but the golf tournament was not over, was not settled. I was feeling a little down in the mouth about the outcome—especially since I wasn't going to be there the next day."

The next day, Finegan returned to his summer job as a caddie at a local club; Hogan, Fazio, and Mangrum returned to play for the U.S. Open title.

Dey later called 1950 edition "the most memorable" of all the U.S. Opens he witnessed. "I thought Ben was going to pass out on the 12th hole. It was the greatest physical accomplishment I've ever seen. Hogan pushed himself beyond the limits of endurance that day."

It has been written in some later accounts that Hogan and Middlecoff took six hours to play the final round, but that didn't come from contemporary reports and is incorrect. If that had been the case, they would have finished at eight o'clock, Peskin's photo would have looked considerably darker, the ten twosomes behind them wouldn't have been able to finish before dark, and there would have been no time for the awards ceremony where James McHale received the medal for low amateur.

Championship committee chairman John D. Ames wrote in *USGA Journal* that the average time per twosome on Saturday was three hours and twenty-five minutes. With some of the early starters playing in less than three hours, Hogan's twosome might have taken four hours, but not much more. (That is borne out by comparing the shadow cast by a large tree in Peskin's photo to an almost identical photo of Hogan on the 18th taken the next day by another photographer, since we know that the playoff threesome took four hours, forty minutes and also started at two o'clock.)

It was a timely decision for the USGA to switch to twosomes for the final day this year. With threesomes, the pace of play in Hogan's group might have been slow enough to cause real problems.

Hogan did not technically secure a spot in a playoff when he finished his round; there were still twenty golfers on the course. Only one twosome provided even a remote threat, however, that of Ferrier and Henry Ransom about a half hour behind Hogan. Either of them would have needed a spectacular final nine, but it wasn't entirely out of the question as both had steadied themselves after their rough starts.

A number of curious observers rushed to the 16th green, not all that far away, to await the arrival of that twosome. They saw Ferrier make a birdie there, but it only got him to nine over—no chance to beat seven-over 287. Ransom was the last player with a chance, coming through the 16th at eight over for the tournament, one under for his back nine. Later in the year, he would win the rich World Championship of Golf. But he was unable to play the spoiler role at Merion, a bogey on the 17th knocking him out of contention. Ferrier and Ransom both finished at 289, tied for fifth with Kirkwood.

In the meantime, Hogan had climbed the stairs to the second-floor locker room. Invited to the bar by a friend, Hogan responded, "Thanks, but I'm headed for a big drink of water."

He continued to his locker, while a crowd of reporters made an alley for him to pass through. The USGA had not followed the Los Angeles Open's lead, so players weren't called to the press area. The locker room was too cramped for the number of writers that wanted to get a word with Hogan, and they formed an awkward scrum around him, trying to hear what he had to say.

The *Bulletin* reported that Hogan sat with a pitcher of ice water on the bench and "held brief court for the few who could make the squeeze play."

He was asked about twisting his knee on the 12th hole, and denied it.

"Listen men, I'm tired of reading about my accident and all that goes with it and I'm sure everyone else is," Hogan said. "I want to be treated like just another golfer up there swinging."

He lamented his tee shot that unexpectedly found a bunker on the 17th and he complained about his putting. "I have to get me a new putter tomorrow," he said.

Then, saying he "felt fine" for the playoff, he excused himself and walked off. Skee Riegel told Hogan biographer James Dodson that as Ben accepted congratulations from several pros, "he looked completely beaten, as bad as I've ever seen a man look after a tournament. I wouldn't have bet you a buck he was capable of playing any more golf that week."

But Hogan looked refreshed by the time he posed for photos with the dashing Mangrum and balding Fazio, all three sporting friendly grins and Hogan still holding his glass of water. After that,

Hogan might have headed out for a radio interview. At some point, he returned to a less crowded locker room.

In 1997, Byrod told Joe Juliano of the *Inquirer* that he sat with Hogan as he removed the bandages from his legs during that second stop in the locker room. "We talked for 30 or 40 minutes about a lot of things, particularly how much pain he was in," Byrod said. "He said he reached one point where he didn't think he'd be able to continue."

This conversation was either tacitly or explicitly considered to be off the record. But the wording of Byrod's report in the *Inquirer* is interesting.

"Asked afterward if he had twisted his leg driving on the 12th, Ben said: 'No, and I'm tired of reading all this stuff about my injuries. Let's forget about it,'" Byrod wrote.

So, Hogan denied a specific question about "twisting" his leg. True enough, if it wasn't a twisted knee that caused him to nearly fall. And he didn't say he wasn't in pain, he said he was tired of reading about his injuries.

Hogan later told Price that "my legs were killing me" down the stretch. To Trinkle in 1971, he said, "I didn't like to talk about my legs because it's no good when you feel that people feel sorry for you."

Hogan's final round might have been heroic in a sense, but it was not a thing of beauty. He didn't make a single birdie, instead grinding out fourteen pars and four bogeys for a 74. He used the putter 38 times (it would officially count as 37 putts under today's standards because he used the putter from off the green on the 12th), and did not make a putt longer than four feet.

But his putting was not quite as awful as it sounds. Playing conservatively, he had only two realistic birdie chances, on the fourth and 11th holes. There wasn't much excuse for the short-range miss on 15, but he did make tense four-footers on 16 and 18 that got him into the playoff. And he had putted well in the morning.

The three-over finish on the last seven holes was certainly disappointing, but perhaps not surprising coming at the end of a long day. In fact, he also played those seven holes three over in the third round and he was two over for that stretch in the second round. He was one under in the first round, but even then told a reporter that he tended to tire on the last four holes.

Mangrum and Fazio were the beneficiaries of Hogan's poor finish. After lamenting how he had blown the tournament, Mangrum got word that after making a couple of bogeys Hogan needed to par the last three holes to win outright. Mangrum walked out to the 18th and sat down to wait next to the large bunker to the left of the fairway.

Before Hogan made his walk up the 18th, an official on the final green announced that Hogan had bogeyed the 17th and now needed a par just to tie.

"What do you think about your chances now, Lloyd?" Mangrum was asked.

"I sure thought I could do it today," he replied without changing expression. "I don't know about tomorrow."

As Hogan came up the 18th, Mangrum turned to Sarazen, who was standing nearby, and remarked, "I guarantee you there'd be nobody happier than I am if he made a three."

Hogan made a four, of course, and Mangrum abandoned an empty Tom Collins glass and went to shake hands with the man he would meet in a playoff.

Fazio hadn't won nearly as many tournaments as Mangrum, but, perhaps buoyed by his excellent final round, struck a more optimistic tone.

"All pro golfers feel they might win any tournament," Fazio said with his arm around his eleven-year-old daughter, Rosalie. "I felt that way here and I had a right to, because I know this Merion course. Anyhow, I was hoping and feel pretty good over the results."

The top ten after the regulation 72 holes looked like this:

Ben Hogan	72–69–72–74—287
Lloyd Mangrum	72–70–69–76—287
George Fazio	73–72–72–70—287
Dutch Harrison	72–67–73–76—288
Joe Kirkwood Jr.	71–74–74–70—289
Jim Ferrier	71–69–74–75—289
Henry Ransom	72–71–73–73—289
Bill Nary	73–70–74–73—290
Julius Boros	68–72–77–74—291
Cary Middlecoff	71–71–71–79—292
Johnny Palmer	73–70–70–79—292

Snead narrowly missed the top ten, finishing in a tie for 12th at 294. An indication of how tough the course was playing was that he moved up twenty-three spots in the standings with rounds of 72 and 74 on Saturday.

Afterward, he talked to Grantland Rice. "I'll tell you about these Opens when you've missed (winning) a few years. They get tougher and tougher on the mental side," Snead said. "You keep remembering the mistakes you made in the past that cost you an Open title. I guess you keep trying too hard."

Snead lamented not winning an Open early in his career, the way Middlecoff had the year before, because "when you are young, you don't know how tough it is. Cary Middlecoff is a fine golfer. In the course of things he was due to win the Open in six or seven years. But he wins his third time out. And I can't win it in my fifteenth time out [actually it was his tenth] and neither can Jimmy Demaret, who has been around a few years also. Cary doesn't know how lucky he was."

Snead was joined in 12th place at 294 by locals Riegel (79–73 on Saturday) and Al Besselink (76–75), veteran Henry Picard (79–73), a fading Bulla (78–76), and future Open champion Dick

Mayer (73–72). A stroke further behind came Skip Alexander, who shot 77–76 on Saturday.

First-round sensation Lee Mackey closed quietly with rounds of 75 and 77 to tie for 25th at 297, saying afterward, "Everyone has been nice to me here."

His traveling companion from Alabama, Harold Williams, finished one stroke ahead of him in a tie for 20th at 296, also shooting 75–77 in the last two rounds. Also finishing at 296 were Demaret (71–76) and Toski (80–74).

Even in 2009, it still stuck in Toski's craw that he earned the same $100 as those who finished well behind him. When the USGA added $5,000 to the purse, it did so in a top- and bottom-heavy manner. First prize doubled from $2,000 to $4,000 and second place jumped from $1,500 to $2,500. The remaining $2,000 was dedicated to paying $100 each to the players who would have been out of the money before, those in 31st to 50th place.

In between, the prizes remained the same. The six players tied for 12th earned a whopping $133.33, and after that it was $100 for everybody else who made the cut whether they finished at 295 or in last place at 316.

Also earning $100 was Wally Ulrich. The Minnesota pro signed an incorrect scorecard in the third round for a score lower than he actually made, which would have gone unnoticed by anyone had he not looked at the scoreboard after the final round and noticed the error. He turned himself in and was disqualified, but officials awarded him the $100 for making the cut.

The fifty-five-year-old Cruickshank finished respectably, tied for 25th at 297, beating out Sarazen, who was back in the pack at 302 after an 82-76 finish.

"Oh, boy, I'm glad that's the last one," Sarazen was heard to exclaim after driving from the 18th tee.

Philadelphia's McHale rallied with a 35 on the back nine for a 74 to take low amateur honors at 302. A struggling Frank Stranahan finished with a 78 for 306. Boatwright was in the driver's seat for amateur honors after a 36 on the front nine, but for the second time that day he found the back nine too much, struggling to a 43 and a 307 total. He did beat two professionals, though, George Bolesta finishing at 311 and John O'Donnell, who shot 83–85 on Saturday to end up at 316.

⟪⟫

1: Hogan wrote in his 1957 instruction book, *Five Lessons: The Modern Fundamentals of Golf,* a collaboration with Herbert Warren Wind, that he hit a two-iron to the 18th green in the final round at Merion. Reminiscing with a group of reporters in 1969, he also said he used a two-iron. Fort Worth's Jenkins, the writer who was closest to Hogan, said that Hogan later told him it was a two-iron, and on one occasion even said it was a three-iron. (Jenkins, just getting his start as a newspaper writer in 1950, didn't make his first trip to the U.S. Open until 1951, so he missed Merion.)

However, the weight of the evidence lies with it being a one-iron. Byrod in the *Inquirer* and Werden in the *New York Times* both wrote in their reports for the next day's paper that it was a one-iron. Hogan told Price a couple of weeks after the Open that it was a one-iron. Those are the accounts closest in time to the event.

Later, when the confusion arose, Merion members wrote to Hogan, asking for clarification on the club he used for the famous shot, as well as for particulars on another story about his one-iron and golf shoes being stolen.

"It was a one-iron I played to the 72nd green," Hogan wrote back. "After hitting my shot, my one-iron was stolen. I haven't seen it since. Also, that night my shoes were stolen out of my locker and I haven't seen them either." (There is evidence that Hogan hit the one-iron in the playoff, which would place the theft a day later.)

Much later, Price asked Hogan why, if he used a one-iron, he didn't have the mistake corrected in later editions of *Five Lessons*. "I didn't think it was important," Hogan replied.

The missing one-iron ended up being returned to Hogan in 1983 after a club collector in North Carolina named Bob Farino purchased an old MacGregor one-iron and suspected it might have been Hogan's. He noticed that the clubface was worn in a spot that was unusually small, an indication that its original owner had made contact on the same spot on the clubface every time. And, tellingly, that worn area was toward the heel of the club—Hogan had his clubs made with the sweet spot toward the heel.

Farino passed the club to tour pro Lanny Wadkins, an acquaintance who was on the Hogan Company staff, and Wadkins brought the club to Fort Worth on his next visit to the Hogan facility. "It is nice to see my old friend back," said Hogan, confirming that the club was his, and that only the grip had been changed.

He immediately decided to give it to the USGA, and did so after changing the grip to one like the original; the club is still displayed in the USGA museum in Far Hills, New Jersey.

21

PLAYOFF

IT WAS WELL into evening by the time Ben Hogan returned to the Barclay Hotel in Philadelphia after the double round on Saturday. A late room-service dinner became even later because Hogan had to sit in a hot bath for an hour to soak his legs. He told a writer six months later that his legs swelled so much that day that it took a hectic evening of massage and bathing to get them in a condition where he might be able to play the next day.

His wife, Valerie, later recalled that she "had given up on his being able to tee off in the playoff, but I couldn't tell him that."

Meanwhile, back in Fort Worth, Ben's brother Royal was frantically trying to figure out how to send a putter to Pennsylvania for morning arrival. He heard a radio report about Ben's putting woes in the final round, and thought about the brass putter that Ben left in his garage at home in favor of a blade model he had been using for the last three months since picking it up during an exhibition in Memphis. Royal reached his brother by telephone at the hotel and said he could send the putter to New York with an airline pilot friend. But Ben didn't think he had anyone who could pick up the putter for him, so he told Royal to forget it. Instead, Royal went to work on arranging for a messenger to take the putter from New York directly to Merion.

Valerie Hogan said that during the night she woke up to the noise of jackhammers in the street below, but Ben was sleeping so soundly he never heard them. In the morning, Valerie recalled, he was "fresh as a daisy."

"Isn't it a nice day?" he said.

Hogan got a break because the playoff didn't start until 2 p.m. due to Pennsylvania blue laws governing events on Sundays. That gave him more time to recover from Saturday's 36-hole ordeal, and meant he did not have to wake up exceptionally early to go through his morning soaking routine.

It also meant there was no chance of a second straight 36-hole day if there was a tie. (That's what happened in the 1946 Open at Canterbury, where Lloyd Mangrum, Byron Nelson, and Vic Ghezzi tied in an 18-hole playoff in the morning and went 18 more in the afternoon, Mangrum winning.)

When the Hogans reached the lobby of the hotel on their way to Merion, they received a surprise—a group of newsmen was waiting for Ben. They had probably gathered to be able to check Hogan's condition and get a comment from him if it turned out he was unable to play in the playoff. Seeing that he would not only play, but was moving well and in good spirits, they cheered him and some said, "Go get 'em, Ben."

Newspaper estimates of the playoff gallery ranged from 6,000 to 10,000, but again that was high. Daily tickets were offered at $3.00, but only 1,440 were sold (compared to 6,088 the previous day). Weekly tournament tickets remained good for the playoff. If all the 3,865 people who purchased tournament tickets attended the playoff, it would have brought the number to above 5,000, but some of those people undoubtedly had other commitments.

Still, several thousand people following one threesome repre-sented a formidable challenge for the marshals. The players had to wait on every hole for the gallery to settle into place, which Championship Committee chairman John D. Ames later estimated took five minutes per hole. There was a photo in the next day's paper of Hogan, Fazio, and Mangrum on the 14th tee, with the caption noting they were "taking a rest." Hogan is taking a drag on a cigarette while sitting on what appears to be a "shooting stick" type of chair that presumably was being carried in his golf bag, Fazio is sitting on a folding chair that he may have borrowed from a gallery member. Mangrum is standing, looking impatient. They must have been waiting on an "all clear" signal from the marshals.

Not *everyone* was rooting for Hogan in the playoff. Fazio not only had a group of family and friends watching, he was also being cheered on by a contingent of some 150 members of his club, Woodmont, who had arrived from Washington, D.C., by car, plane, and train, according to the *Washington Post*.

"Win or lose, we're going to have a big 'Welcome Home' banquet and reception for him Tuesday night," said Woodmont President Arthur Sundlun.

Other than that, though, Hogan had the gallery in the palm of his hand. Mangrum had to settle for only polite applause when he hit a good shot or made a birdie.

Shirley Povich wrote in the *Washington Post* that, unlike in the past, the usually dour and aloof competitor Hogan was actually feeding off the gallery.

"Hogan was the least tense of any of the three men in the playoff," Povich wrote. "He was gallery-conscious, and they liked it. For the first time in his career, he was probably trying to win for the gallery as well as for Hogan."

Povich had observed a changed Hogan the previous week at the National Celebrities Tournament in Washington. Admittedly it was more of a fun event than a serious competition, but still Hogan's friends noted that it was the first time they remembered seeing him smile on the first tee of a tournament. "He found himself even manning the loudspeaker during the antics of Danny Kaye and

Milton Berle and Bob Hope and (Arthur) Godfrey, and having fun," according to Povich.

"Hogan didn't know that things like this could ever happen on a golf course," said one of his friends. "It is loosening him up, and I hope he keeps this mood the next week at the Open."

Hogan certainly appeared to be in a good mood as he arrived at the course on Sunday. "I feel fine," he stated while sitting in the locker room—an assertion he was liable to make in any case, but it really did seem to be true.

It is likely that with only three competitors they were allowed to warm up by hitting shots into the 14th fairway instead of having to go to the West Course, followed by some strokes on the practice green. Just before tee time, Hogan's brass putter arrived by messenger.

A scriptwriter would have Hogan delightedly grab his old familiar weapon and go on a putting spree that netted him the Open title. Unfortunately, Royal's best efforts were for naught. The club arrived too late for Ben to even try it on the practice green, so he stuck with the one he had warmed up with.

Fazio was a big underdog, but looking back on it he said he felt he had a chance to win. He told Al Barkow in *Gettin' to the Dance Floor* that the only player he ever felt he couldn't beat was Byron Nelson. "With everybody else I felt I might be able to out luck them, they might get a bad bounce or I might hit a lucky shot or something—even Hogan. Like in that playoff for the '50 Open. I was first up on the first tee, and when I went to put it down I was shaking. When Ben went I was looking at him tee it up and he was shaking, too, so I said, 'This is not too bad.' Mangrum liked to play the cool cat, but he was shaking, too."

Mangrum at least had one thing going for him. He had been in a three-way U.S. Open playoff before, and had won.

Mangrum had a prickly relationship with Hogan, however. In a *Sport* magazine profile of Hogan in 1953, Bob Brumby wrote that there was a long-standing personal feud between the two, though each had a healthy respect for the others' ability. At the time of the article, Mangrum had just been quoted with a remark that was seen as disparaging Hogan. When it was related to Hogan that Mangrum said he was misquoted, Hogan responded, "He has never liked me and the feeling is mutual." Mangrum, on the other hand, said the two had gotten along fine until a couple of years before.

In truth, it was probably just a lack of mutual understanding by two men who were difficult to get to know. They had little to say to each other, and each may have misinterpreted the sometimes blunt comments both were liable to make in the press.

Fazio and Hogan got along well; indeed, George had joined Ben for his first practice round at the Los Angeles Open when he returned to the tour after an 11-month absence. Fazio was the only gregarious member of the trio, but he knew there would be little conversation that day, which was fine. "Hogan is the most perfect gentleman on the golf course that I ever played with," he told Barkow. "I mean, he's not going to do anything *for* you, but he's not going to do anything against you. You play your game, he plays his."

The first hole was a short par four of 360 yards, but it was no pushover at the Open, playing as the seventh toughest hole. Hogan and Mangrum calmed their nerves and made routine pars, while Fazio showed signs of an inability to control his adrenaline. For the first of three times on the front nine, his approach shot went over the green, and it resulted in a bogey.

Fazio got the stroke back with a birdie from 20 feet on the par-five second, while Mangrum moved in front by planting his approach three feet from the hole and making a birdie to go one under. Hogan was still getting his bearings. His drive was on the fringe of the right rough, and his second shot with an iron found the left rough. Still, he hit his next one on the green and made a par.

Mangrum pulled his tee shot on the par-three third. While it found the fringe instead of the deep rough, he was unable to get up and down, his par putt catching the lip and staying out. With regulation pars by Hogan and Fazio, all three were now at even par after three holes. They remained that way after the par-five fourth, where Hogan and Fazio hit into the rough with their second shots. Hogan hit the green from there to join Mangrum in two-putting for pars, while Fazio missed the putting surface but chipped close and made his par putt. All three emerged unscathed from the dangerous par-four fifth, with Fazio again one-putting for a par while the other two both hit the green. All three players were even par through five holes.

Things began to unravel for Fazio on the par-four sixth, where his approach shot went long into a bunker. This time he couldn't get up and down, and made a bogey.

The par-four seventh and eighth holes were birdie opportunities—if you could keep your tee shot in the fairway. But Fazio was wild off the tee on the seventh, hitting it out of bounds to the right and making a bogey. The winner of only two tour events in his career seemed to be succumbing in the pressure-cooker of a playoff for the national championship.

In that out-of-bounds area to the right of the seventh, hundreds of spectators perched on the framework of a house being built near the green. The ground slopes down sharply to the left of that green and the eighth tee is immediately behind the putting surface, making viewing impossible from either spot, so enterprising fans utilized the partially built home as a chance to see the action on an otherwise difficult spectator hole. Fortunately for both the spectators and the property owner, the frame did not collapse under the fans' weight.

Hogan took the lead for the first time in the playoff by hitting his short-iron approach to within four feet and making the birdie putt on the seventh, after missing a birdie try from a similar distance on the previous hole. Mangrum, after a routine par on the sixth, caught a bunker with his approach on the seventh. He avoided losing two strokes to Hogan, coming out of the sand to within four feet and making the putt to save par.

On the eighth hole, Hogan hit what was to be his only poor shot of the round, finding a fairway bunker with his tee shot. Even then, it wasn't so much a poor swing as a poor club selection.

"I made a mistake," Hogan said after the round. "We couldn't feel the wind there, and I used a No. 1 iron when I should have hit a brassie [three-wood]."

Wait a minute! A one-iron? Didn't Hogan later say his one-iron had been stolen after the fourth round?

Hogan missed the green on his shot from the fairway bunker and ended up with a bogey, dropping back to even par. Meanwhile, Mangrum had another solid par, while Fazio bounced back from his two consecutive bogeys with a birdie on the eighth, holing a nine-foot putt.

On the par-three ninth, Fazio missed the green yet again, finishing in a bunker, but escaped with a par. It completed a scrambling nine where he hit a scant three greens in regulation, but one-putted five holes to keep himself in the thick of things with a one-over 37, just a stroke behind his companions.

"I was too keyed up for that playoff," Fazio recalled. "I usually drove even with Hogan for length, and that day I was 10 and 15 yards ahead of him. But I'd forget I was keyed up and knock the approach shots over the greens."

Hogan and Mangrum, in contrast, were solid on the front nine, Hogan hitting eight greens and Mangrum seven. Both shot even-par 36s with one birdie and one bogey, the birdies coming on short putts.

The back nine would be a different story, at least for Mangrum. While Hogan continued his relentless, error-free play, knocking it down the fairway and onto the green hole after hole, Mangrum had one of the wilder nine-hole rides ever seen in a U.S. Open playoff. Over the next seven holes, Mangrum made only one par, and became involved in a pair of strange incidents that turned the tide in Hogan's favor.

The yo-yo act started on the 10th hole, where Mangrum's tee shot ended up in the same bunker that had caught Middlecoff and Hogan in the fourth round. The USGA's Richard Tufts, who had suggested the bunker, must have been smiling.

Mangrum missed the green and made a bogey on the 10th, but he came right back on the 11th with an approach to five feet and a holed birdie putt. He walked to the 12th tee tied with Hogan, while Fazio was still one stroke back. Mangrum hit his drive into the 12th fairway and then entered the Twilight Zone. Mangrum's second shot flew over the heads of the amazed gallery, past Ardmore Avenue, and came to rest in the rough just past the 13th tee, at least 30 yards over the 12th green.

There was some question whether the ball was out of bounds. It had crossed over an out-of-bounds road, but was sitting on the property of the golf course, which could have allowed for an interpretation that it was in bounds. USGA rules chairman Isaac Grainger ruled that it was out.

In truth, that was a break for Mangrum, especially with the distance-only penalty. He would have faced an exceptionally difficult shot from where his ball lay near the 13th tee, back across the road to a hard and fast green sloping away from him. Making par from there would have been almost impossible, while double bogey was a definite possibility. Instead, he dropped one in the fairway, and using the correct club this time found the green and walked off with a bogey.

This extraordinary turn of events was glossed over in the newspaper accounts. The *New York Times* said that Mangrum hit a five-iron "too strongly as the breeze faded and the ball flew over the crowd." While mentioning the out-of-bounds approach shot, all of the reports simply state that Mangrum made a five on the hole without any further description. But a fading breeze could hardly explain the ball flying that far past its target. In an interview with Merion historian John Capers in 1986, Grainger offered a more plausible explanation. Mangrum, he said, asked his caddie for a nine-iron. The caddie handed him a six-iron instead, and Lloyd somehow didn't notice.

It's hard to imagine a player escaping scrutiny for such a gaffe today. But the playoff wasn't televised and post-round press interviews were more perfunctory than they are now. Also, an even more unusual incident on the 16th hole would overshadow this one, and that's what reporters asked Mangrum about after the round.

Hogan, meanwhile, pounded out routine pars on the 10th, 11th, and 12th, as did Fazio, who was getting his ball-striking (and nerves) under control. Through 12 holes, Hogan was even par, with Mangrum and Fazio a stroke behind. Still tight. It remained that way through the 13th, where they all hit the green off the tee and two-putted that par three.

Hogan found himself with a little bit of breathing room after the par-four 14th. Continuing to play like a machine, he drove in the fairway and hit the green for yet another par. His long game straightened out, Fazio's putting now began to go sour as he three-putted for a bogey. An erratic Mangrum hit his second shot into a greenside bunker and also bogeyed the hole. Hogan pulled two strokes ahead of both of his fellow competitors.

Mangrum cut Hogan's lead to one on the 15th. His drive nearly went out of bounds, but he hit an outstanding shot from the rough to within 12 feet of the cup and sank the birdie putt. Fazio, however, fell three behind with his second consecutive three-putt. Either his new putting method let him down at the end, or he reverted to old habits under pressure.

The feared 16th hole claimed Mangrum as a victim in the playoff, but in truth it was Lloyd who did himself in. Or perhaps some blame should be placed on what Mangrum described as a "bug fly" that landed on his ball while he was about to putt it.

Mangrum, his Achilles heel (shaky driving) continuing to haunt him, sprayed his drive into the right rough. With a not-so-good lie in the deep stuff and some trees in the way, Mangrum made his one smart decision on the back nine by laying up short of the quarry.

He figured he could still make a par with a nice third shot and a one-putt. He hit a decent shot to the green, leaving himself with a 15-foot putt to salvage a four. Mangrum marked his ball because it was in the line of Fazio, who was on his way to a third straight bogey after missing the green. Mangrum then replaced his ball, and here is how Associated Press writer Gayle Talbot described the scene:

"He addressed his ball carefully several times, bobbed his head back and forth the way golfers are supposed to do, and then stopped dead still. He planted his putter in front of the pellet to 'mark' it, lifted the sphere and blew upon it gently to dislodge the unwelcome guest [the 'bug fly'], then replaced it as the gallery laughed."

The USGA's Grainger wasn't laughing, though. He knew that Mangrum had just incurred a two-stroke penalty for lifting his ball. Not until 1960 were players allowed to lift and clean their ball on the green. In 1950, they were allowed to mark and lift their ball on the green in stroke play only if it interfered with or might assist another player.

Mangrum rolled in the putt for what nearly everyone thought was a par. Hogan had a birdie putt from 10 feet, but he missed. It was high drama, with Mangrum apparently managing to stay right on Hogan's heels just when it looked like he was going to lose one or two strokes.

Mangrum strode confidently to the 17th tee, and prepared to tee off (he had the honor from his birdie on the 15th.) Then Grainger appeared on the tee and the drama was drained from the event, replaced by confusion and an altered scoreboard that showed Hogan's lead grow from one stroke to three.

Grainger later said in a USGA oral history that he had trouble getting to the 17th tee to inform Mangrum of the penalty because of the rush of the gallery. When he arrived, he delivered the bad news. "Lloyd, I'm sorry to tell you, but I have to enact a penalty of two strokes because you lifted and cleaned your ball on the previous hole."

As Grainger recalled, "He immediately realized that he had done that, and put the club back into the bag and made the statement, 'Well, I guess I can still feed the children,' or something like that."

For Mangrum, it was a matter of Ike Grainger giveth and Ike Grainger taketh away. In the 1946 U.S. Open, Grainger had been the one to levy a one-stroke penalty on Byron Nelson when his caddie inadvertently kicked his ball in the fairway after emerging from under a gallery rope. The penalty dropped Nelson into a playoff, which Mangrum won.

Knowledgeable spectators knew something was up when they saw that Mangrum wasn't going to play first. Everyone quickly became aware of the penalty—though not necessarily what it was for—when the chalkboard showing the standing of the players was changed, with Mangrum going from one over to three over.

It was a shame it had to happen coming down the stretch of a U.S. Open playoff that was so closely contested, especially on the heels of Mangrum making a great scrambling par that would have kept the pressure on Hogan. Mangrum's absentminded move still ranks as one of the all-time golf blunders.

It has been suggested that cleaning the ball on the green was allowed as a local rule at PGA tournaments at the time, so Mangrum might simply have let instinct take over and forgotten that he couldn't pick up the ball at a USGA event. But the PGA had stopped using this local rule. A pro named Pete Cooper lost a tournament just two months after the U.S. Open because he missed a short putt due to having a piece of chewing gum on his ball (ironically, in that case Cooper would have been allowed to remove the gum because it was a man-made object).

Mangrum's comments after the round show that it wasn't a PGA vs. USGA issue. The problem didn't arise because he temporarily forgot he was in a U.S. Open, it was because he thought blowing off a fly was OK.

"I had the idea you could get off anything like a bug or snake," he said, admitting that he didn't know the rule.

He was wrong, but in a way he was ahead of his time. According to the USGA's current Decisions on the Rules of Golf, a live insect can be removed from a ball in play because it is not considered to be adhering to the ball. But in 1950, the interpretation was different. At that time, a live insect *was* considered to be adhering, so he wouldn't even have been allowed to remove it without touching the ball. Thus, Mangrum breached the rules twice, once for lifting and once for cleaning, but there was no double jeopardy so he incurred only a single two-stroke penalty.

Mangrum earned praise for the equanimity with which he accepted the ruling that practically destroyed his hopes for a second Open championship. His only flash of annoyance came at the awards ceremony, where USGA President James Standish referred to the club as Merion Cricket Club instead of Merion Golf Club. When called to the podium to accept his runner-up medal, Mangrum said, "Well, the brass might not know where they are, but they sure know the rules."

Mangrum didn't hold a grudge. A photographer had taken a picture of Mangrum and Grainger walking down a fairway at Merion during the Open, and Lloyd later sent it to Grainger with this inscription:

To Ike
May we never have
bugs again—Love & kisses
Lloyd Mangrum

Back on the 17th tee, everyone, probably even including Hogan, could agree that this was no good way to determine the Open champion. On this hole, Ben would do his best to make sure the two-stroke penalty wasn't the deciding factor. Or maybe Hogan was happy to have a three-stroke lead any way he could get it. *Life* ran a second U.S. Open spread a week after Peskin's famous 18th-hole photo, and a shot of Hogan walking toward the 17th green in the playoff showed him with a big smile, a rarity during competition.

Minutes later, Hogan would have even more reason to smile. Facing a 50-foot uphill putt from the front level of the 17th green, Hogan hit it perfectly and watched it go into the hole for a birdie, the longest putt he made all week. Another *Life* photo shows Hogan in an uncharacteristically demonstrative gesture, doffing his cap and bowing to the crowd. The fans responded with a loud and prolonged cheer.

Just like later Arnold Palmer roars at the Masters, you didn't have to be on the scene to know who the cheering was for and what it was all about. Those sitting by the 18th green or the clubhouse knew that Hogan had done something great and that he must have clinched the U.S. Open.

With routine pars on the final two holes, Mangrum finished with a 73. Fazio parred 17, but ended with his fourth bogey on the last five holes as he overshot the green yet again on the 18th and limped in with a 75. After earning his way into the playoff with spectacular back nines of 32 and 33 on Saturday, Fazio gave away his chances on Sunday by stumbling home in four-over 38.

Hogan hit his drive in the fairway—where else?—on 18. He was only a little bit beyond his drive of the previous day, but this time he hit a five-iron. Years later, he explained to Hogan Company vice president Doug McGrath that the breeze was behind him and he felt his adrenaline running. Pumped up instead of leg-weary, Hogan's five-iron bounced over the green.

Standing behind Hogan, a photographer named Alex Bremner reprised Peskin's shot of the previous day. Never printed in a national magazine, the shot appears in Merion's club history, right under Peskin's famous photo. Bremner's photo also shows Hogan frozen in his follow-through, this time wearing a sweater on a day that was not so warm. The crowd is smaller, and has not encroached on the field of play as it did on Saturday. Instead of forming a line on the fairway side of the bunker ahead of Hogan, the gallery has politely stayed to the outside of it.

Hogan finished in style, chipping to seven feet and holing the putt for a par and a one-under 69. An enthusiastic crowd rushed in like they wanted to raise Hogan onto their shoulders the way the gallery did with amateur Francis Ouimet when he won the Open in a major upset in 1913. The Haverford Township police were having none of that.

"There was a mad crush and several persons were knocked down in the melee," the *New York Times* reported. "A cordon of police saved Hogan from the happy jam of well-wishers."

On the clubhouse porch, Valerie Hogan celebrated in a more quiet fashion. Just as she had done the previous three days, she sat sipping iced tea for the entirety of Ben's round. Valerie heard the cheer from the 18th green and heard somebody say, "Ben Hogan won."

She began to cry. The couple at the next table came over and asked, "Is there anything we can do for you?"

"I'm all right," she replied. "I'm just happy for my husband. I'm crying with joy."

Hogan's storybook return from his auto accident and Mangrum's unfortunate blunder attracted most of the attention in the aftermath of the playoff. What got lost in the shuffle was the exceptional round that Hogan played to earn the title. The day after 104 rounds had been posted on the East Course with only one of them under par, Hogan produced a 69 with the U.S. Open title on the line. He did it with an impressive display of controlled golf. The accident may have humanized him, but he played the playoff with almost robotic precision.

His lone mistake, the tee shot into the bunker on the eighth, was the result of misreading the wind and hitting the wrong club. Over the next eight holes, with Mangrum and Fazio nipping at his heels, Hogan methodically hit every fairway and every green, grinding his foes down with eight straight pars. It was effective on the scorecard, and also mentally. As his opponents watched Hogan's relentlessly efficient play, they sensed he wasn't going to make any mistakes or give them any openings. Perhaps that led them into trying to force the issue on the back nine, where Mangrum was wildly up-and-down and Fazio fell apart after holding things together with baling wire on the first nine.

That eight-hole stretch of regulation pars was broken by Hogan's clinching birdie on the 17th. He ended up hitting 16 of 18 greens in regulation, including a meaningless miss on the finishing hole. Hogan's putting held up, too. The blade putter that had served him poorly the previous afternoon was a worthy companion on Sunday. The playoff was his only round without a three-putt, he showed a good touch in getting his long putts close to the hole on Merion's tricky greens, and missed only one short putt (the birdie try on the sixth), finishing the round with 33 putts.

Hogan had told reporters in the hotel lobby before the playoff round, "The trouble with Merion is that it always has you on the defensive. There's no way you can take the offensive against it."

He said it with a tone of frustration, because he preferred to be able to attack. But, like a smart quarterback, Hogan knew to take what the defense gave him. Taking few chances, Hogan played for the center of greens and walked away with the U.S. Open trophy. After the round, Hogan told reporters that he played for the flag only once in 90 holes. That was on the ninth hole of the third round, and his shot ended up in a bunker. He also said that he had made an adjustment in his putting in the playoff, taking the club back more with his left hand instead of his right. "It kept my stroke smoother," Hogan said, though he didn't credit that for making the long putt on the 17th. "That was strictly unconscious."

Hogan didn't hide his excitement at winning the championship: "It's the biggest kick I ever got out of winning a title, including the Open in Los Angeles in 1948."

Hogan's fellow pros were happy for him, too. Johnny Bulla, who had returned home to Pittsburgh, was so antsy about the outcome he called the *Post-Gazette* three times for updates. When told Hogan had won, he said, "That's great. I'm glad to hear little Ben has made it after all he's been through. It's a good thing for golf, too, because Hogan is one of the greatest competitors of all time . . . What a comeback that boy has made!"

A number of pros delayed leaving town, instead heading back to Merion to see the playoff. Skee Riegel remembered sitting in the locker room afterward with Jimmy Demaret, Cary Middlecoff, and others, having a celebratory cocktail. "We all wanted Ben to do it," Riegel said.

A picture taken at the awards ceremony shows runners-up Fazio and Mangrum smiling genuinely and broadly, with the latter applauding. Shortly thereafter, Mangrum said this to Associated Press writer Will Grimsley about Hogan: "He's the greatest of them all."

These days, in a playoff with three or more players, those who don't win finish in an official tie for second. Unfortunately for Fazio, it wasn't done that way in 1950; he got third-place money while Mangrum got second-place money. Even worse, the breakdown was $2,500 for second and just $1,000 for third, a terrible deal for Fazio. Good thing he had a scrap metal business on the side.

It was fortunate for Mangrum that his two-stroke penalty didn't drop him from second to third. For a player who avowedly played for money, losing $1,500 would have been very upsetting. It was bad enough having to look back on two huge mental lapses that cost him a chance at the title (and the $4,000 first prize). Would they have happened if the opponent had been someone other than Hogan? Could playing with the game's toughest competitor have led to a lack of clear thinking?

There was a telling quote in the 1949 *Time* cover story about Hogan.

"Look at that Mangrum," said one pro at a tournament where Hogan wasn't playing. "Steady as a rock out there. He even grins once in a while. But if Hogan were in this tournament, you'd see Lloyd shake when he lit a cigarette. I'm telling you, the guy's got ulcers, and Ben Hogan gave them to him."

Once, it was Hogan who had the reputation of not being able to win the big one. Now Mangrum was the one who was winning tournaments by the handful, but still was stuck on one major championship.

Now, about that one-iron . . . Not only did Hogan say he hit a one-iron from the eighth tee in the playoff, the *Inquirer* reported he hit a "driving iron" (a colloquialism for a one-iron) off the 11th tee that day. How could Hogan have said at the time that he hit a one-iron in the playoff, and later in life said that it was stolen after the fourth round? Did he have a backup one-iron? Not likely—he didn't even have a backup putter. Did he misspeak after the playoff round about hitting the one-iron? Could it really have been a two-iron? Not likely. His comment was specifically about choosing one club over another, so you would expect him to remember which club it was. The most likely explanation is that his memory was wrong later on, and the one-iron was actually stolen after the playoff. Statements at the time carry more weight than memories, which can be fuzzy. Besides, there are other reasons why a post-playoff theft makes more sense than a theft after the fourth round.

There is the fact that the shoes were stolen, too. Hogan later asserted that they disappeared from his locker and the one-iron was taken from his golf bag, but it would be more plausible if they were taken at the same time, and also that they were taken from a public place. Hogan's bag would have been put on a rack outside the clubhouse after each round. After the fourth round, it would have been whisked away to the caddie master's area for storage, but after the playoff it would have stayed there until Hogan was ready to leave. The thief could have done his work while everyone's attention was diverted at the awards ceremony. Hogan would have left his shoes in his locker after the fourth round, but it's easier to see how he might have put them in his golf bag after the playoff. He could have gone to the locker room after the round to change into a jacket and street shoes for the ceremony and then brought his golf shoes down to put in his bag since there was no need to leave them in the locker now that the tournament was over.

A final point: On Saturday night, the thief wouldn't have known what club Hogan hit on the 18th hole of the fourth round. But the Sunday paper reported that he hit a one-iron, so an unscrupulous person looking to steal a historic club would have known which one to take.

We'll never know, of course. Just as we'll never know if Hogan really told his caddie he was going to quit during the fourth round. That story started by word of mouth and was only confirmed by Hogan decades later, which means it could be another hazy memory. We can't be certain it was a one-iron that Hogan hit on the 72nd hole.

Some things we do know for sure. Sixteen months after suffering such severe injuries in an auto accident that there was severe doubt as to whether he would even be able to play golf again, Ben Hogan returned to play in the national championship. Required to play 36 holes in one day on bandage-wrapped legs now ill-suited to the task of carrying him that far, he survived that ordeal and lived to play another day—on which he played stellar golf and won the championship.

As Red Smith wrote in the *New York Herald Tribune*:

"Maybe once in the lifetime of any of us it is possible to say with accuracy and without mawkishness, 'This was a spiritual victory, an absolute triumph of will!' This is that one time."

EPILOGUE

SPEAKING TO REPORTERS after the Sunday playoff at Merion, Ben Hogan admitted the toll that the previous day's double round had taken.

"I'll never play 36 holes again in one day, the way I feel now," he said.

Reminded that his schedule called for him to play 36 holes the very next Sunday at the Palm Beach Round Robin in New York, and that future U.S. Opens would require double rounds, he conceded that he might play 36 holes under some circumstances.

Hogan had already ruled out playing in the PGA Championship, which required five straight double rounds of the players who reached the final. He also realized that he had probably played too much over the first half of 1950, and planned to cut down his schedule in order to preserve his body and maximize his chances of winning the tournaments he did enter.

"I would like to play as much golf as physically possible," he said, "but I guess I will just have to pick my spots for a while. I know I've got to slow down. Not quit, understand, just slow down."

Hogan dutifully showed up at Wykagyl Country Club north of New York City the next week for the Palm Beach Round Robin, honoring a commitment he made in January. In the first-round gallery was twenty-one-year-old Dave Anderson, a college student and future *New York Times* sports columnist who made a two-hour trip from Brooklyn to New Rochelle by subway, train, and bus.

"I went to see the guy who had won the Open, the same way I went to see the great basketball players at the [Madison Square] Garden," Anderson said in 2009. A drained Hogan shot a 76 that day and finished 11th in the elite field of 16 while playing 90 holes for the second consecutive week. Lloyd Mangrum won by a wide margin.

Most of the golf world then convened in Columbus, Ohio, for the PGA Championship just two weeks after the U.S. Open. Hogan was criticized by local newspaper writers and sponsors for not competing, even though it should have been obvious that the potential for playing 216 holes in seven days was too much for him to even contemplate. Chandler Harper, who failed to qualify for the U.S. Open, ended up beating Henry Williams Jr., the little-known Pennsylvania pro who shot a first-round 69 at Merion, in an uninspiring final.

Hogan returned to action the next week at the Motor City Open, finishing 11th. That was his tenth event in the six months since his return, but he wouldn't compete in another until the Seminole Pro-Am nine months later. He told a writer in December that he had played only four rounds in a number of months. He spent a good part of the latter half of 1950 helping with production of the film *Follow the Sun*, which told his comeback story. (Glenn Ford played Hogan.) With the script already written by spring, Hogan's U.S. Open victory wasn't depicted in the movie, which climaxed with the Los Angeles Open.

The U.S. Open was Hogan's only victory in the eight official events he entered in 1950 (if you count the two unofficial pro-ams, he was two-for-ten). Sam Snead finished the year with eleven wins, although none of them were majors, and easily led the money list.

His scoring average of 69.23 not only won the Vardon Trophy, it held up as the best raw scoring average for a single season ever on tour until Tiger Woods bested the mark in 2000 by averaging 68.17. Yet despite Snead's great campaign, Hogan's U.S. Open triumph was so significant that Hogan was named PGA Player of the Year for 1950, based on a vote by the writers. It wasn't even close; Hogan topped Snead 112–43.

Snead never forgot the perceived slight, bringing it up countless times the rest of his life (he died in 2002). He wrote in his 1997 book, *The Game I Love,* that he was so affected by being overlooked for Player of the Year, "I said, 'The hell with it,' and cut back on my playing significantly." Indeed, after playing 30 events in 1950, he entered only 13 or 14 in ensuing years. "It hurts even now," he wrote.

But Snead didn't give up the tour completely until he was sixty-four; remarkably, he finished third in the 1974 PGA Championship at age sixty-two. The good ol' boy from Virginia holds the all-time PGA Tour victory record with 82—but he never did capture that elusive U.S. Open.

Mangrum won five tournaments in 1950. But in a June/July hot streak that saw him win three times in five events, the two he didn't win were the U.S. Open and PGA Championship. Dapper Lloyd would finish his career with 36 victories, but never won another major beside the 1946 U.S. Open, probably the biggest reason he is little remembered today. He died in 1973 at the age of fifty-nine after suffering his 12th heart attack.

George Fazio finished in the top five in the 1952 and 1953 U.S. Opens, but never won another tour event as he cut back his schedule when his Ford dealership started. In the early 1960s he got into in golf design, and was responsible for such courses as Jupiter Hills in Florida, Butler National near Chicago, and a thorough redesign of Atlanta Athletic Club prior to the 1976 U.S. Open. He brought his nephew into the business, and Tom Fazio went on to become one of the top architects in the latter 20th and early 21st centuries. Among Tom's projects was a redesign of Merion in preparation for the 2005 U.S. Amateur.

Tom said in 2009 that George never expressed regrets about the outcome of the 1950 U.S. Open. "I spent almost every day with him from 1963 to the early 1980s [George got out of the business a few years before he died in 1986], and I never heard him say, 'I wish I had won,' or anything like that. He was comfortable in his life."

Dutch Harrison's divorce went through on July 14, 1950, a little more than a month after the U.S. Open, and cost him a large financial settlement. On August 18, he married Thelma Akana, who moved with her four children from Hawaii to the United States. Harrison had great longevity on tour, winning eight times after his fortieth birthday to run his total to eighteen career victories, none of them majors. He even qualified for the 1971 U.S. Open at Merion at age sixty-one.

Once the Joe Palooka movies and television show came to an end in the mid-1950s, so, essentially, did the acting career of Joe Kirkwood Jr. His only non-Palooka role came in the 1960 movie *The Marriage Go-Round*, but he did get a star on the Hollywood Walk of Fame, on Vine Street, next to that of Grantland Rice (who got his star for his radio work). In 1955, he opened the Joe Kirkwood Jr. Driving Range in Studio City, California, operating it with three partners until selling it in 1958. He also developed a golf course in Palm Springs, owned a bowling alley, and had various other real estate investments. Through it all, he continued to play the tour off and on. His last victory was in 1951, but as late as 1965 he was the 36-hole leader at the Speedway Festival Open in Indianapolis.

Kirkwood's penchant for investments took an odd turn in 1966 when he and some partners planned to sink an old troop carrier in some shallows 110 miles off the Southern California coast to make an abalone fishing station and processing plant. However, the vessel sank before it was in position and Kirkwood was one of four men who had to be rescued.

Jim Ferrier went at the tour full-bore from 1946 to 1953 and claimed 16 victories in that span, including five in 1951. He and his ever-present wife, Norma, finally stopped living out of their car in 1954 when Jim took a club job at Lakeside Golf Club outside Los Angeles. Ferrier returned to the tour from 1961 to '63 and claimed his final tour win at age forty-six.

Southern Californian Bill Nary was the swing double for actor Dennis O'Keefe in *Follow the Sun* (O'Keefe played Hogan's fictional friend). Despite making a run at the 1950 U.S. Open, he never won a PGA tour event. "If I knew then what I know now," said Nary in 1997, when he was a teaching pro, "I would have practiced every day like Hogan."

Tragedy struck Julius Boros in September 1951 when his wife, Buttons, who he had married shortly before the U.S. Open at Merion, died of a cerebral hemorrhage days after giving birth to their first child. Boros was so shaken he considered leaving the game, but he returned to the tour, remembering that she had told him he would win in 1952.

Boros did get his first win that year, and it came in the U.S. Open, where he beat out Hogan and hard-luck Porky Oliver. What's more, he also captured the World Championship of Golf, and finished the year as leading money winner and Player of the Year. Despite not joining the tour until age thirty, Boros notched 18 victories, including a second U.S. Open in 1963. He won the PGA Championship in 1968 at the age of forty-eight, making him the oldest player ever to win a major. He continued to post top-ten finishes into his mid-fifties, and was known for his statement about retirement: "Retire to what? I already play golf and fish for a living." Boros remarried in 1954 and had six more children. All four boys became golf pros, including Guy, who won a PGA Tour event.

With Snead playing a little less and Hogan a lot less, Cary Middlecoff was the most prolific winner on tour from 1951 until Arnold Palmer came along in the late 1950s. "Doc" won 28 times in the 1950s and 39 times in his career, an impressive total since he didn't start until he was twenty-six years old and had to quit at forty-two because of back problems.

Middlecoff never really captured the imagination of the public the way Hogan and Snead had before him or the charismatic Palmer did after him. But while not a particularly dynamic player, he was well-spoken and had a long career as a television commentator after his playing days, which meant he never had to go back to practicing dentistry—though he did keep up his license, as a matter of pride.

Skip Alexander endured a terrible crash and staged a remarkable comeback of his own. Just three weeks after the promising pro scored his third PGA tour victory, he was taking a Civil Air Patrol plane from the Kansas City Open to his North Carolina home in September 1950. The CAP was in the process of making a deal with the tour to fly two players each week to an exhibition the Monday after a tournament, and officials offered Alexander a ride home when he told them that his tee time on Sunday didn't allow him to make it to the airport in time to make a commercial flight.

The plane crashed in Evansville, Indiana, on its approach to an emergency landing due to mechanical failure, and burst into flames. The two pilots and a CAP official were killed; Alexander, the sole survivor, was burned on seventy percent of his body, including his hands, in addition to breaking an ankle. Alexander underwent seventeen operations in the ensuing months. In one of them, doctors permanently bent his pinkies into the position of a golf grip so that he could eventually play golf. He earned a spot on the 1951 United States Ryder Cup team because he played so well in 1950 that he finished 10th in points over the two-year qualifying period. Alexander returned to play a few tournaments in the fall of 1951, a year after the crash. At the Ryder Cup, he ignored bleeding hands to defeat England's John Panton in a stirring 36-hole singles match.

However, Alexander's career as a competitive golfer was essentially over. His broken ankle never healed completely, and he wasn't able to walk well enough to play 72-hole tournaments. He settled into a club pro job in St. Petersburg, Florida, and raised a son, Buddy, who won the 1986 U.S. Amateur and is now the golf coach at the University of Florida.

Bob Toski came into his own in 1954 when he won four of his five career titles and led the tour in victories. One of those wins came in the World Championship of Golf, where the first prize had risen to a stunning $50,000 (five times the next highest first prize). Toski couldn't follow up on that success; instead, finding his calling as a instructor, he became one of the most respected teaching pros in the game.

Lee Mackey never became a regular on the PGA tour, playing in only a few isolated events. Not even his 64 in the U.S. Open attracted any financial backers. "There weren't any sponsors in those days and I had to go to work," Mackey said in 1971. "I think I could have made a go of it on the tour if I had been able to play it with any degree of regularity."

Mackey's tie for 25th at Merion remained his career best finish on tour. In scattered appearances afterward, his best was a tie for 26th in the 1955 Baton Rouge Open. Instead of going the club pro route, Mackey got a job as a salesman for a concrete company and settled into a 9-to-5 working life. Still a member of the PGA, he won one Southeastern PGA and three Alabama PGA titles before becoming ineligible when the association restricted its events to those making a living from golf.

The 64 in the U.S. Open helped him some in his sales business, Mackey said, but hurt him in first-tee negotiations. "People remind me of it so they can get more strokes from me," he said in that 1971 interview.

(Mackey, by the way, wasn't interviewed out of the blue in 1971. That was the year the U.S. Open returned to Merion for the first time since 1950, so there was interest in what had happened to him.)

The differences between the 1950 and 1971 Opens at Merion were far greater than those between the 1934 and 1950 Opens. The tour and the U.S. Open had grown by leaps and bounds in two decades, fueled by Palmer and television. Having progressed greatly since its primitive beginnings in mid-century, by 1971 television coverage now required a production compound. The area adjacent to the 16th hole used for parking in 1950 had been purchased from Haverford College and turned into the club's practice range in the 1950s; that's where the television compound was placed.

Once again, the players would have to practice on the West Course, but that now meant the establishment of an official range area on one of that course's fairways and a shuttle service to get players there and back. Thanks in large part to Hogan's example, players were practicing a lot more by that time. And with purses rising, the birth of the PGA Tour as a separate organization, and the increased profile of tour golf, players' needs had to be attended to; there would be no asking them to drive back and forth to the practice range, nor would they be kept out of the members' locker room.

Public parking was moved to lots at Haverford College and three miles away at Villanova University, with shuttle buses bringing spectators to Merion. U.S. Opens were now drawing close to 20,000 spectators on the weekend (which after 1965 meant the third round on Saturday and fourth round on Sunday), but with Merion's small acreage making for less room between fairways, tickets had to be limited to 14,000 a day. (Even in 1950, *Golf World* had sniffed that Merion East was a magnificent test of golf but "hardly satisfactory as a sports arena.")

Artistically, the 1971 U.S. Open was a blockbuster, with Lee Trevino beating Jack Nicklaus in an 18-hole playoff. That success led to the 1981 Open being awarded to Merion, which David Graham won thanks to a nearly flawless final round. But by then it was clear the U.S. Open was outgrowing Merion and its 127 acres hemmed in by residential areas. In coming years, ever more space would be needed for corporate tents and a huge merchandise tent. Typical U.S. Opens came to draw more than 30,000 spectators; even with increased use of grandstands, Merion couldn't accommodate more than 20,000. And at 6,544 yards, the course had become too short as driving distance continued to increase due to improved technology.

But in 2013 the U.S. Open will return to Merion for the first time in 32 years. Developments leading to this were a lengthening of the course to 6,868 yards by architect Tom Fazio, cooperation from Haverford College in providing space for corporate tents, and acquisition of a six-acre property adjacent to the sixth hole to provide some extra room. Ticket sales will, of course, be limited, but the USGA is operating on the philosophy that for certain special courses, inconveniences and less-than-maximum on-course revenue will be tolerated. So, a fortunate player will be able to take a victory stroll up the same 18th fairway where Hogan hobbled to his historic victory 63 years before.

The 1950 U.S. Open was probably Hogan's most famous victory. It was also the most special to him. Later in life, he picked his Merion triumph as his most satisfying victory to interviewers for both *Golf* and *Golf Digest*.

After 1950, Hogan would never play more than five official events in any year—and usually just three or four (plus a couple of unofficial pro-ams). In 1951, he finally won his first Masters and added his third straight U.S. Open title (not counting the one he couldn't enter in 1949) with one of the greatest final rounds ever, a 67 at brutally difficult Oakland Hills. For good measure, he also won the World Championship, just to show he could play for money as well as for trophies.

In 1952, he won only the Colonial, but 1953 was a year to remember. Hogan won all four official events in which he teed it up—and you can make that all five, because the British Open retroactively counts as an official win though it wasn't considered so at the time. It was Hogan's only appearance at the British Open.

Hogan was the first player to win three modern majors in one year (the only one to join him since was Tiger Woods in 2000), as he also claimed the Masters and U.S. Open in 1953. But, for two reasons, he couldn't even attempt the Grand Slam. It was an impossible feat for anyone because the PGA Championship and British Open overlapped—the seven-day PGA marathon ended on a Tuesday, the same day as the second day of qualifying for the British Open, which all entrants were required to compete in. Also, it was impossible for Hogan in any case, because winning the PGA still required five days of double rounds (it switched to stroke play in 1958).

The triple crown of 1953, achieved at the age of forty, was practically Hogan's last hurrah. He won only one more tournament, his hometown Colonial, in 1959. Perhaps his incompletely repaired shoulder, his un-operated on knee, and his poor-circulation legs became more of a factor. But the biggest reason for his decline was probably putting—it got to the point where Hogan was so afraid of missing short putts he could hardly bring the putter back and would stand frozen over the ball. The biggest disappointments of this period came at the 1955 U.S. Open, where he lost in a playoff to unheralded Jack Fleck, and the 1960 U.S. Open, where his bid ended with a shot in the water on the 71st hole as Arnold Palmer claimed the title.

Hogan started a golf-equipment company in 1954, and put much of his attention toward that business. At occasional tournament appearances, which continued until 1970, he was viewed reverently by younger pros, who would gather to watch him practice. After that, public appearances were few and far between, which, if anything, served only to increase his legend.

Once Hogan cut back on his time in the office, he spent his days at Shady Oaks Country Club in Fort Worth. When he could play no longer, he still enjoyed hitting balls on the range, which had always been his passion. Finally, Hogan couldn't even do that anymore, and spent his time at a particular table in the dining room, looking out over the course. He would occasionally be visited there by golf pilgrims, including six-time major champion Nick Faldo, who asked him how to win the U.S. Open (a major Faldo never was able to capture). "Shoot the lowest score," Hogan pithily responded.

Hogan died in 1997 at the age of eighty-four.

How Hogan's 1949 car-bus crash affected his legacy is a fascinating question. Looking at the numbers, it certainly cost him a lot of victories. He ranks fourth to Snead, Jack Nicklaus, and Tiger Woods with 64 career PGA Tour wins. Considering that he missed nearly the entire 1949 season at a time when he was winning tournaments at an extraordinary pace, and played in very few events each year after that, it's safe to say he would have accumulated more than Nicklaus's total of 73 and probably would have threatened or surpassed Snead's record of 82.

The accident didn't seem to hurt his major championship victory total very much, since he won only three majors before it and six after. Still, his injuries deprived him of chances in the PGA Championship, where he was unable to compete. (His major total was also hurt by the lost World War II years and the fact that he played in only one British Open. Clearly, Hogan is undervalued by looking only at his number of major titles.)

On the other hand, the crash and comeback made Hogan well-known to the entire public, not just golfers. It lifted his 1950 U.S. Open victory at Merion to mythic proportions, making it an inspirational event that will be celebrated for generations to come, not a mere victory in a national championship.

For hard-core golfers and golf fans, the comeback only enhanced the Hogan Mystique. Here was a man whose father committed suicide, who had a decidedly unprivileged upbringing, who stubbornly ignored early evidence that he wasn't good enough for the tour, who dug his game out of the dirt by pure hard work and indomitable will, who overcame potentially crushing failures in a couple of majors. Not even a head-on collision with a bus was able to stop him.

At the same time, the accident humanized Hogan. Following the crash he was no longer just an unsmiling golf robot with poor public relations skills. He was a husband who, seeing the headlights of a bus bearing down on him in the fog, dove to protect his wife. He was a player who had to wrap his legs in elastic bandages and drag his uncooperative lower appendages around the course in pursuit of championships. From 1950 on, he was embraced by the galleries in a way he never had been before.

Without the accident, Ben Hogan could have been the winningest golfer in the history of American golf. With the accident . . . well, maybe that's exactly what he was.

ACKNOWLEDGMENTS

BEN HOGAN'S VICTORY at Merion happened 60 years ago, but fortunately a wealth of material exists about the tournament and the players who were the key figures. I was able to find much of this material in one place at the United States Golf Association library in Far Hills, New Jersey, under the direction of Nancy Stulack. Besides a large collection of periodicals and books, its files on players and U.S. Opens also proved a good resource.

Merion Golf Club also has extensive archives, dedicated not only to the history of the club but also to ancillary material on the 1950 U.S. Open and other tournaments contested at Merion. Historian John Capers and archivist Wayne Morrison are both dedicated to preserving this history, and were helpful in offering both the club's resources and their own insights.

I was fortunate to be able to talk to people who were on hand at Merion in 1950: players Bob Toski, Doug Ford, Al Besselink, Bill Campbell, and Jacques Houdry and spectator Jim Finegan. Others who were able to provide insight into aspects of the story were Dan Jenkins, Dave Anderson, Tom Fazio, and Tim Cronin.

The Internet is a boon to researchers these days, with some newspaper archives beginning to appear on Google and articles from magazines, newspapers, and Web sites findable via searches. In addition to articles circa 1950, later articles about the players involved were often very useful.

Among mid-20th-century periodicals, *Golf World* was the main source, particularly for information on the other tournaments and tour news in the period covered in this book, 1948 through 1950. *Sport* magazine helpfully profiled most of the leading players around that time and the USGA publication *Golf Journal* had some inside stuff on the U.S. Opens. *Time* had a cover story on Hogan, *Esquire* and *Collier's* also had some golf coverage, and *Life* sent photographer Hy Peskin to the 1950 U.S. Open. Periodicals that didn't exist in 1950 but later had articles on some of the players involved include *Golf Digest*, *Golf*, and *Sports Illustrated*.

The primary sources for newspaper reports on the 1950 U.S. Open were the *Philadelphia Inquirer* and *Philadelphia Bulletin*, supplemented by the *New York Times*, *New York Herald Tribune*, and *Washington Post*. Reports on other tournaments and news came from the *Los Angeles Times*, *Augusta Chronicle*, and wire services Associated Press, United Press International, and International News Service. On Ben Hogan's crash and recovery, the *Chicago Tribune* had a three-part series from Charles Bartlett, who visited Hogan in the hospital, while a couple dozen other newspapers had useful articles on various players.

On Ben Hogan's life, the main biographies are by Gene Gregston (*Hogan: The Man Who Played For Glory*), Curt Sampson (*Hogan*), and James Dodson (*Ben Hogan: An American Life*). Other books with useful biographical information are Martin Davis's *Ben Hogan: The Man Behind The Mystique* and Jimmy Demaret's *My Partner, Ben Hogan*.

On other players, several of them told their stories to author Al Barkow in *Gettin' to the Dance Floor*. Other books of note on players include *Slammin' Sam*, by Sam Snead with George Mendoza; *The Education of a Golfer*, by Sam Snead with Al Stump; *Mr. Dutch:*

The Arkansas Traveler, by Beach Leighton; and *Jimmy Demaret: The Swing's The Thing*, by John Companiotte. Other book sources included *The History of the PGA Tour*, by Al Barkow; *The Official U.S. Open Almanac*, by Salvatore Johnson; *The U.S. Open: Golf's Ultimate Challenge*, by Robert Sommers; and *Pinehurst Stories*, by Lee Pace.

As far as getting this book off the ground and seeing it through, thanks go to editor Mark Weinstein at Skyhorse Publishing. At home, the support and patience of my wife, Ludmila, and children Michael and Sophia enabled me to put in the time necessary in my home office to get this finished, and for that and much more I give them thanks.

—DAVID BARRETT
White Plains, New York

ABOUT THE AUTHOR

DAVID BARRETT has been a professional golf writer for three decades. For 18 years, Barrett served as an editor at *Golf,* where he coordinated the magazine's major championship coverage. He presently contributes to GolfObserver.com and has his own website, davidhbarrett.com, that is part of TheAPosition.com. He graduated from Haverford College, just across the road from Merion Golf Club, and has covered 25 U.S. Opens. The author of three previous books, he lives in White Plains, New York.

INDEX